◆ BUSINESS STATIONERY GRAPHICS 2 ◆

BUSINESS STATIONERY GRAPHICS 2

First published in Japan 1994 by: **P·I·E BOOKS**
*Villa Phoenix Suite 402, 4-14-6, Komagome, Toshima-ku,
Tokyo 170, Japan
Tel: 03-3949-5010 Fax: 03-3949-5650*
ISBN 4-938586-48-7

First published in Germany 1994 by: **Nippan**
*Nippon Shuppan Hanbai Deutschland GmbH
Krefelder Str.85 D-40549 Düsseldorf 11 (Heerdt) Germany
Tel: 0211-5048089 Fax: 0211-5049326*
ISBN 3-910052-37-1

Printed in Hong Kong

CONTENTS

◆

序文
◆ Preface ◆
Vorwort

序　文

現在は、企業やショップ等を設立する場合に個々のマーケティング・アイデンティティの企画立案と並行して、ロゴやマーク、コーポレートカラーに代表されるビジュアル・アイデンティティを考えていくことがＣＩ形成の大切な役割であるという意識が定着しているようです。そのようなビジュアル・アイデンティティの中でも、レターヘッド、封筒、名刺といったステーショナリーは、送り手が受け手に対してまず見せたいと思っているイメージを通してコミュニケートする行為を、最も明快にできるチャンスを秘めたグラフィックツールといえるでしょう。

ビジネスで使用されるステーショナリー・システムのアイテムやバリエーションは様々ですが、まず欠かせないレターヘッドの概念を考えてみます。サイズは現在はほとんどがＡ４版、これはＯＡ機器への対応、書類のファイリング等の事務処理においてより効率的なサイズとして世界共通で浸透しつつあります。またレターヘッドはメッセージを書き入れるために存在し、その後折りたたまれて封筒に挿入されるプロセスが待機されている、いわばこれから使われる為のツールです。如何なるメッセージをどのように書き入れるのか、デザインに合う機能的な紙は何か、同様に封筒はどうマッチングさせるか等を考慮する必要性があります。グラフィック・アイテムとしてみた場合、他のものとはビジュアル的に最終ではない点において特異な存在と言えます。言い換えれば、その構成要素や諸事情に規制の多いのがレターヘッドです。

本書がVol.1に引き続き２を出版することになったポイントにはまず、社会背景及びビジネスのあり方が変容し、それに伴いステーショナリー・デザインもリニューアルし変わってきているということがあります。加えて、Vol.1以上に多彩な国々の作品を掲載しています。その数は17か国、それぞれの国民性や文化、デザイン傾向の違いなどを楽しみながらイマジネーションを刺激できるのではないでしょうか。もう一つ、今回はスペシャルプログラムと銘打ってFax用紙を紹介しています。ステーショナリーの中で例えばレターヘッドとFax用紙を比較してみますと、本来の目的及びふさわしい内容において双方は対極の違いを備えており、デザイン的には前者の方がはるかに時間とコストをかけて制作されていることは顕著です。が、Faxにおいてはワールドワイドな視野から今後さらに合理的になるであろうビジネス・コミュニケーションの可能性を多大に持ち合わせています。すなわち、レターヘッド・デザインが数年で変わっていったのと同様に、Fax用紙のデザインに関する認識と理解はますます深まっていくのではないかと推測されます。これらの事情に注目して、"Fax headers"のプログラムを楽しみながら見て触発されてください。現状ではモノクロが主体であり、簡素なフォルムながらも斬新な要素を含んでいる作品を本書ではチョイスしてみました。おそらく初めての試みであろう当プログラムが、これからのビジネス・ステーショナリー・アイデンティティのサポートとなれば幸いです。また印刷技術の発達により、様々な特殊効果を使った新しいタイプのステーショナリーも数多く登場しています。本書で掲載している作品の中からそのテクニックのいくつかを列記してみますと、盛り上げ印刷、箔押し、型押し（エンボス）、メタリック・インク、ラバースタンプ、ニス状の上塗り、型抜き等があります。またテクニックと相乗して、紙の扱いや紙質の選び方もステーショナリーを構成する大切な要素として見逃せません。ベースに薄く色柄をひいたもの、裏面全体をプリントしたもの、グラデーショントーン使い等のデザイン効果や、和紙、トレーシングペーパー、表裏の色が違う紙等、数々の表情のある紙を選んでいます。実際現物の感触をお届けできないのが残念な所ですが、それらの新鮮なアイデアソースは、もちろんクライアントの事業内容がベースとなっています。本書はクライアントの業種で大きくグルーピングし、個々のステーショナリーに事業内容を表記してあります。

ビジネス・ステーショナリーにおいての優れたデザインは、先に述べたようにクライアントのビジュアル・アイデンティティ意向に伴って、様々な制約のある中でどれだけ機能的なものに仕上げるかというのが最大のポイントです。これは、パーソナリティの表現方法も然り、ビジネスにおいてそれぞれのステーショナリーの扱いをきちんと押さえた上で、コミュニケーション・ツールとしてデザインをどう反映させるかということです。本書をご覧いただく読者の方々が、これから登場するステーショナリー・グラフィックスのオリジナリティと美しさを感じとるのと同時にその機能美も理解していただけることを期待しています。

ピエ・ブックス編集部

Preface

*T*oday, Almost everyone is aware of the importance of creating a strong visual identity in the public mind. Logos, trademarks, corporate colors and so on are among the primary tools in this undertaking, along with the more conventional approach of establishing specific, individual identities for given target markets. Stationery, such as letter heads, envelopes and business cards, is a system of communication tools that constitutes a key element in the making of a corporate identity. And because stationery incorporates graphic tools, it has the potential to carry an image of the sender directly and intimately to the recipient.

There is a wonderful diversity of items included in business stationery systems used today. Consider for a moment the letterhead, which is still probably the anchor of any stationery system. The most common size is A4, now widely used all over the world. This international standard has proven efficient for various applications, including use in OA devices, filing, correspondence and so forth. The letterhead exists to carry a message and, inherent in the object, there is the process, whereby it is written on, folded and inserted into an envelope. In other words, the letterhead is nothing before it is used, but when it's time comes, the letterhead is more than just the sum of its parts. The unique quality of the letterhead is that, visually speaking, it is not a final product: it is the user who puts the finishing touches on it. Thus, it is necessary for the designer of a letterhead to consider how the message will be presented - the format and style of the actual words that will be written on the page, the type of paper that will optimize the function of the letter and so on. Also, how will it coordinate with the envelope and other elements in the stationery system?

One of the reasons we decided to produce Volume 2 of Business Stationery Graphics, after the success of Volume 1, is that since that first issue was published, both the social background and the business community have undergone a major shift, and we have discovered that stationery design on the whole has moved as well: it has been renewed. Volume 2 also carries graphic design works from a broader field than Volume 1: seventeen countries are represented in this volume. We are confident that these work, collected from around the world, will more, delight and inspire you. You will appreciate the fine differences in national characteristics, cultural influences and design inclinations among these pieces. Another special feature of this volume is the inclusion of fax cover sheets.

Among the various stationery items, notice that letterheads and fax cover sheets are quite the contrary of each other in their original objectives and the contents they are supposed to carry. From a design point of view, the former often carries very distinctly higher "production values" than does its cousin, the fax cover sheet. We can easily imagine, however, that these rather utilitarian, monochrome designs will blossom in the future, somewhat the way letterhead design has over the past couple of decades. The importance of the fax cover sheet as a front line of visual communication is being recognized even now, and a revolution is already underway. Keeping these points in mind, we hope you will enjoy our "Fax headers" feature. Fax cover sheet design is generally in monochrome, and we selected designs with relatively simple formats but which were, nevertheless, during in some way. This feature is probably the first of a kind, and we hope will serve to invigorate the development of new possibilities in business stationery.

Another point to be noted is that, with advances in state of the art printing technology, we are seeing numerous new types of stationery items that use spectacular special effects. To list a few that are shown here, you will see thermography, foil stamping, embossing, metallic inks, rubber stamps, varnishing and engraving. In happy collaboration with all this technology is the paper itself, and the choice of paper stock continues to be the foundation of any stationery system. The items shown in this book employ all manner of media, including screen tints, paper with printing covering the entire back surface and design effects such as tone gradation. We are also seeing various types and textures of paper such as traditional rice paper, tracing paper and paper with different colors on front and back. We have done our best to bring you the actual texture of these tactile treats by sparing nothing in our reproduction techniques.

The best identities are always based upon the clients' actual business activities. In this volume, the works are grouped according to the type of business the client is engaged in, and this information is clearly indicated for each item.

The most crucial point in any design for business stationery is its serviceability: is it functional and, at the same time, does it faithfully reflect the visual identity of the client? Just as in the expression of individual personalities, the heart of the matter is how well the design can facilitate communication of a specific, individual message within the scheme of an overall, coordinated framework.

Finally, it is our hope for this volume, that it will help our readers better appreciate the beauty of functionality while enjoying the artistic verve of the stationery graphics contained here.

P·I·E BOOKS Editorial Department

Vorwort

Heute ist fast jedem die Bedeutung einer starken visuellen Identität im öffentlichen Bewußtsein bekannt und Logos, Warenzeichen, Firmenfarben und dergleichen sind die wichtigsten Werkzeuge in diesem Unterfangen im Einklang mit konventionellem Ansatz um dieses Marktziel zu etablieren. Geschäftsdrucksachen wie Briefbogen, Umschläge und Visitenkarten bilden ein System von kommunikativen Medien, das die Schlüsselposition bei der Einrichtung einer Corporate Identity besetzt. Und weil Geschäftsdrucksachen graphische Elemente inkorporieren haben sie das Potential, das Image des Senders direkt und unmittelbar zum Empfänger zu transportieren.

Es gibt mittlerweile eine wunderbare Vielfalt im Bereich Geschäftsdrucksachen. Denken Sie einmal an den Briefbogen, der nach wie vor der Schwerpunkt von Geschäftsdrucksachen ist. DinA 4 ist mittlerweile das gebräuchlichste Format. Dieser internationale Standard zeigt sich bei unterschiedlichsten Anwendungen als sehr effektiv inklusive in der Anwendung aller Formen von Computern, Ablage, Korrespondenz usw. Der Briefbogen existiert um eine Nachricht zu transportieren und inkorporiert bereits den Prozess des Beschreibens, Faltens und Einkouvertierens. In anderen Worten ist der Briefbogen ein Nichts bevor er verwendet wird und wenn er seine Zeit gekommen ist, mehr als die Summe der Teile. Die einzigartige Eigenschaft des Briefbogens ist daher, im visuellen Kontext, daß er kein endgültiges Produkt ist: wer ihn verwendet, fügt die letzten Feinheiten hinzu. Daher kann der Designer nicht außer Acht lassen, wie die Nachricht präsentiert werden wird - das Format und der Schriftstil, mit dem die Seite dann tatsächlich beschrieben wird, die Papiersorte, die die Funktion des Briefes optimieren soll usw. Natürlich ist auch zu beachten, wie die Koordination mit dem Umschlag und anderen Bestandteilen der Geschäftsausstattung vorsich geht.

Einer der Gründe, warum wir uns mit BUSINESS STATIONARY GRAPHICS 2 zur Fortsetzung des erfolgreichen ersten Bandes entschlossen haben ist, daß sich seit der Veröffentlichung des ersten Bandes sowohl der soziale Hintergrund und die Geschäftswelt massiv verändert haben, und wir beobachten konnten, daß die Geschäftsdrucksachen in gleichem Maße verändert und oftmals erneuert wurden. Band 2 reflektiert außerdem eine Auswahl von Designs, die mit insgesamt 17 Herkunftsländern wesentlich breiter angelegt ist. Wir sind sicher, daß sich diese internationalen Arbeiten dazu eignen, Sie zu motivieren, zu erfreuen und zu inspirieren. Sicherlich werden Sie die jenen Nuancen in nationalem Charakter, kulturellen Einflüssen und Designströmungen zu schätzen wissen. Eine weitere Besonderheit ist die Berücksichtigung von Telefax-Deckblättern.

Unter den verschiedenen Bestandteilen der Geschäftsdrucksachen sind Briefbogen und Telefax-Deckblatt sicherlich - unter Berücksichtigung - von Form und Inhalt - das Paar mit den größten Gestaltlichkeiten. Unter Designgesichtspunkten ist der Briefbogen sicherlich oft mit dem größten Produktionsunrwert ausgestaltet, als das Fax-Deckblatt. Aber wir können uns gut vorstellen, daß diese zweckorientierten, einfarbigen Designs sich in Zukunft ebenso entwickeln werden wie Briefbogen in den letzten Jahrzehnten. Die Bedeutung das Fax-Deckblattes als vorderste Linie der Kommunikation wird eigentlich gerade jetzt erst entdeckt, und das hat die Designs schon revolutioniert. Unter diesen Gesichtspunkten hoffen wir, daß die Sektion "Telefax-Deckblätter" Sie sowohl anregen als auch informieren wird. Telefax-Deckblätter sind bisher generell einfarbig und wir haben relative einfache Formate ausgewählt, die vom Design her jedoch recht kühn sind. Diese Sektion ist wahrscheinlich die erste ihrer Art, und wir hoffen, daß sie Ihnen hilft, neue Bereiche in der Gestaltung von Geschäftsgpapieren zu entdecken.

Eine weitere Besonderheit ist, daß wir den Fortschritten in der Drucktechnik Rechnung zu tragen hatten, und wir stellen zahlreiche Geschäftsdrucksachen mit speziellen Effekten vor. Um nur einige Techniken zu nennen: Thermographie, Folienprägung, Prägung, Metallic-Druckfarben, Flexdruck, Lackierung und Stahl (Kupfer) - Stich. In erfreulicher Zusammenarbeit mit diesen Techniken finden sich die verwendeten Papiere, und die Papierwahl wird immer stärker zum ausschlaggebenden Kriterium bei Geschäftspapieren. Die vorgestellten Objekte zeigen eine große Vielfalt u.a. Siebdruck, rückseitig vollflächig bedruckte Papier - oder Farbverläufe. Wir sehen auch verschiedenste Arten von Texturen von Papier von traditionellen Sorten aus Reisstroh zu Zeichenpapier und Papieren mit unterschiedlich gefärbten Vorder - und Rückseiten. Wir haben versucht, diese Effekte und faktilen Eigenschaften mit der besten Reproduktionstechnik sichtbar und nachvollziehbar zu machen.

Die erfolgreichsten Firmenidentitäten basieren in der Regel immer auf den tatsächlichen Geschäftsaktivitäten des Kunden. In diesem Band sind die Arbeiten nach Geschäftsbereichen gegliedert und jedes objekt ist mit der entsprechenden Information versehen. Der ausschlaggebende Punkt bei jedem Design von Geschäftsdrucksachen ist die Benutzbarkeit, ist sie funktional und - gleich - zeitig - reflektiert sie die visuelle Identität des Auftraggebers? Ebenso wie der individuelle, persönliche Ausdruck, ist der Kernpunkt, wie das Design die Kommunikation einer spezifischen individuellen Nachricht in einem allgegenwärtigen, koordinierten Rahmen unterstützt. Abschließend ist es unsere Hoffnung für diesen Band, daß er den Lesern hilft, die Schönheit der Funktionalität zu erkennen und gleichzeitig die künstlerische Verve der vorgestellten Geschäftsdrucksachen zu genießen.

Die Herausgeber von P·I·E BOOKS

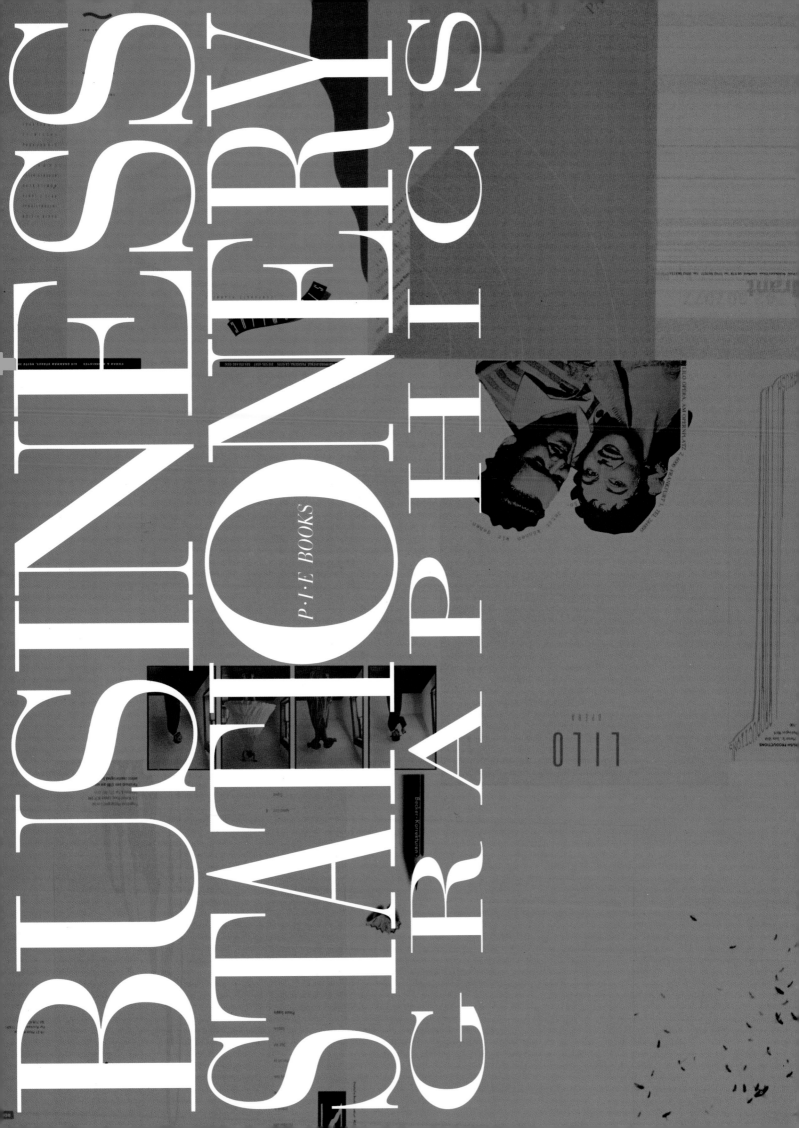

BUSINESS STATIONERY GRAPHICS

P·I·E BOOKS

THE DESIGNERS REPUBLIC   Graphic Design and Art Direction   グラフィックデザイン, アートディレクション   UK 1991

AD, D: The Designers Republic   D: Mark Ross / Peter Ward   DF: The Designers Republic

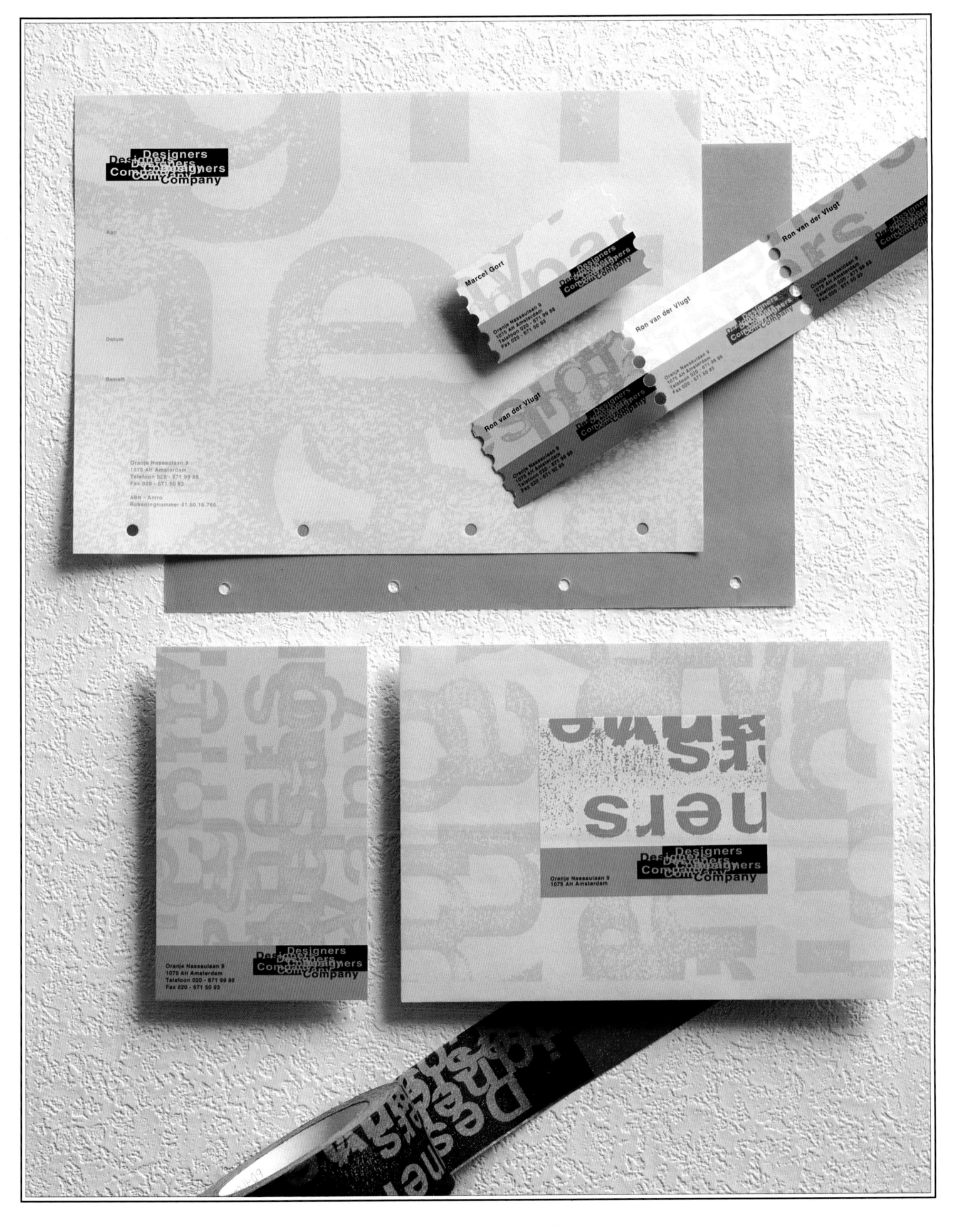

DESIGNERS COMPANY Graphic Design グラフィックデザイン THE NETHERLANDS 1993 AD, D: Marcel Gort DF: Designers Company

I COMME IMAGE   Graphic Design   グラフィックデザイン   FRANCE 1990   AD, D: Jsan Jacques Tachdjian   DF: I Comme Image

facsimile sheet

to   date

from

Phone. 06 532 7280 Facs. 06 532 7285
701. 1-6-20, KITAHORIE, NISHI-KU, OSAKA 550 JAPAN.

of pages   ing this page

KINEMA MOON
Evo. DESIGNING

KINEMA MOON
Evo.
DESIGNING
1993

中川勇一
Art Director
Yuichi NAKAGAWA

KINEMA MOON
Evo. DESIGNING

Advertising
Planning
Direction
All Printing Media

KINEMA MOON DESIGNING Graphic Design グラフィックデザイン JAPAN 1993 AD: Yuichi Nakagawa D: Sachiko Kitani DF: Kinema Moon Designing

MIKE SALISBURY COMMUNICATIONS Graphic Design グラフィックデザイン USA 1993 AD: Mike Salisbury D, I: Regina Grosveld DF: Mike Salisbury Communications

ESQUISSE INC. Goods Design グッズデザイン JAPAN AD, D: Tatsuomi Majima ARTIST: Bob Zoell DF: Majima Design

RENO DESIGN GROUP Graphic Design and Consultancy グラフィックデザイン、コンサルタント AUSTRALIA 1990 AD, D: Graham Rendoth CW: Reno Design Group DF: Reno Design Group

REMY PAGART Architecture and Interior Design 建築設計、インテリアデザイン FRANCE 1992 AD, D: Jean Jacques Tachdjian DF: I Comme Image

CHARLES S. ANDERSON DESIGN COMPANY Graphic Design グラフィックデザイン USA 1991 AD, D: Todd Hauswirth DF: Charles S. Anderson Design

MELIA DESIGN GROUP　Graphic Design　グラフィックデザイン　USA　1990　AD, D: P. Michael Melia　D: Mark Skingcuber / Jordan Louie　DF: Melia Design Group
Special Effects: Trademark and margin have been embossed.　マークと中の枠が型押しされている。

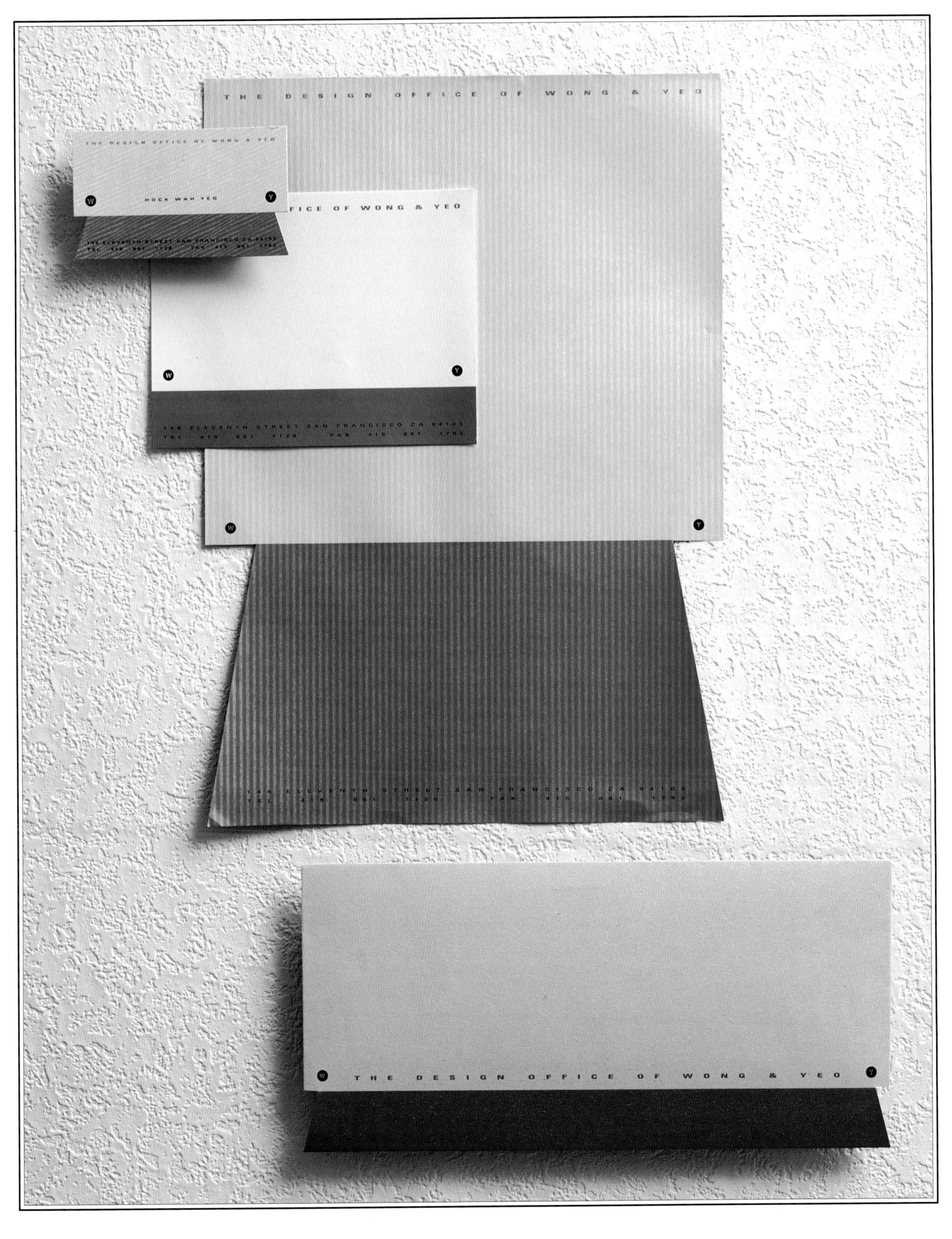

THE DESIGN OFFICE OF WONG & YEO Graphic Design グラフィックデザイン USA 1993 AD, D: Hock Wah Yeo D: Cary Chiao DF: The Design Office of Wong & Yeo
Special Effects: Striped metallic paper has been used. ストライプの入ったメタリック紙を使用。

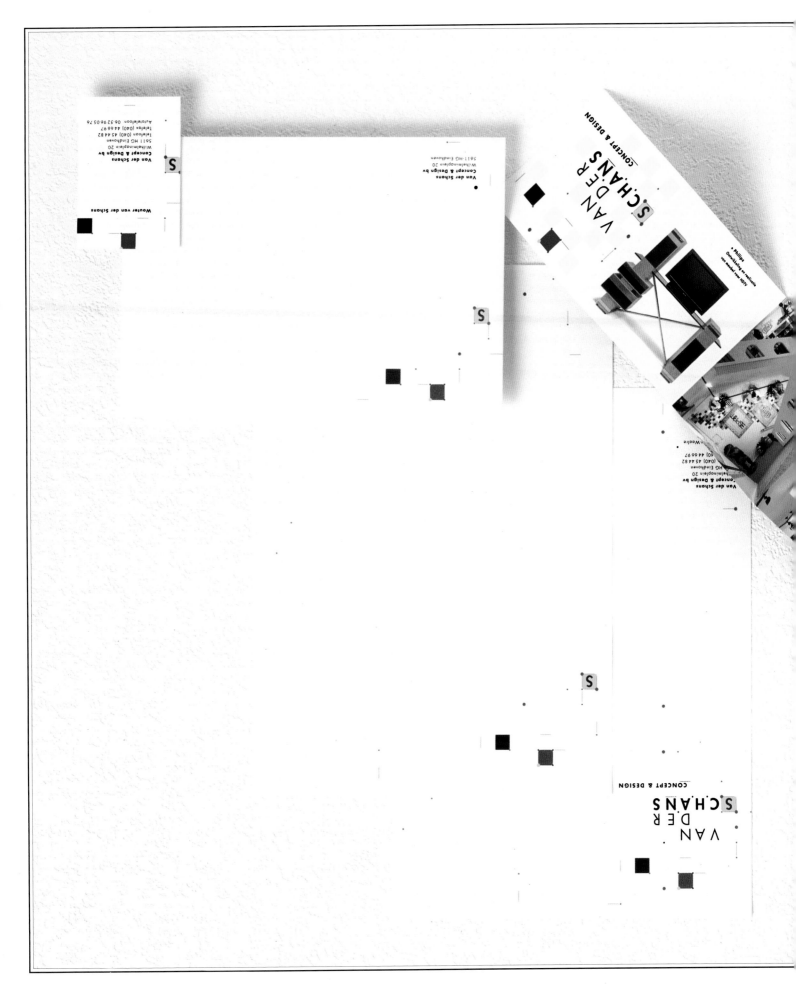

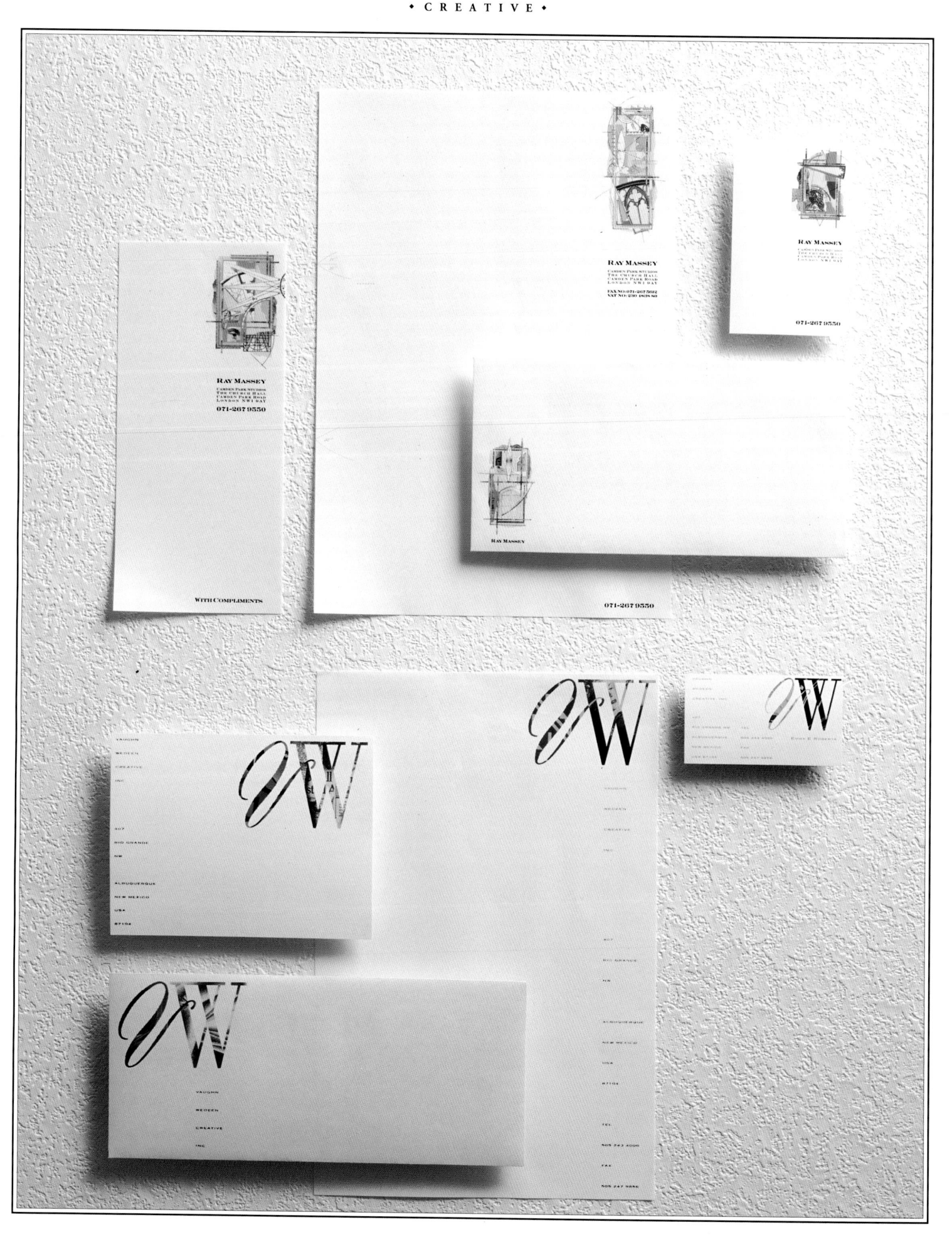

RAY MASSEY PHOTOGRAPHY   Photography   写真   UK 1991   AD, D: David Tyrell   I: David Loftus   DF: David Tyrell

VAUGHN WEDEEN CREATIVE   Graphic Design   グラフィックデザイン   USA 1991   A, D: Rick Vaughn / Steve Wedeen   DF: Vaughn Wedeen Creative

DAVID LOFTUS ILLUSTRATION llustration イラストレーション UK. 1993 D, I: David Loftus

GULLIVER CO., LTD. Printing ガリバーティッシュ JAPAN 1992 CD: Seiji Koseki AD: Tatsuomi Majima D: 1, Yukio Ikoma / 2, Masami Shimizu

GULLIVER CO., LTD. Printing フリップフロップ JAPAN 1992 CD: Seiji Koseki AD: Tatsuomi Majima D: 1. Yoshiro Kajitani / 2. Shin Matsunaga

EYE STUDIO   Photography / Design   写真 / デザイン   HONG KONG 1992 AD, D: Ching Lai Shan   P: Kam Ming, Ng   DF: Eye Studio

MARZENA Photographer's Representation　写真家の代理・演出　USA 1992　CD: Robert Bergman-Unger　D: Liong The

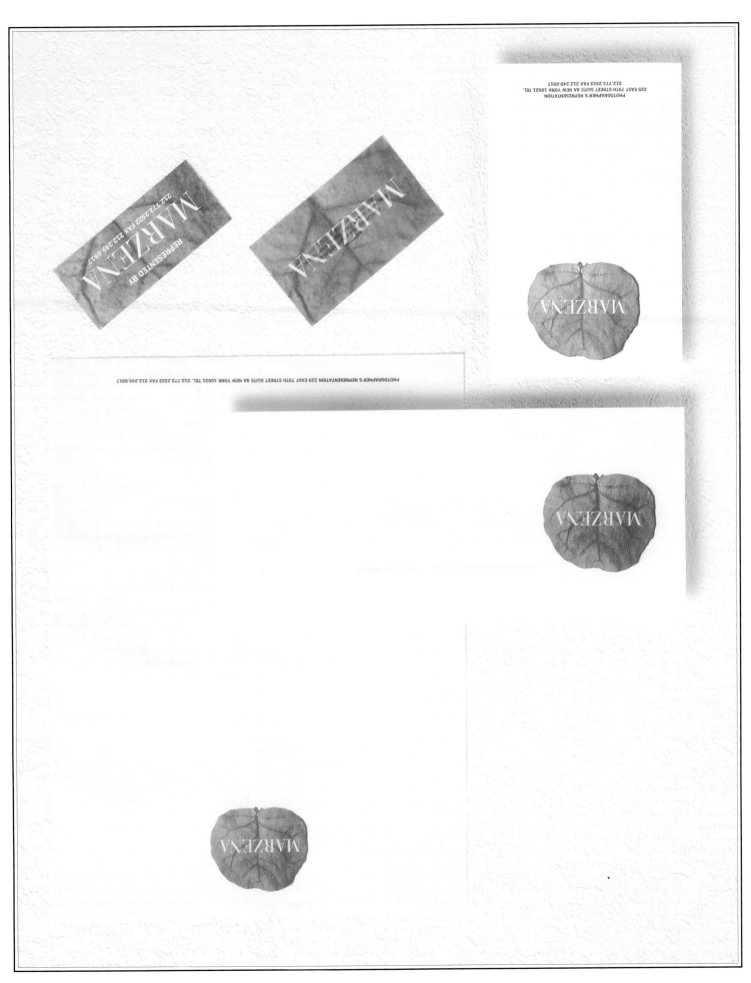

CESAR RUBIO PHOTOGRAPHY Photographic Studio 写真スタジオ USA 1992 D: Raul Cabra P: Cesar Rubio DF: Cabra Diseño

PENDULUM DESIGN Graphic Communication グラフィックデザイン AUSTRALIA 1993 AD: John Sellitto D: David Blyth P: Tim Scott

ART KANE Photographer 写真家 USA 1991 AD, P: Art Kane AD, D: Miho DF: Miho

RYOICHI SAITO Photographer 写真家 JAPAN AD, D: Tatsuomi Majima P: Ryoichi Saito DF: Majima Design

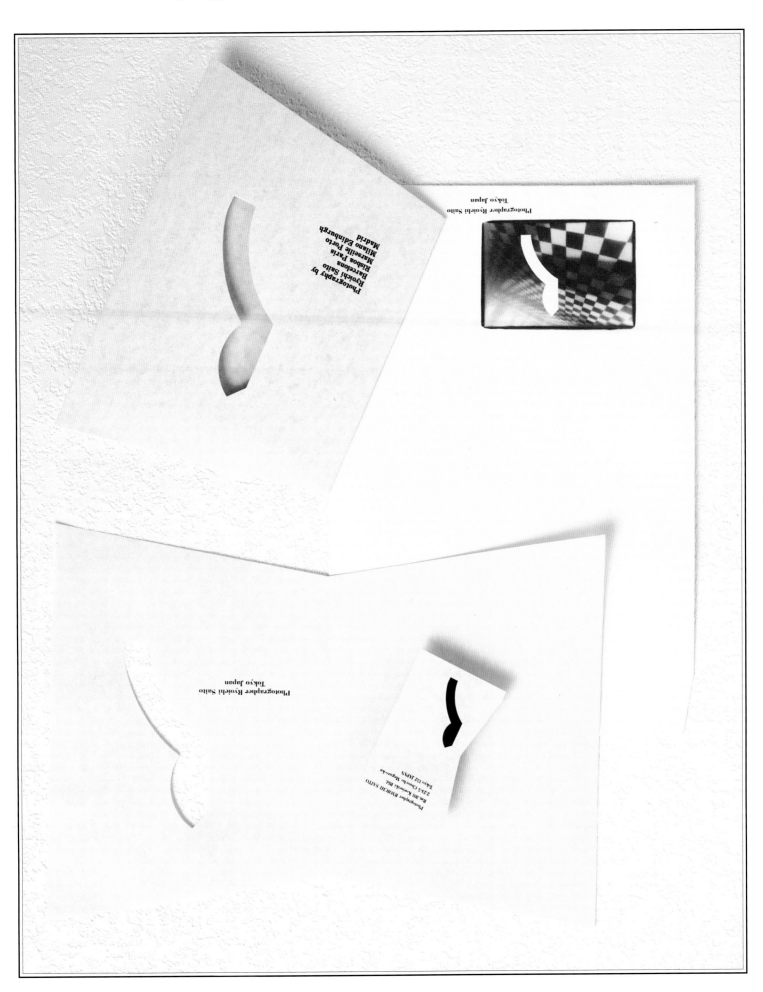

SHIN SUGINO PHOTOGRAPHY　Photographer　写真家　CANADA 1991　AD, D: Del Terrelonge　P: Shin Sugino　DF: Terrelonge Design

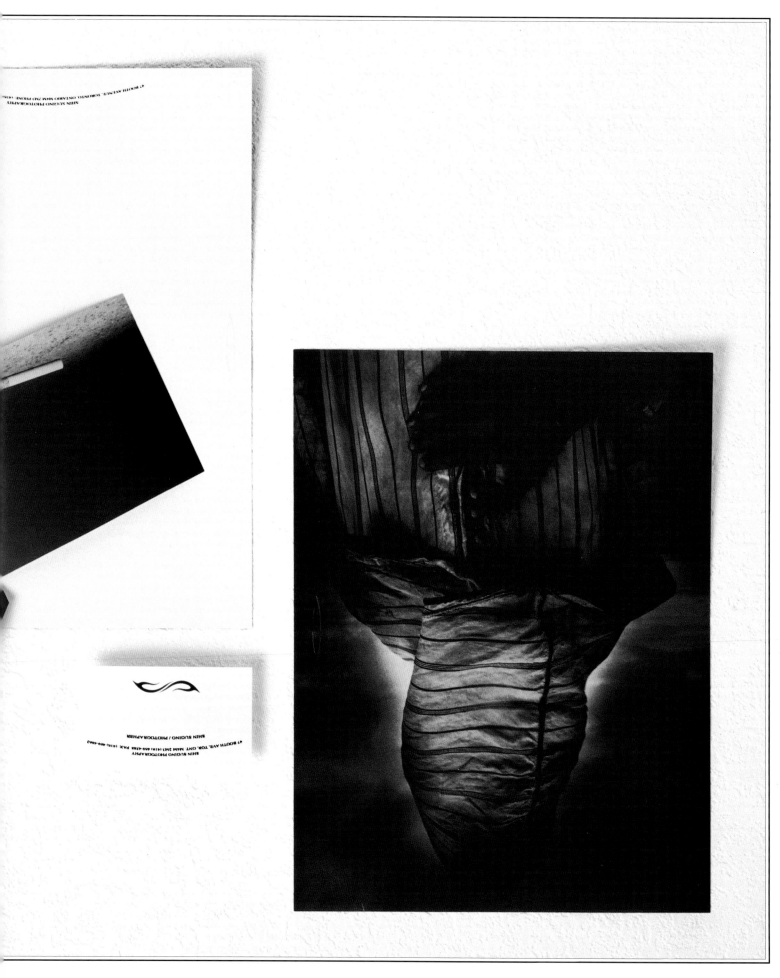

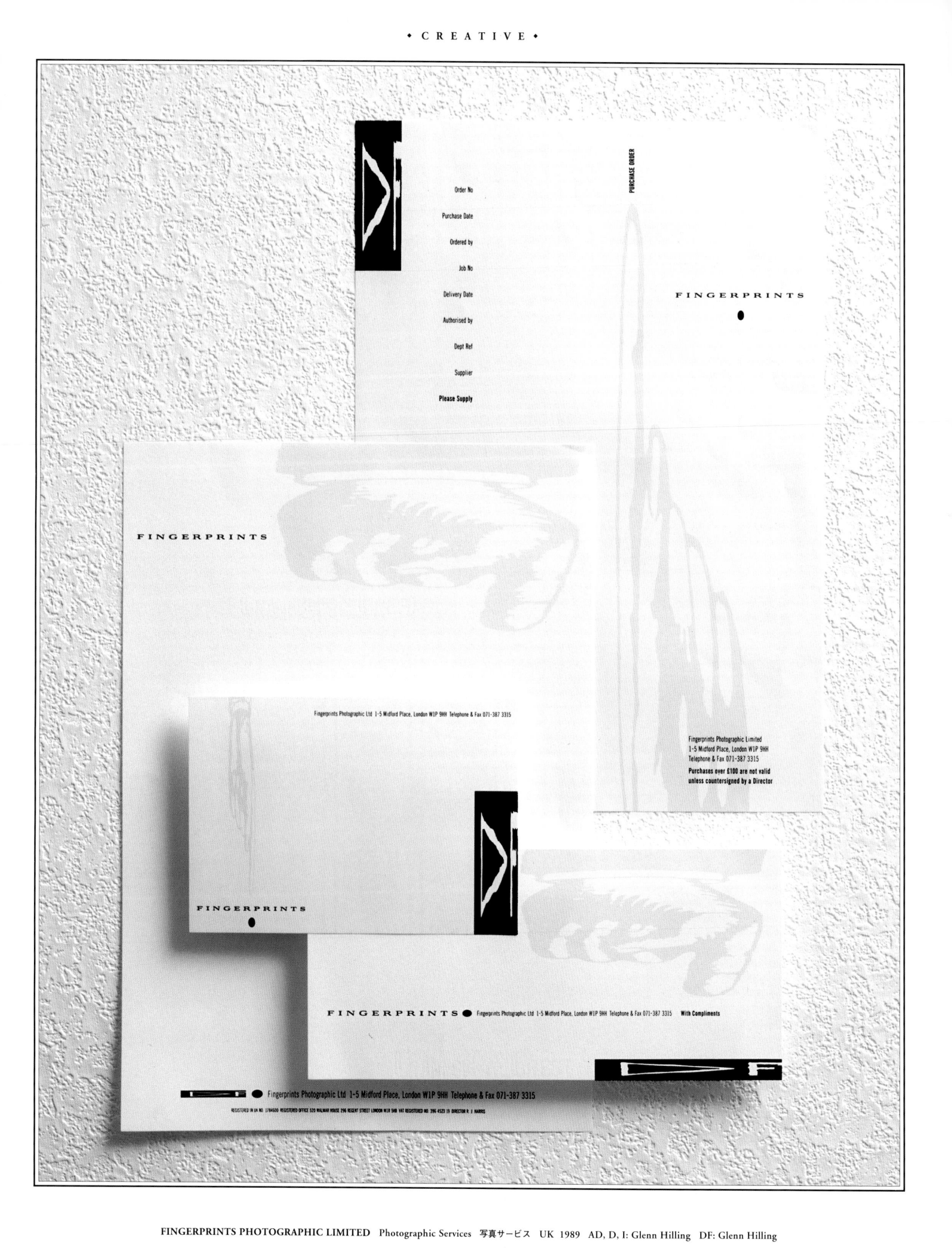

FINGERPRINTS PHOTOGRAPHIC LIMITED   Photographic Services   写真サービス   UK 1989   AD, D, I: Glenn Hilling   DF: Glenn Hilling

CALLAHAN & COMPANY　写真サービス　USA 1987　AD, D, P: Dianne Yanovick　DF: Yanovick & Associates

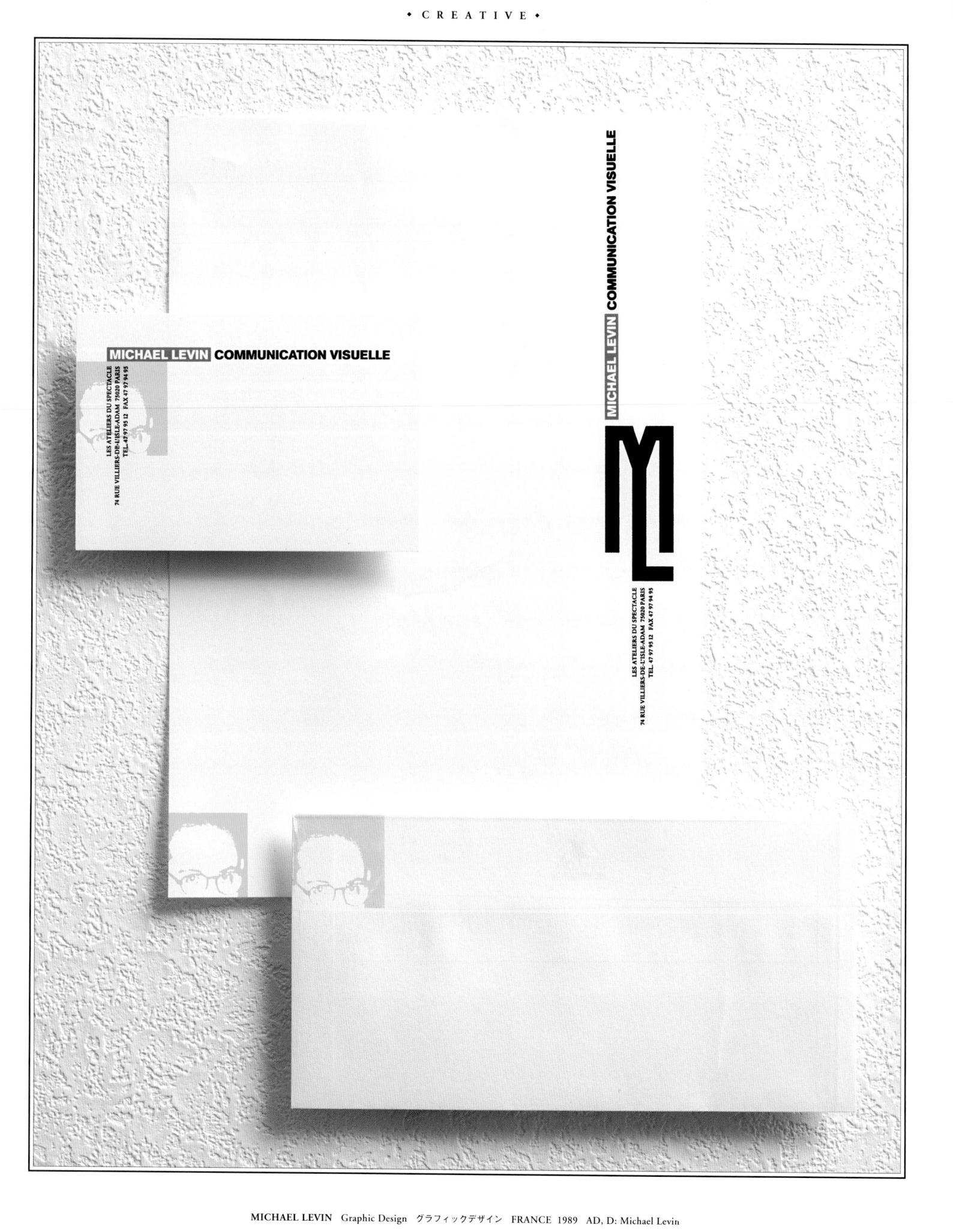

MICHAEL LEVIN   Graphic Design   グラフィックデザイン   FRANCE 1989   AD, D: Michael Levin

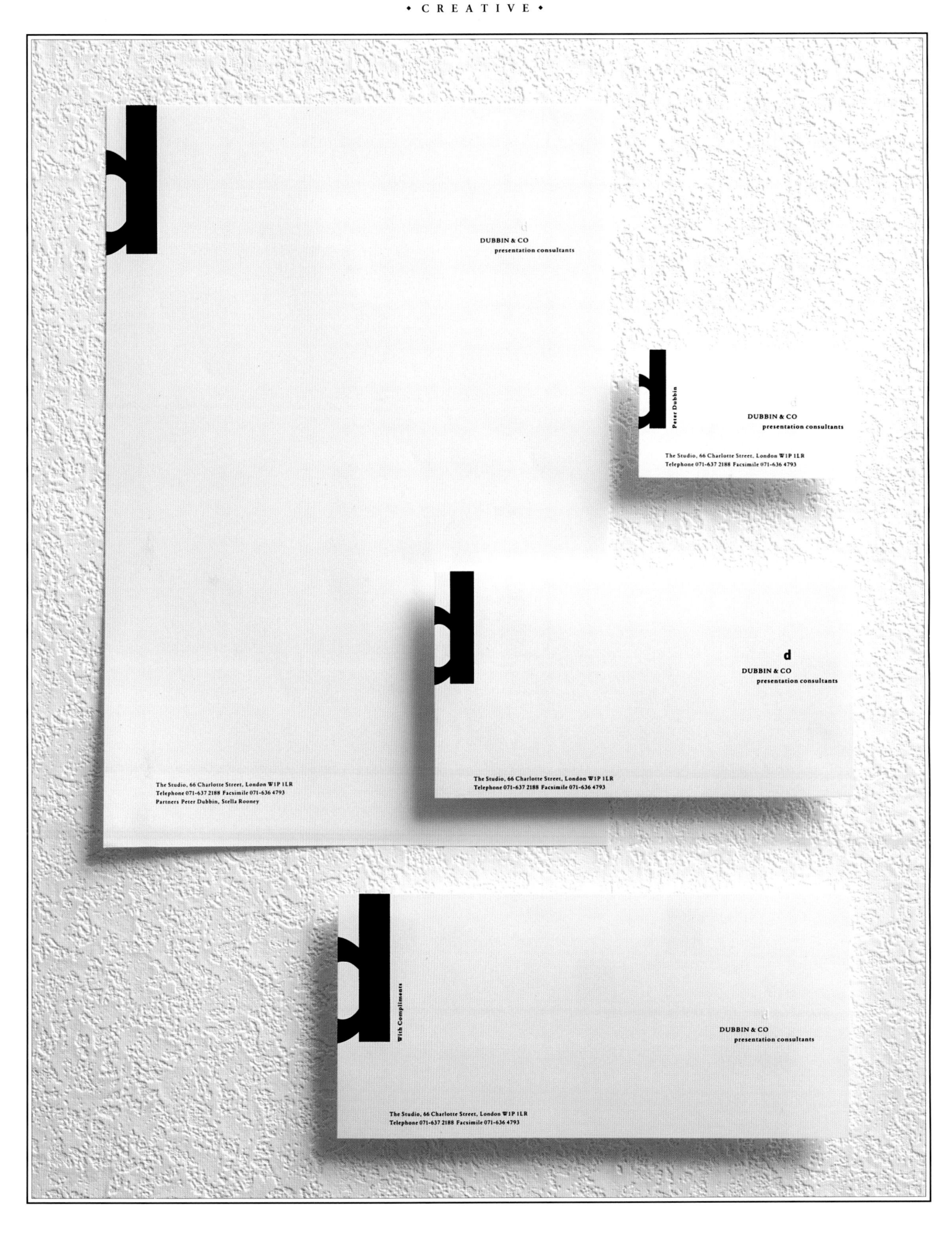

DUBBIN & CO PRESENTATION CONSULTANTS Presentational Graphics プレゼンテーション・グラフィックデザイン UK 1991 AD, D, I, CW: Glenn Hilling DF: Glenn Hilling

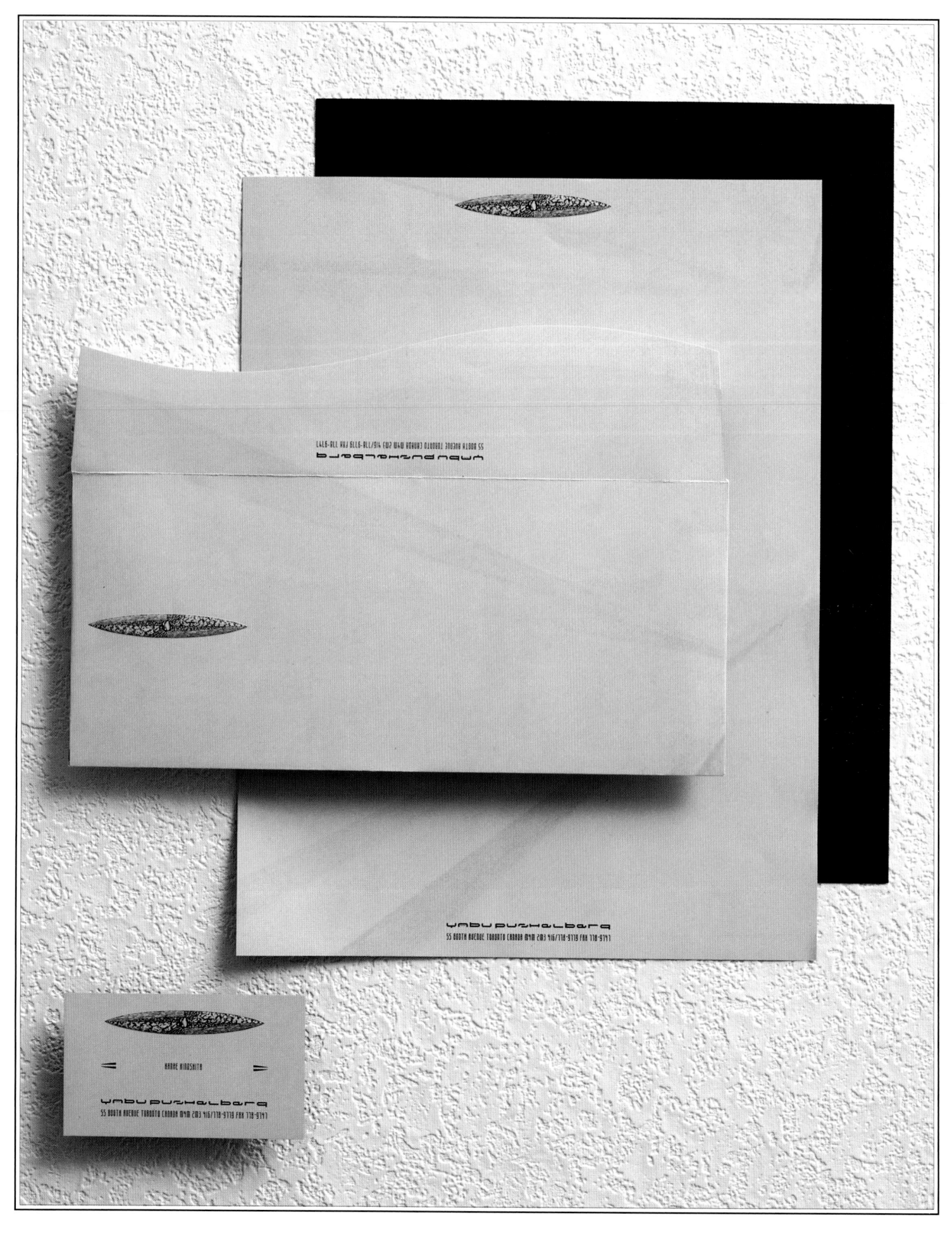

YABU PUSHELBERG Interior Design インテリアデザイン CANADA 1990 AD, D: Del Terrelonge DF: Terrelonge Design
Special Effects: Trademark has been embossed. マークが型押しされている。

ROBERT BERGMAN-UNGAR Art Direction アートディレクション USA 1993 CD: Robert Bergman-Ungar D: Liong The

H. M. BRANDSTON & PARTNERS Lighting Design 照明デザイン USA 1991 AD, D: Richard Poulin DF: Richard Poulin Design Group
Special Effects: Clear varnish has been used for the upper portion. 上部の枠内にニス状の上塗りをしてある。
RICK WAHLSTROM Photographer 写真家 USA 1986 AD, D: Jennifer Morla Special Effects: Logomark has been embossed. マークが型押しされている。

STUDIO SEIREENI Design and Advertising デザイン、広告 USA 1991 CD: Richard Seireeni AD, D: Romane Cameron P, I: Geof Kern DF: Studio Seireeni

ELLEN ROSENBERG Interior Design インテリアデザイン USA 1993 D: Jilly Simons / Cindy Chang DF: Concrete, Chicago

MARK ZINGARELLI Illustrator イラストレーター USA 1989 AD, D, P, I, CW: Art Chantry DF: Art Chantry Design

MORLA DESIGN Graphic Design グラフィックデザイン USA 1987 AD, D, CW: Jennifer Morla CW: Michelle Mitchell

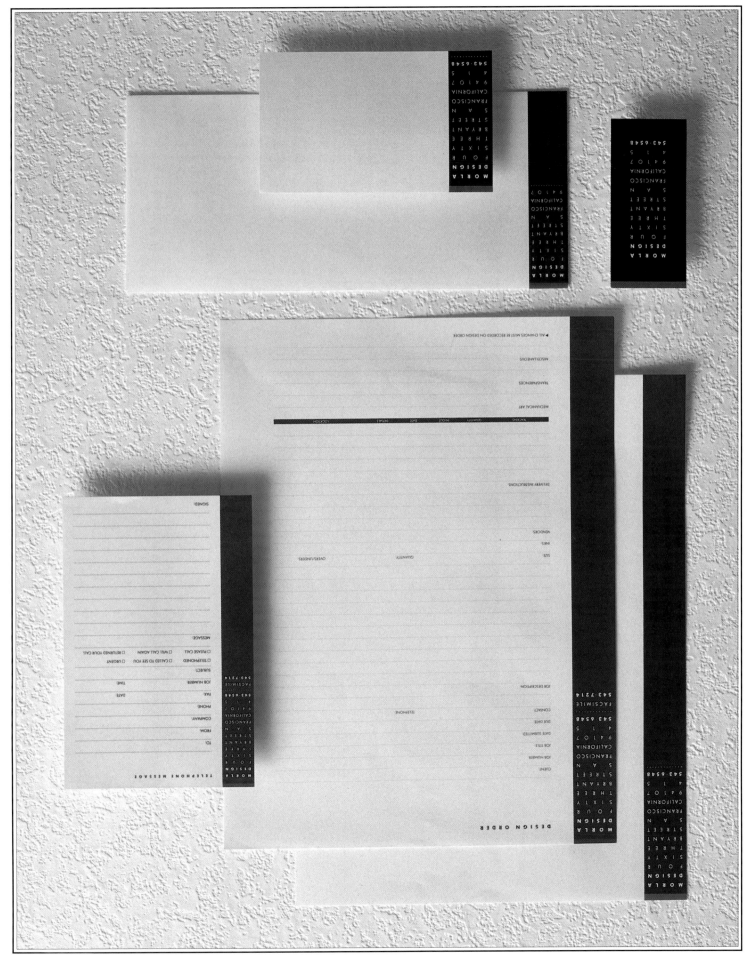

CAHAN & ASSOCIATES Graphic Design グラフィックデザイン USA 1990 AD: Bill Cahan D, I: Talin Gureghian / Stuart Flake DF: Cahan & Associates

FORSYTHE DESIGN Graphic Design グラフィックデザイン USA 1989 AD, D: Kathleen Forsythe   D: Julie Steinhilber   DF: Forsythe Design

SAGMEISTER GRAPHICS VIENNA Graphic Design グラフィックデザイン HONG KONG 1990 AD, D: Stefan Sagmeister DF: Sagmeister Graphics

7

TOM SCHIERLITZ Photographer 肖草鏊 HONG KONG 1989 AD, D: Stefan Sagmeister DF: Sagmeister Graphics

CREATIVE

FHA DESIGN　Graphic Design　グラフィックデザイン　AUSTRALIA　1993　AD, D: Richard Henderson　D: Julia Jarvis　DF: FHA Design Australia

CLIF SPARKMAN　Photographer　写真家　USA　1991　AD, D: P. Michael Melia　DF: Melia Design Group

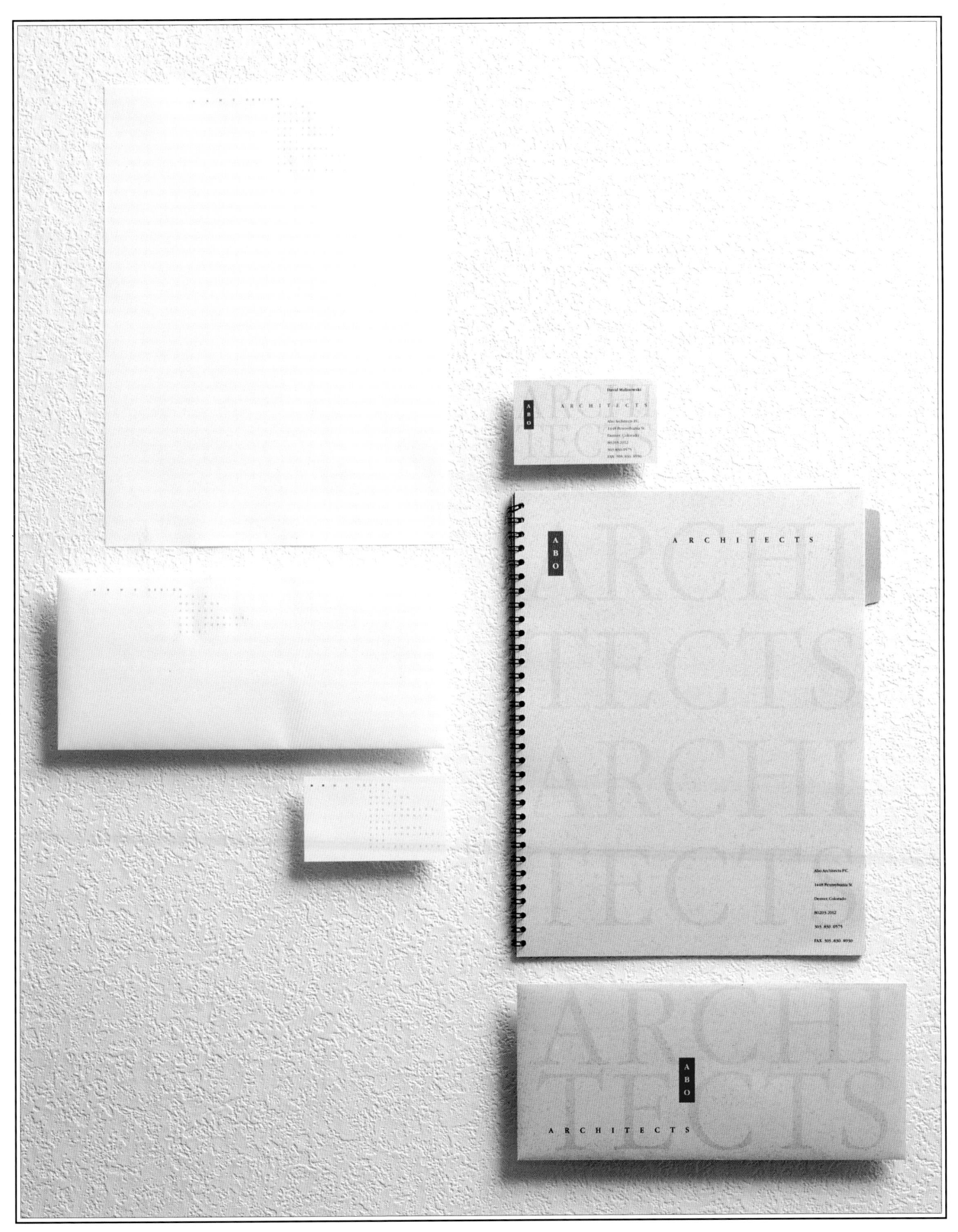

M. E. DESIGN, LOS ANGELES Design デザイン USA 1986 AD, D: Rebeca Méndez

ABO ARCHITECTS Architecture 建築設計 USA 1992 AD, D: David Warren DF: David Warren Design

NUMBER ONE DESIGN OFFICE Graphic Design グラフィックデザイン JAPAN 1991 AD,D: Kenichi Samura DF: Number One Design Office

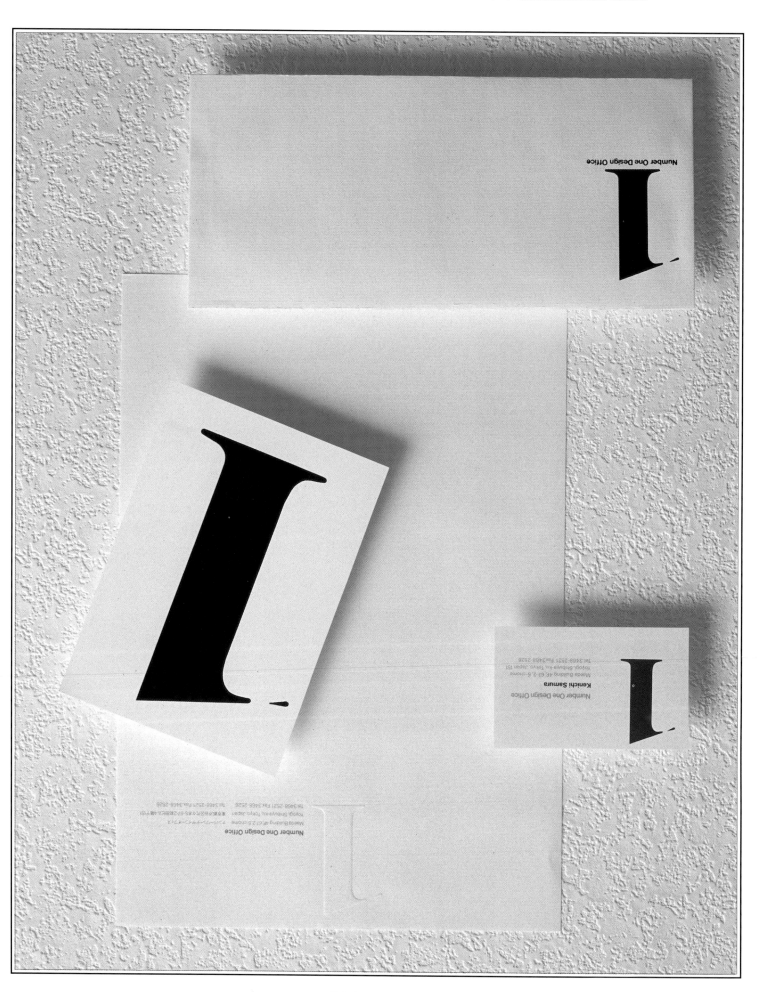

STEWART TILGER Photography 写真 USA 1991 AD, D: John Hornall D: David Bates DF: Hornall Anderson Design Works

LATCHEZAR BOYADJIEV Art Glass Design アートガラス・デザイン USA 1992 AD, D: Iva Frank DF: Iva Frank Graphic Design

REKTA REKLAM TASARIM Advertising and Design 広告、デザイン TURKEY 1991 AD: Hakan Poroy D: Goskun Türk DF: Rekta Reklam Tasarim

studio alfalfa

studio alfalfa

House 5
46 Grove End Rd
London
NW8 9NN
Telephone
071 289 5560
Facsimile
071 286 8008

Andrea Lennon
Stefano Azario

House 5
46 Grove End Rd
London
NW8 9NN
Telephone
071 289 5560
Facsimile
071 286 8008

Vat No
523 1069 81

ALFALFA Children's Fashion Photography 子供のファッション写真 UK 1990 AD, D: Teresa Roviras DF: Teresa Roviras
Special Effects: Positive film has been pasted on. ポジフィルムが貼られている。

JOE TRELEVEN   Photographic Studio   写真スタジオ   USA 1991   AD, D: Todd Nesser   DF: McCool & Company

ART DIRECTORS CLUB OF METROPOLITAN WASHINGTON   Art Direction   アートディレクション   USA 1992   AD, D: Supon Phornirunlit   P: Barry Myer   DF: Supon Design Group

LEONARD CURRIE DESIGN Typographic Design タイポグラフィック・デザイン UK 1989 D, TYPOGRAPHER: Leonard Currie DF: Leonard Currie Design

ALLYSON ANTHONY Stylist スタイリスト USA 1990 AD, D: Jennifer Morla DF: Morla Design

ZIMMERMANN CROWE DESIGN Graphic Design グラフィックデザイン USA 1991 AD, D: Neal Zimmermann / Dennis Crowe DF: Zimmermann Crowe Design

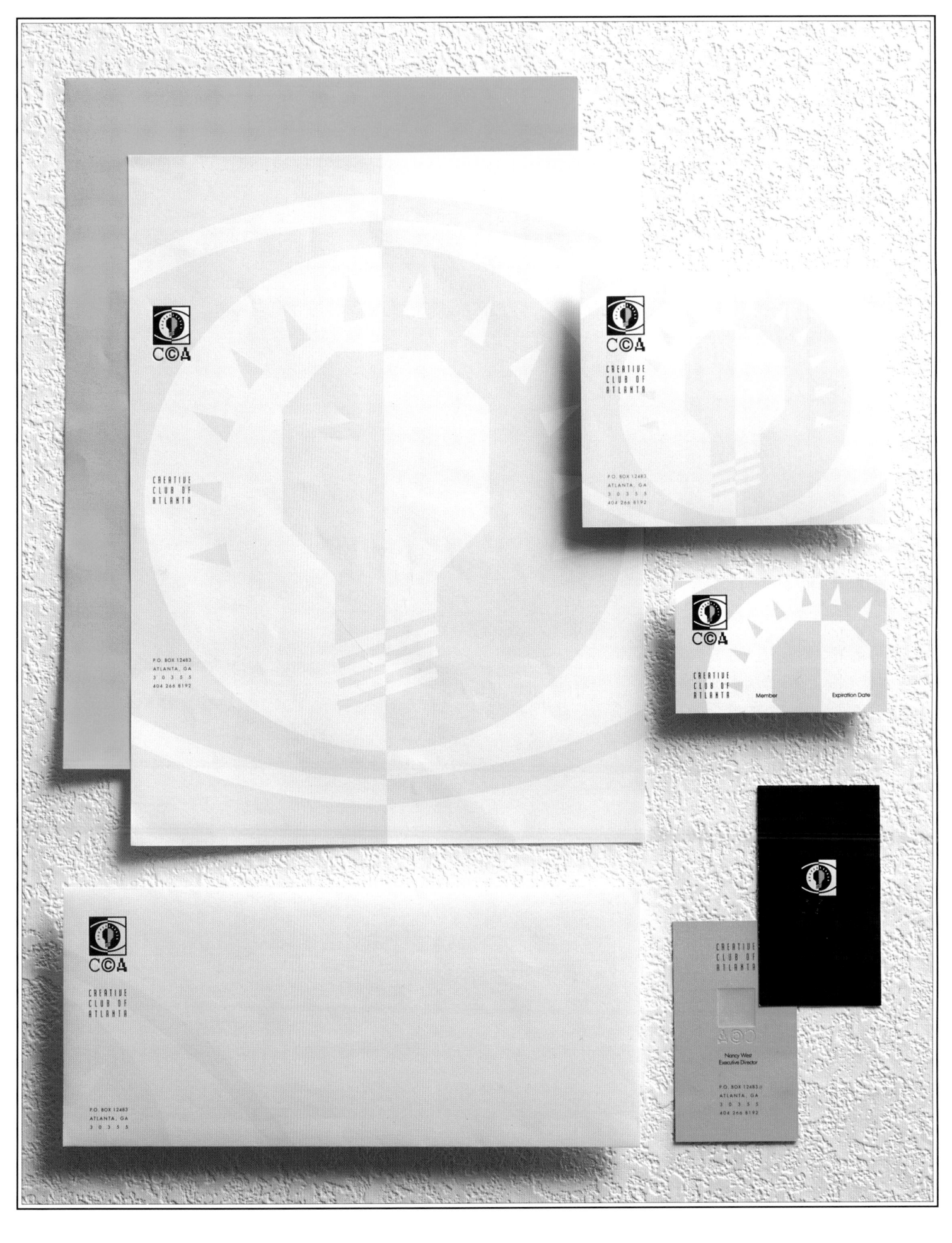

CREATIVE CLUB OF ATLANTA Advertising and Graphic Design 広告、グラフィックデザイン USA 1990 AD, D: P. Michael Melia D: Lisa Farmer DF: Melia Design Group

THE DESIGN OFFICE, INC.   Graphic Design   グラフィックデザイン   USA 1987   D: Joseph H. Feigenbaum   DF: The Design Office

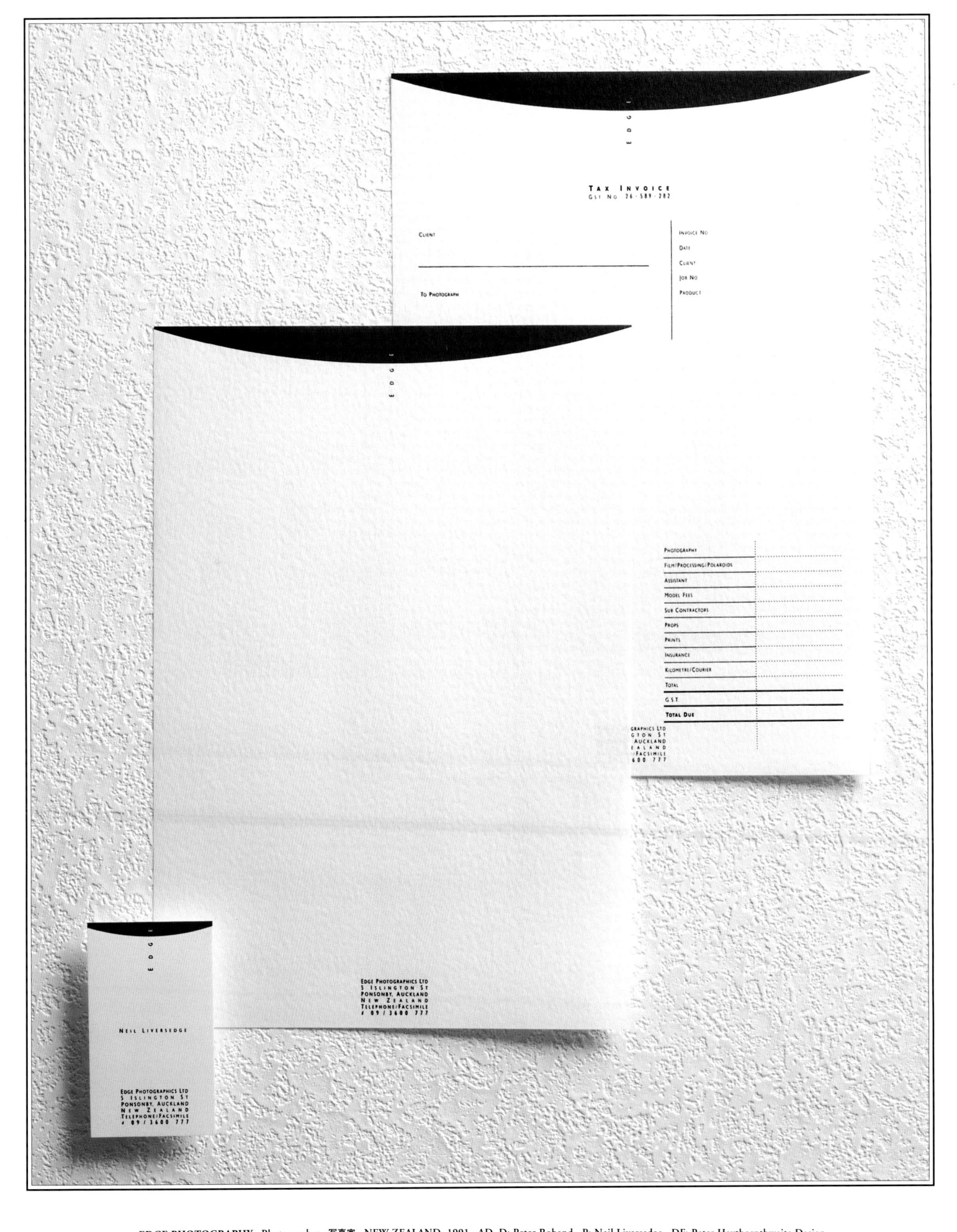

EDGE PHOTOGRAPHY Photographer 写真家 NEW ZEALAND 1991 AD, D: Peter Roband P: Neil Liversedge DF: Peter Haythornthwaite Design

ANDY IP   Design   デザイン   CANADA   D, I: Andy Ip
LINDSTROM PHOTOGRAPHY   Commercial Photography   商業写真   USA   D, I: Lauren Smith   DF: Lauren Smith Design

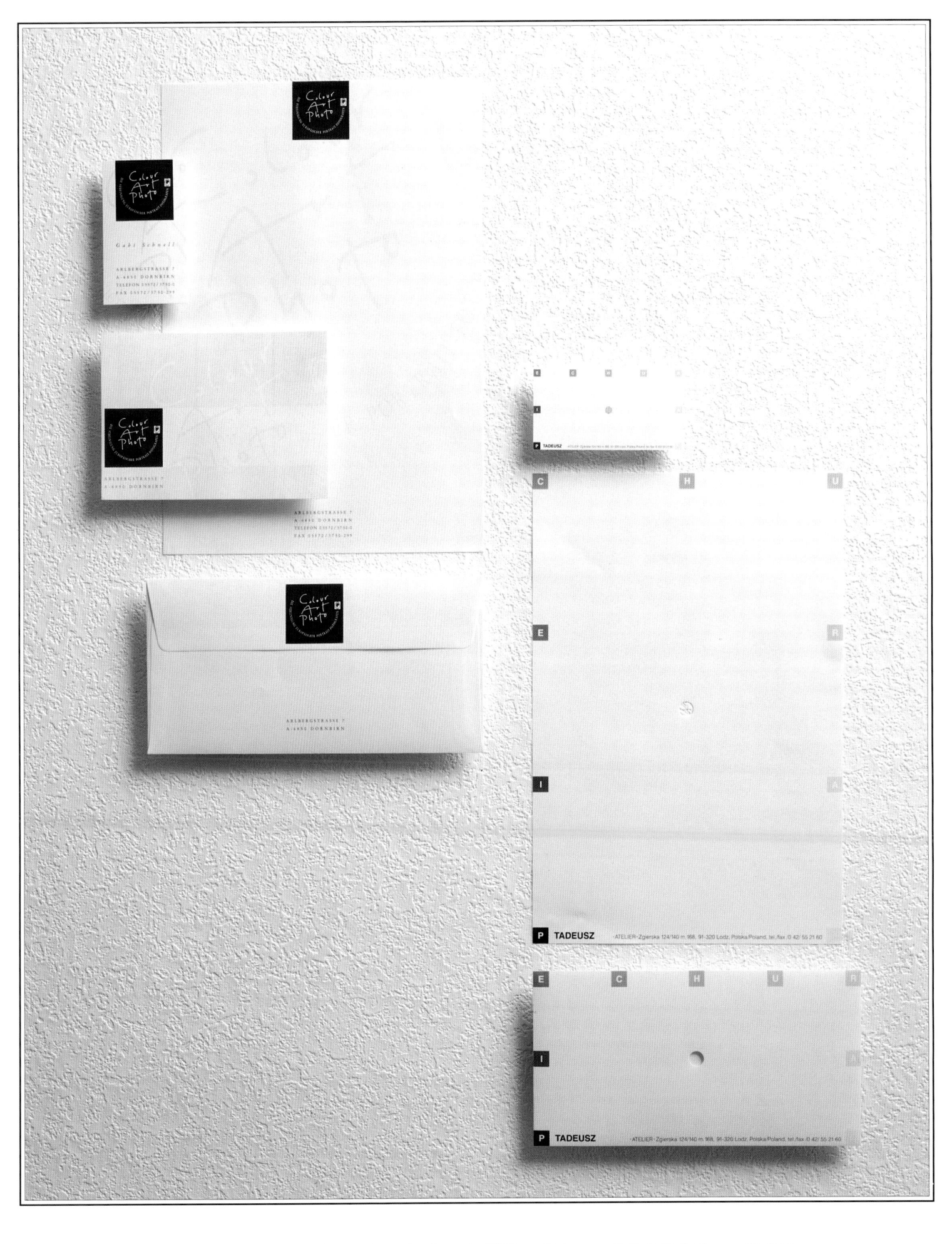

KODAK PHOTO SERVICE Professional Portrait Photographs ポートレイト専門写真 AUSTRIA 1992 AD, D, I, CW: Sigi Ramoser DF: Sigi Ramoser

TADEUSZ PIECHURA Graphic Design グラフィックデザイン POLAND 1989 AD, D: Tadeusz Piechura DF: Aterier Tadeusz Piechura

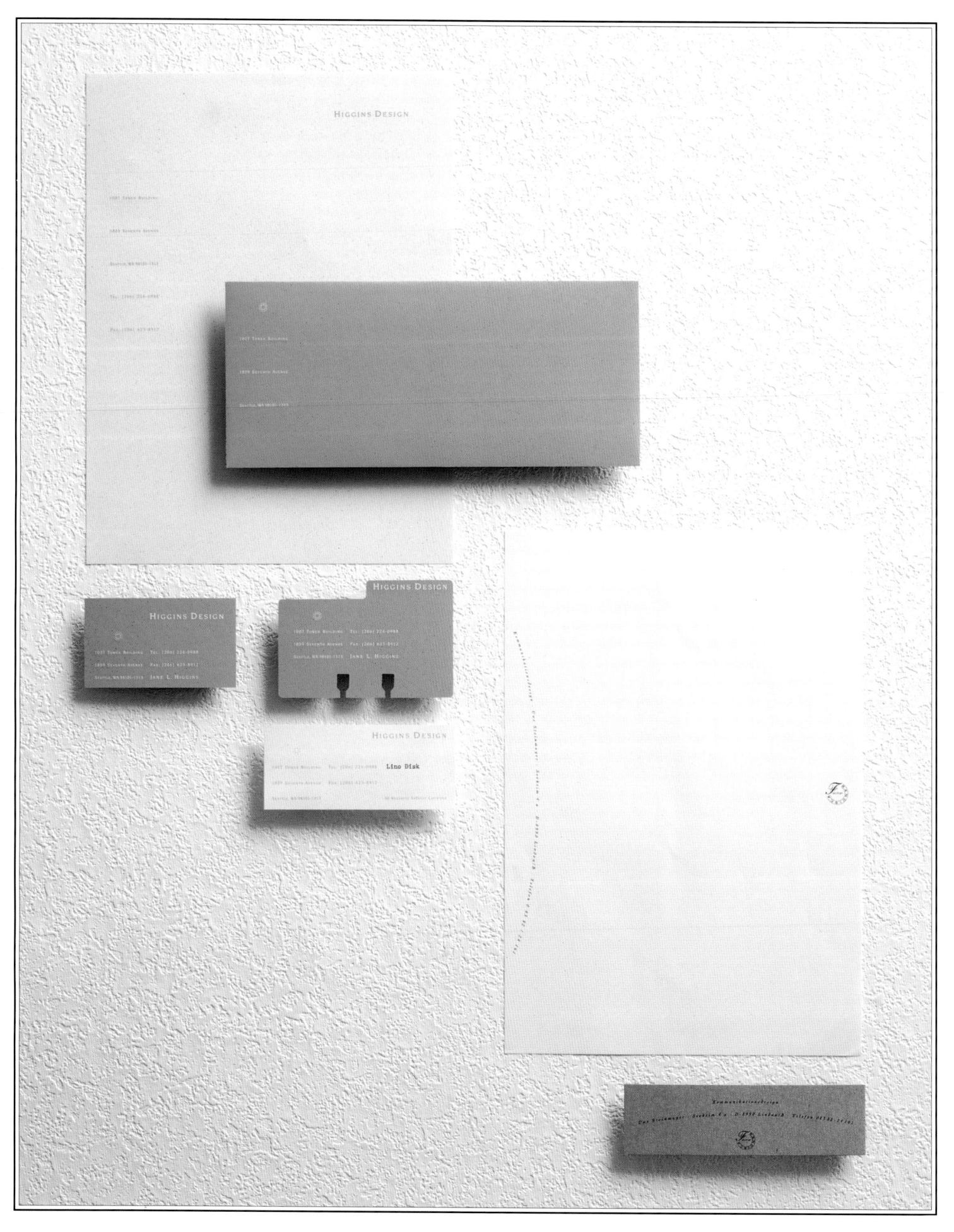

HIGGINS DESIGN Graphic Design グラフィックデザイン USA 1992 CD, D: Jane Higgins DF: Higgins Design
UWE STEINMAYER Graphic Design グラフィックデザイン GERMANY 1992 AD, D: Uwe Steinmayer

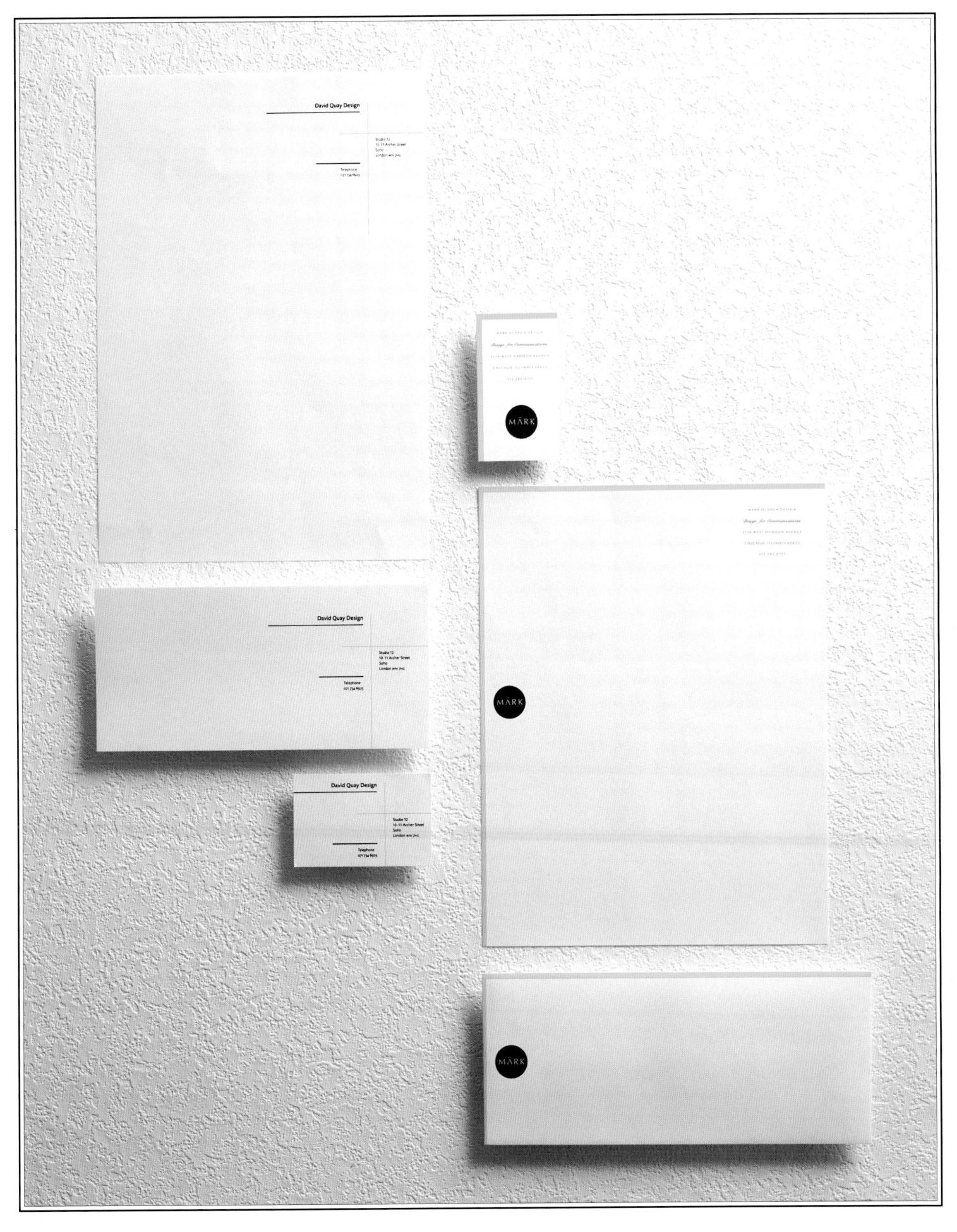

DAVID QUAY DESIGN Design デザイン UK 1991 D: David Quay DF: David Quay Design

MARK OLDACH DESIGN Graphic Design グラフィックデザイン USA 1990 AD, D: Mark Oldach DF: Mark Oldach Design

LIMAGE DANGEREUSE BV Graphic Design グラフィックデザイン THE NETHERLANDS 1991

CD: Arie V Baarle AD: Theo Seesing D, I: Limage Dangereuse CW: Taco Sipma DF: Limage Dangereuse

WATERS DESIGN ASSOCIATES, INC. Graphic Design グラフィックデザイン USA AD, D: John Waters D, I: Dana Gonsalves DF: Waters Design Associates

MICHAEL HAZARD ARCHITECTS   Architecture   建築設計   USA 1991   AD, D: David Warren   DF: David Warren Design

KORAKOT SRIVIKORN Textile Design テキスタイルデザイン UK 1990 AD, D: Teresa Roviras DF: Teresa Roviras

GLENN HILLING Graphic Design グラフィックデザイン UK 1989 AD, D: Glenn Hilling DF: Glenn Hilling

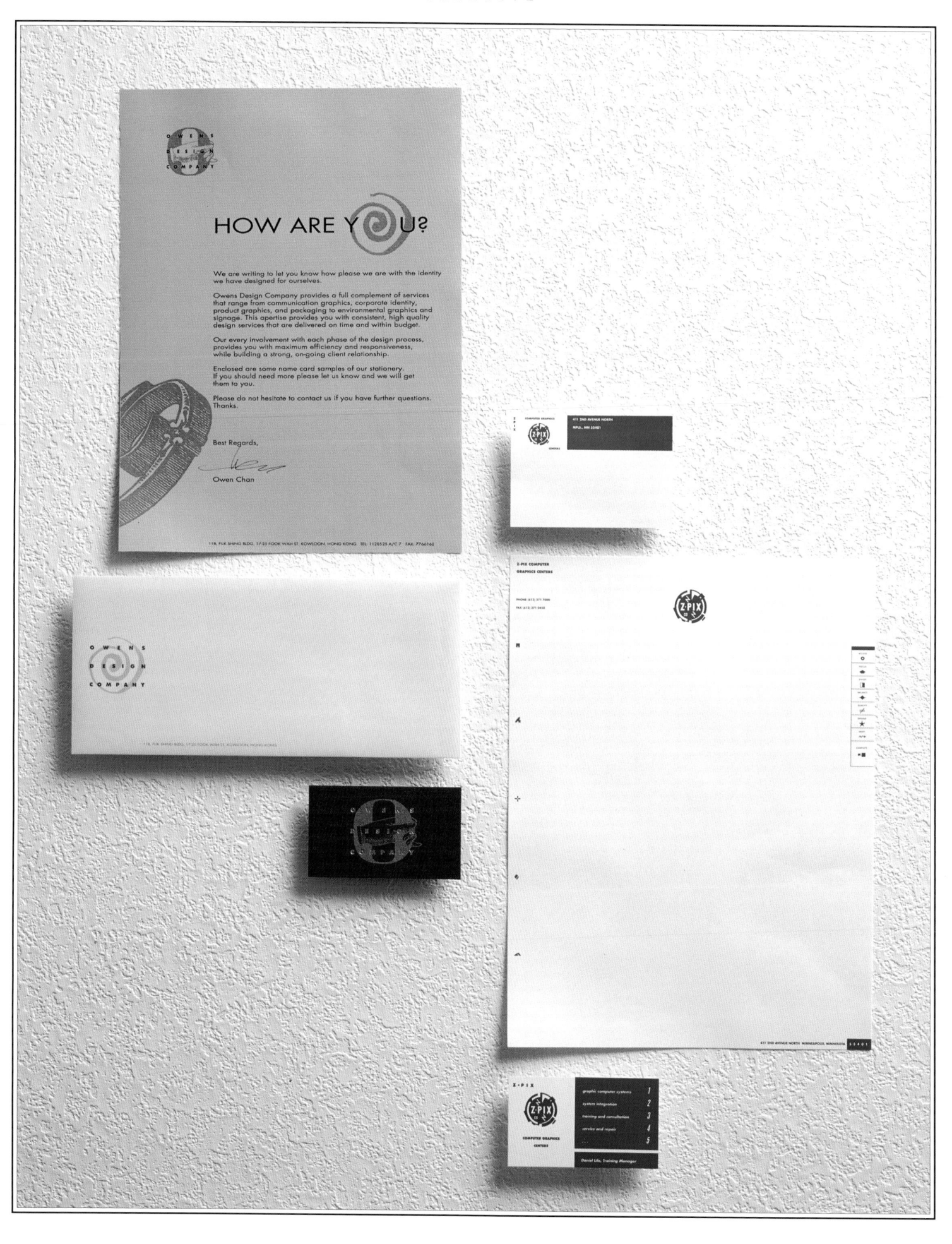

OWENS DESIGN COMPANY   Graphic Design   グラフィックデザイン   HONG KONG 1992   AD: Owen Chan   D: Frankie Chan   DF: Owens Design

Z - PIX, INC.   Computer Graphics   コンピューターグラフィックス   USA 1990   AD, D: Charles Spencer Anderson   D: Daniel Olson   DF: Charles S. Anderson Design

SOCIETY FOR ENVIRONMENTAL GRAPHIC DESIGN   Non-profit Environmental Graphic Design Organization   非営利環境グラフィックデザイン協会   USA 1993

AD, D: Clifford Stoltze   DF: Clifford Stoltze Design

PEPE ORBEIN + ASSOCIATES   Graphic Design / Signs   グラフィックデザイン / サイン   USA 1991   AD, D, I: Pepe Orbein   DF: Pepe Orbein + Associates

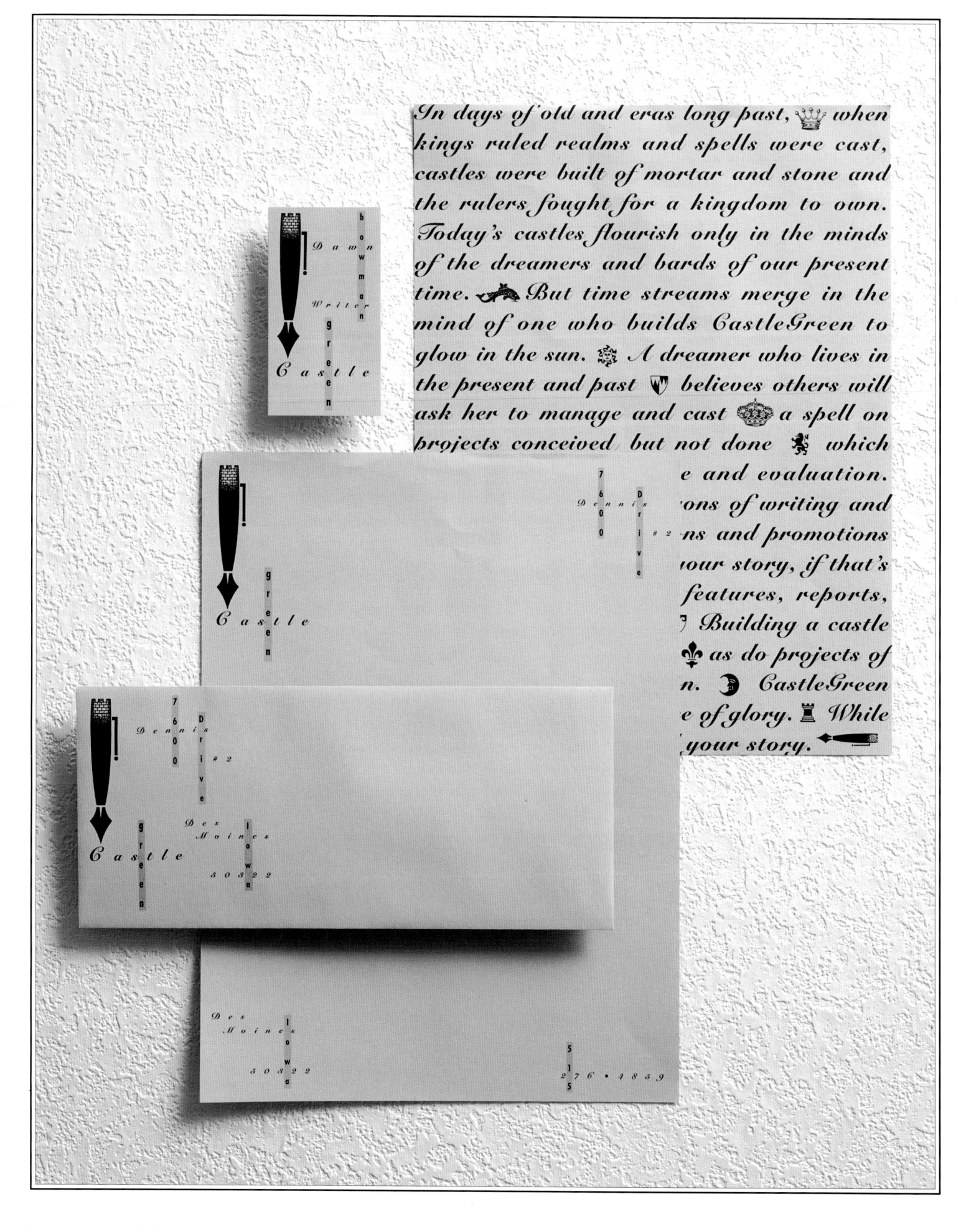

CASTLE GREEN   Freelance Copywriter   フリーランス・コピーライター   USA 1993   AD, D, I: John Sayles   CW: Dawn Bowman   DF: Sayles Graphic Design

SEEGERS EN GOMBEER VORMGEVING Graphic Design グラフィックデザイン BELGIUM 1992 CD, D: Wim Gombeer AD: Marloes Seegers DF: Seegers En Gombeer Vormgeving

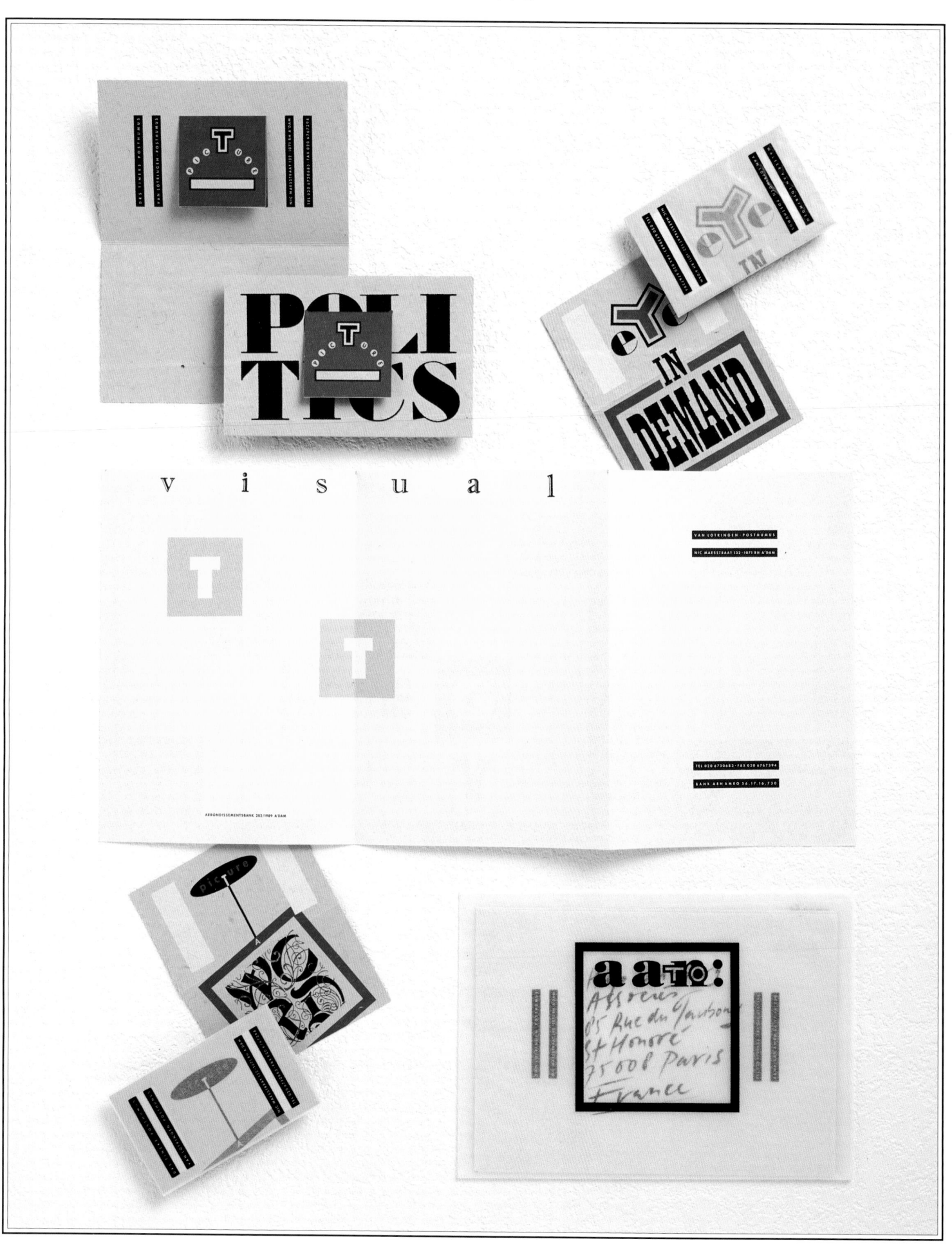

WALTER VAN LOTRINGEN / TINEKE POSTHUMUS Freelance Illustrator / Art Historian フリーランス・イラストレーター / 美術歴史学者 THE NETHERLANDS 1991

AD: Teun Anders VBAT   D: Marc Lochs   CW: Walter van Lotringen

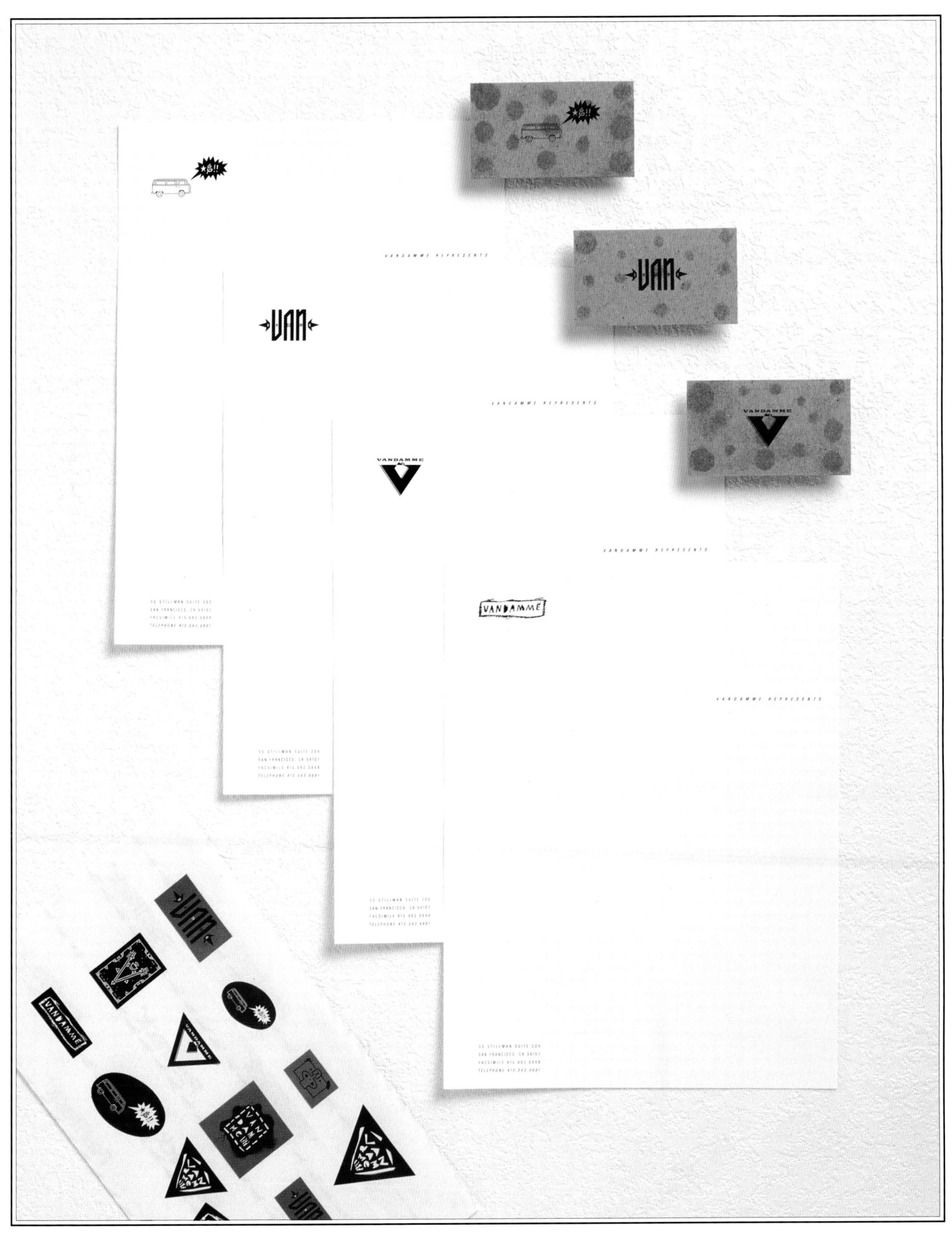

VANDAMME REPRESENTS Artist アーティスト USA 1990 AD, D: Dannis Crowe / Neal Zimmermann D: John Pappas DF: Zimmermann Crowe Design

CAVU DESIGN   Graphic Design and Marketing   グラフィックデザイン、マーケティング   USA 1993 D: Barry Kettery   DF: Cavu Design

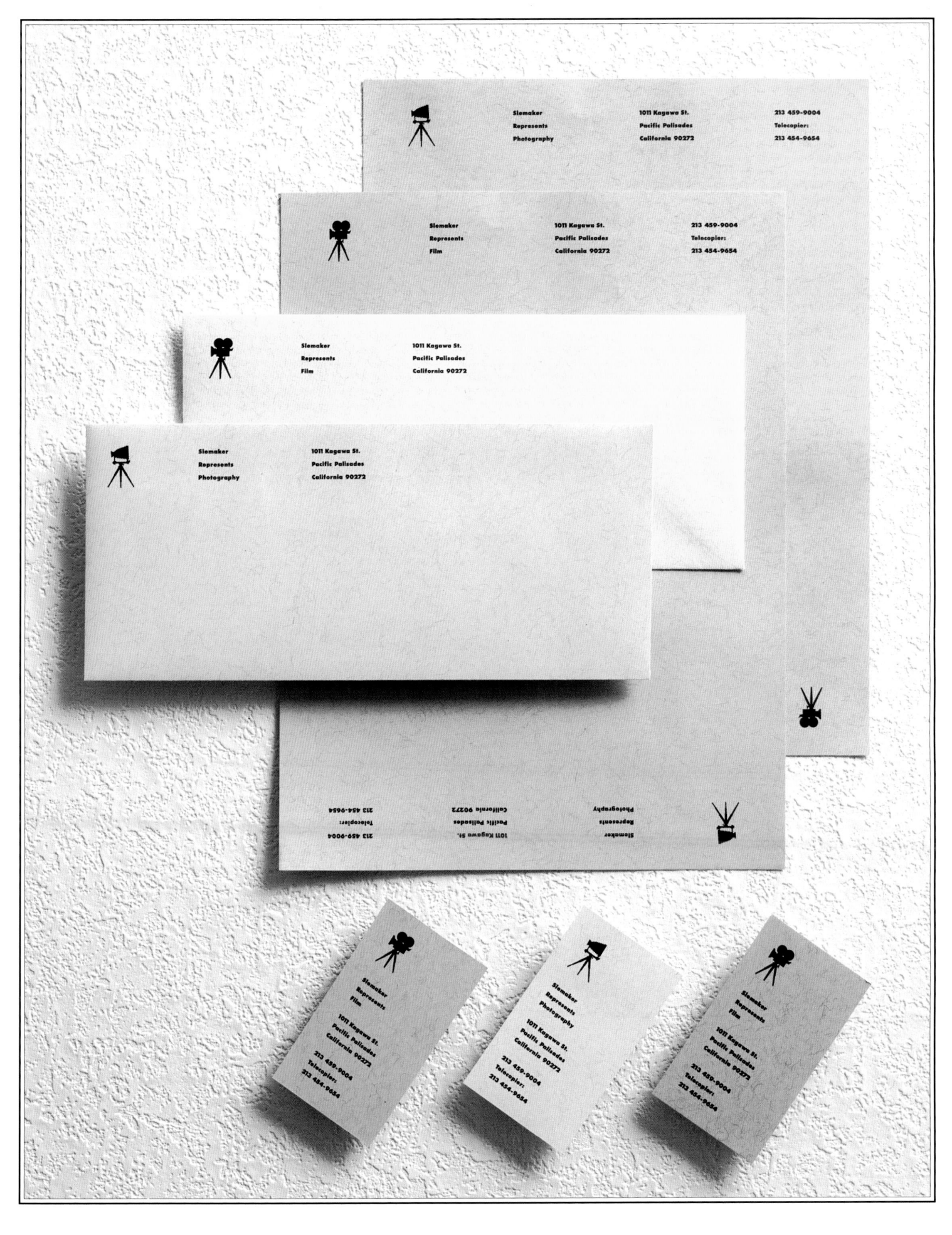

SLEMAKER REPRESENTS Photographic and Film Representative 写真、映画演出 USA 1991 AD, D, I: Joe Baratelli DF: Joseph Baratelli Design

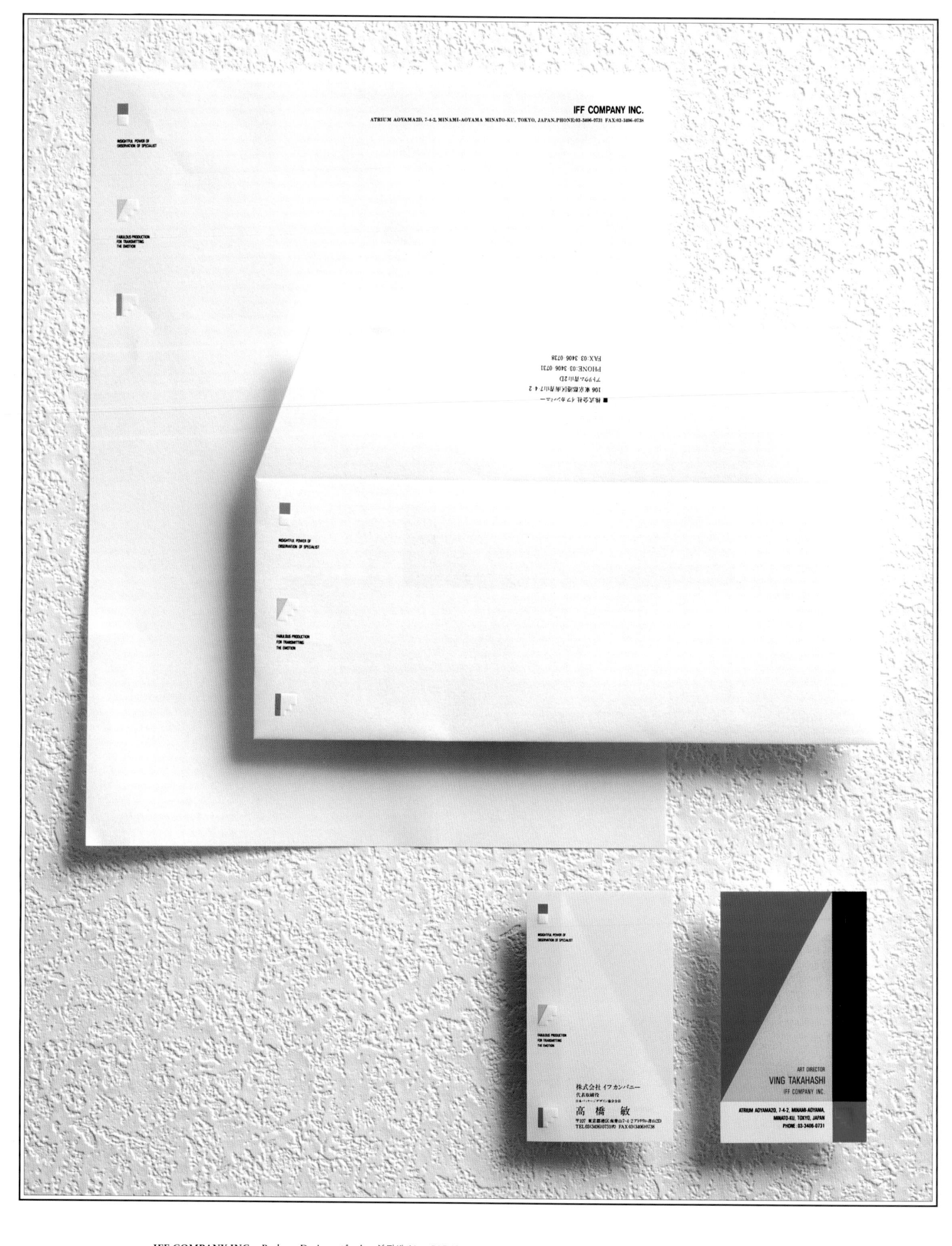

IFF COMPANY INC.　Package Design　パッケージデザイン　JAPAN　1992-1993　AD: Ving Takahashi　D: Masakazu Tagawa / Tomoko Masuda

CONCEPT WORKS SHIGOTOBA INC. Advertising and Graphic Design 広告企画・制作、CI・VI 計画 JAPAN 1991 CD: Masamori Tani AD: Tetsuya Daimatsu D: Asami Nakada

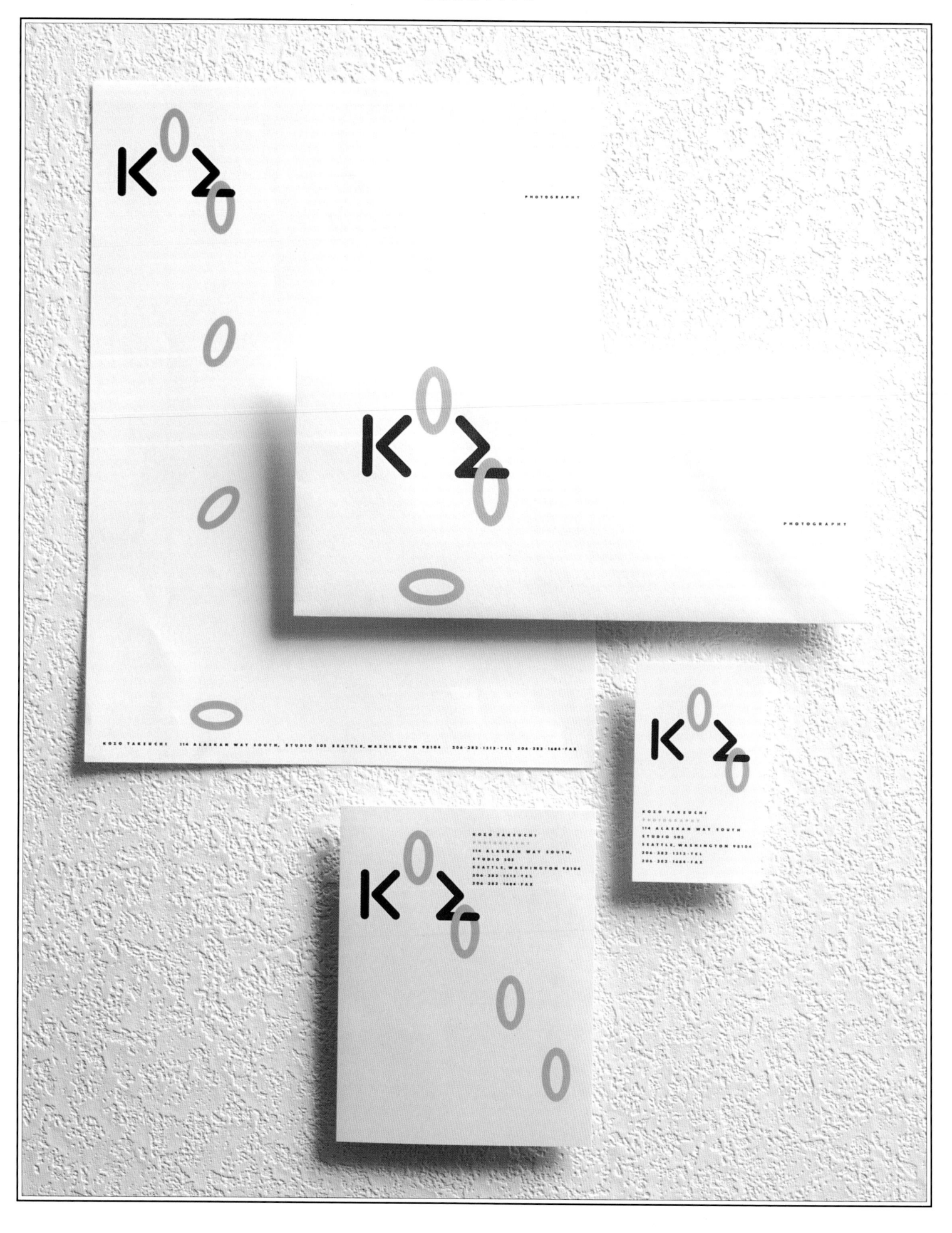

KOZO TAKEUCHI Photographer 写真家 JAPAN 1992 AD, D: Yoshiro Kajitani D: Michiko Arakawa DF: Kajitani Design Room

TASTE INC Graphic Design グラフィックデザイン JAPAN 1992 AD, D: Toshiyasu Nanbu

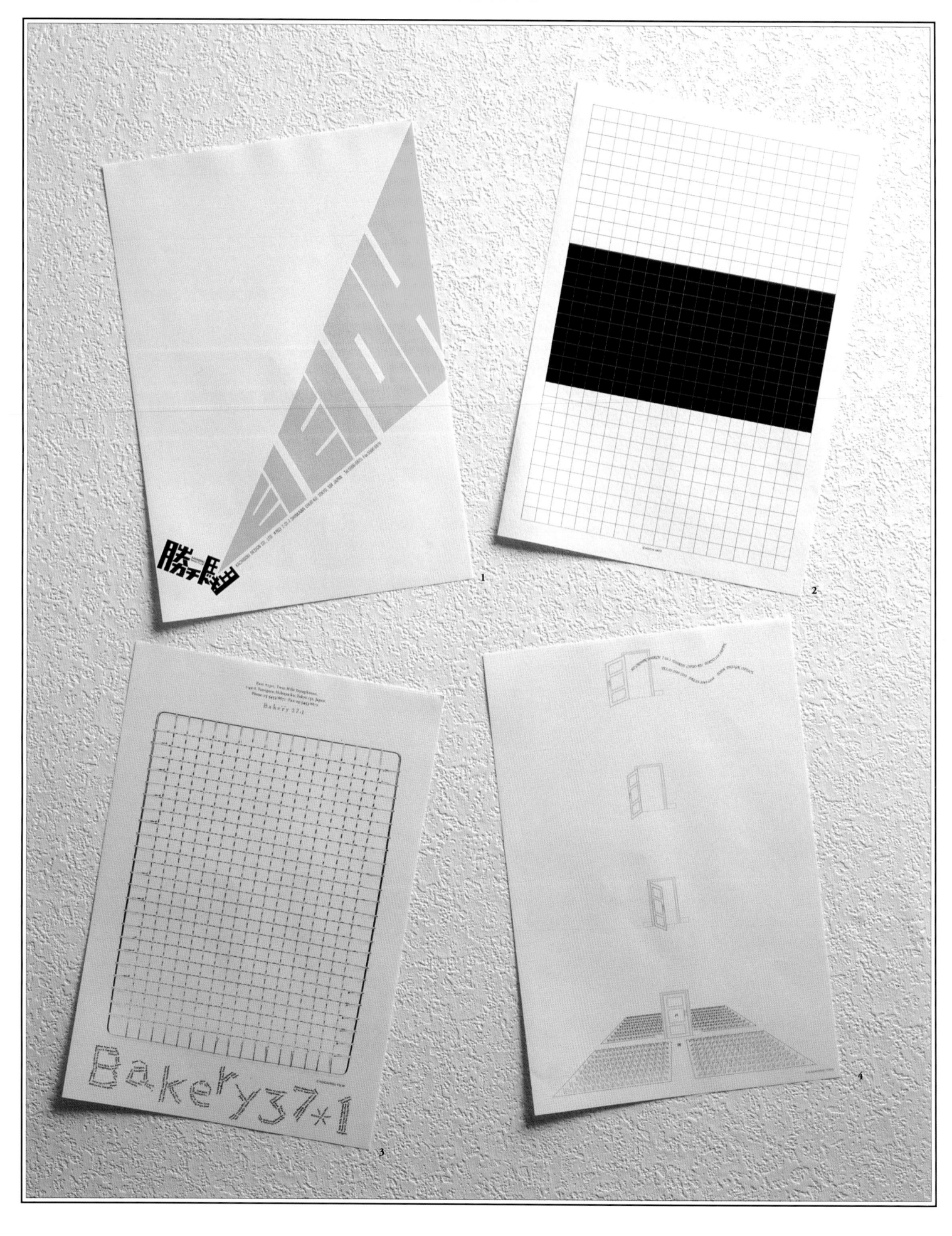

GULLIVER CO., LTD. Printing プリンティング JAPAN 1992 CD: Seiji Koseki AD: Tatsuomi Majima D: 1. Takashi Nomura / 2. Koichi Sato / 3. Yoichirou Fujii / 4. Masatoshi Toda

GULLIVER CO., LTD. Printing プリンティング JAPAN 1992 CD: Seiji Koseki AD: Tatsuomi Majima   D: 1. Teruhiko Yumura / 2. Nobuo Nakagaki / 3. Keisuke Konishi / 4. Yukimasa Okumura

KOWALSKI DESIGNWORKS, INC.   Graphic Design   グラフィックデザイン   USA 1991   AD: Stephen Kowalski   D: Janél Apple   P: George Post   DF: Kowalski Designworks

DESIGN LABORATORY Graphic Design グラフィックデザイン JAPAN 1992 AD, D: Tsuyokatsu Kudo P: Satoru Ebina DF: Design Laboratory

HUNDRED INC.　Graphic Design　グラフィックデザイン　JAPAN　1992　AD, D: Yuko Araki　DF: Hundred

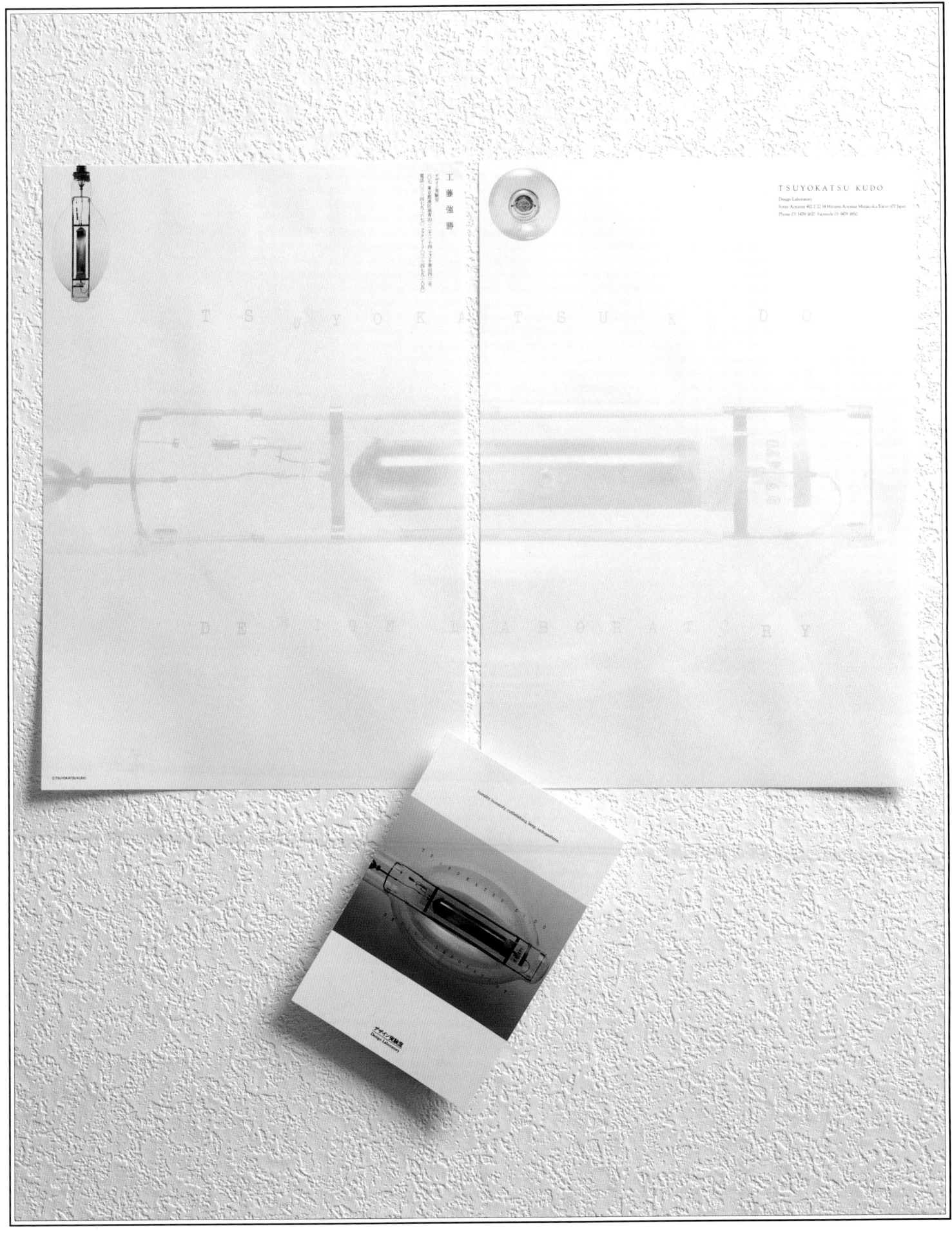

TSUYOKATSU KUDO *Graphic Design* グラフィックデザイン JAPAN 1992 AD, D: Tsuyokatsu Kudo P: Satoru Ebina DF: Design Laboratory

CD, D, I: Bradford Lawton   AD, D, I: Jody Laney   AD: Jennifer Griffith Garcia   DF: The Bradford Lawton Design Group

BRADFORD LAWTON DESIGN GROUP Graphic Design   ブラッドウドデザイン   USA 1992

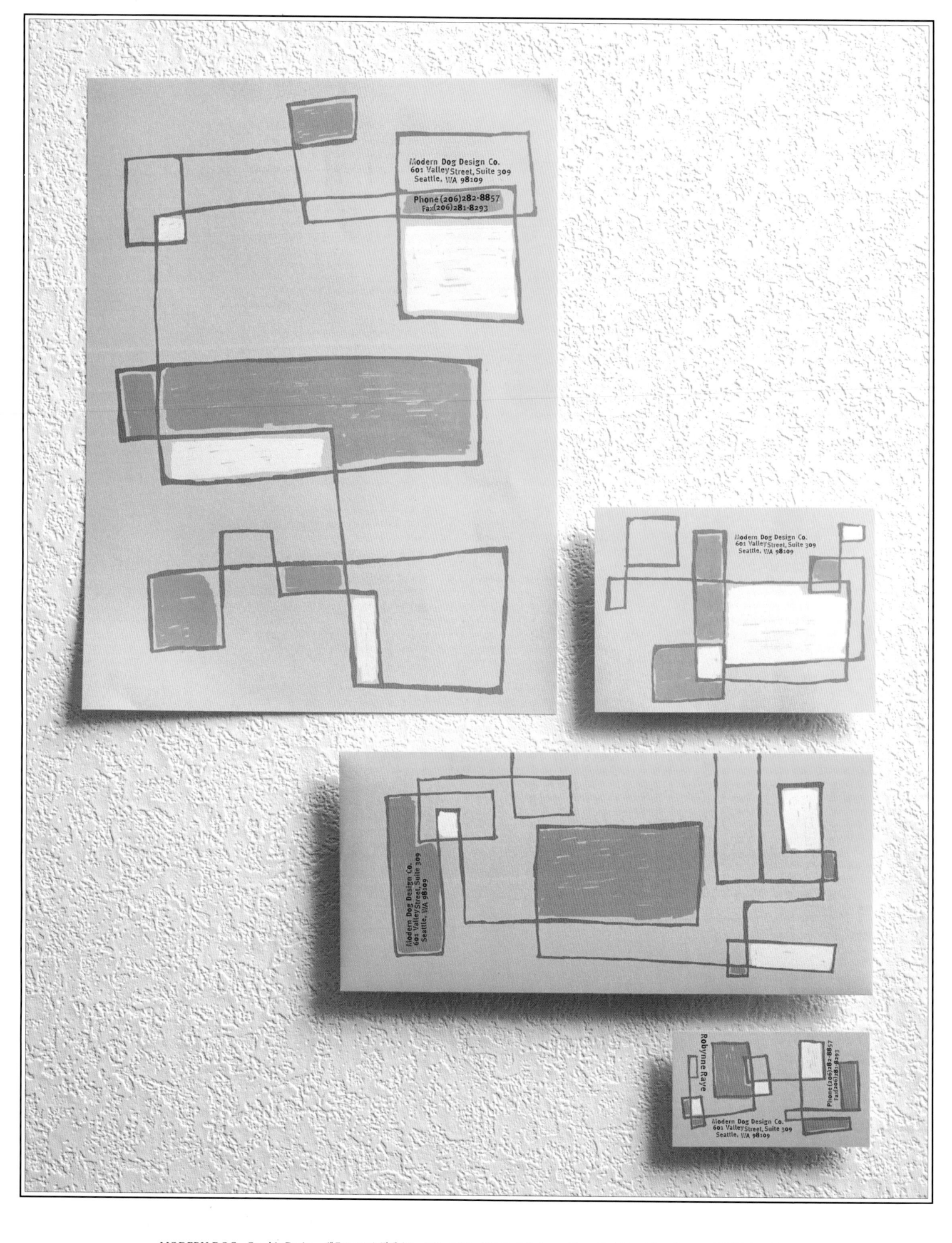

MODERN DOG Graphic Design グラフィックデザイン USA 1993 AD, D, I: Robynne Raye D: Michael Strassburger DF: Modern Dog

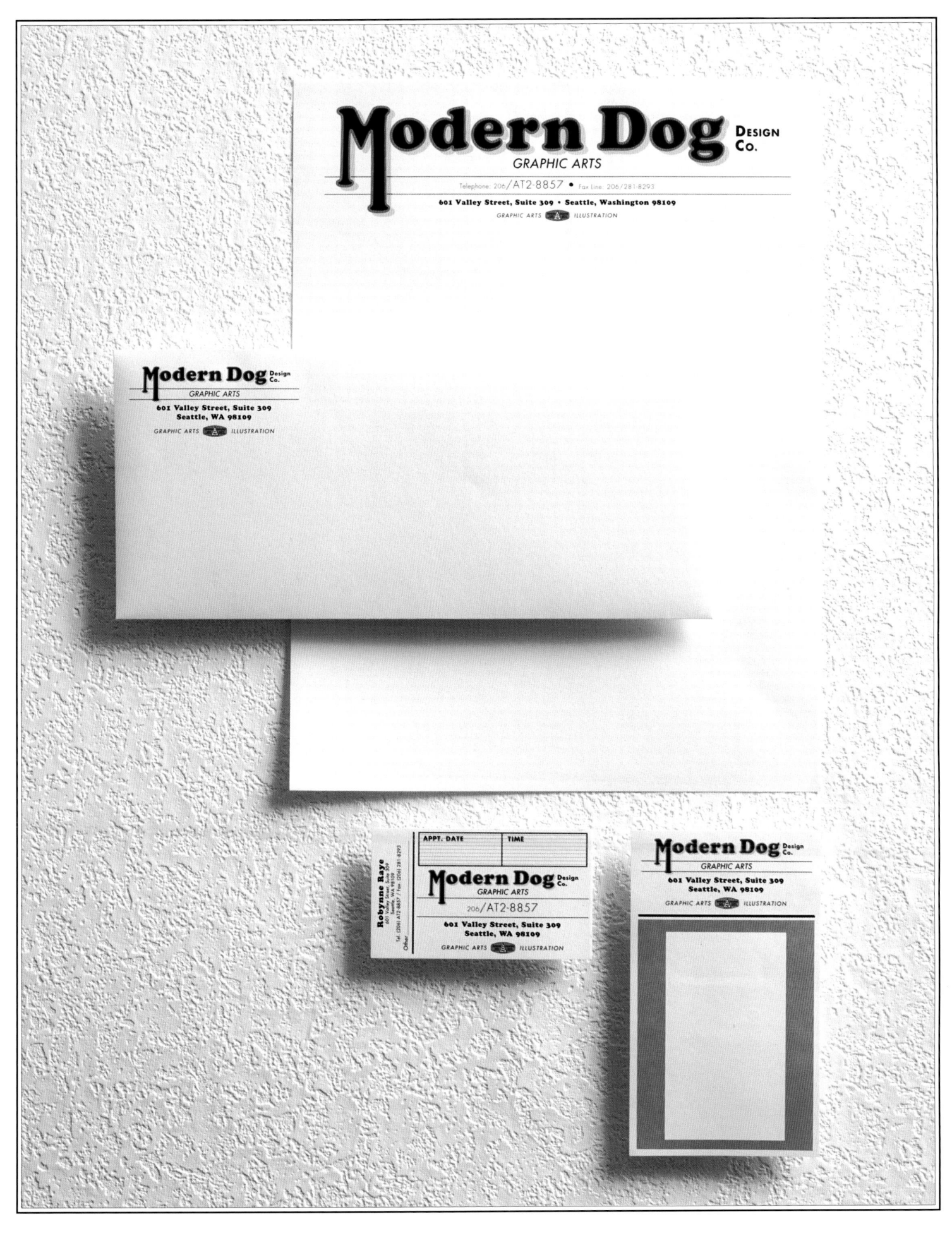

MODERN DOG   Graphic Design   グラフィックデザイン   USA 1993   AD, D, CW: Michael Strassburger   DF: Modern Dog

KEES KASANDER   Film, Television and Theater Production   映画、TV、劇の制作   THE NETHERLANDS 1990   AD, D, I: Ruud van Empel   DF: Ruud van Empel

CHUCKIE-BOY RECORDS   Record Co.   レコード会社   USA 1990   AD, D, P: Art Chantry   I: Peter Bagge   DF: Art Chantry

KRONEN AUDIO   Audio Engineering and Production   オーディオ技工、製作   USA 1988   AD, D: Steve Wedeen   DF: Vaughn Wedeen Creative

LA 4ÈME DIMENSION   Communication Agency   通信機関   FRANCE 1991   AD, D: Jean-Jacques Tachdjian   DF: I Comme Image

ACACIA AGENCY Magazine Agency　雑誌取次　FRANCE 1991 AD, D: Jean-Jacques Tachdjian DF: I Comme Image

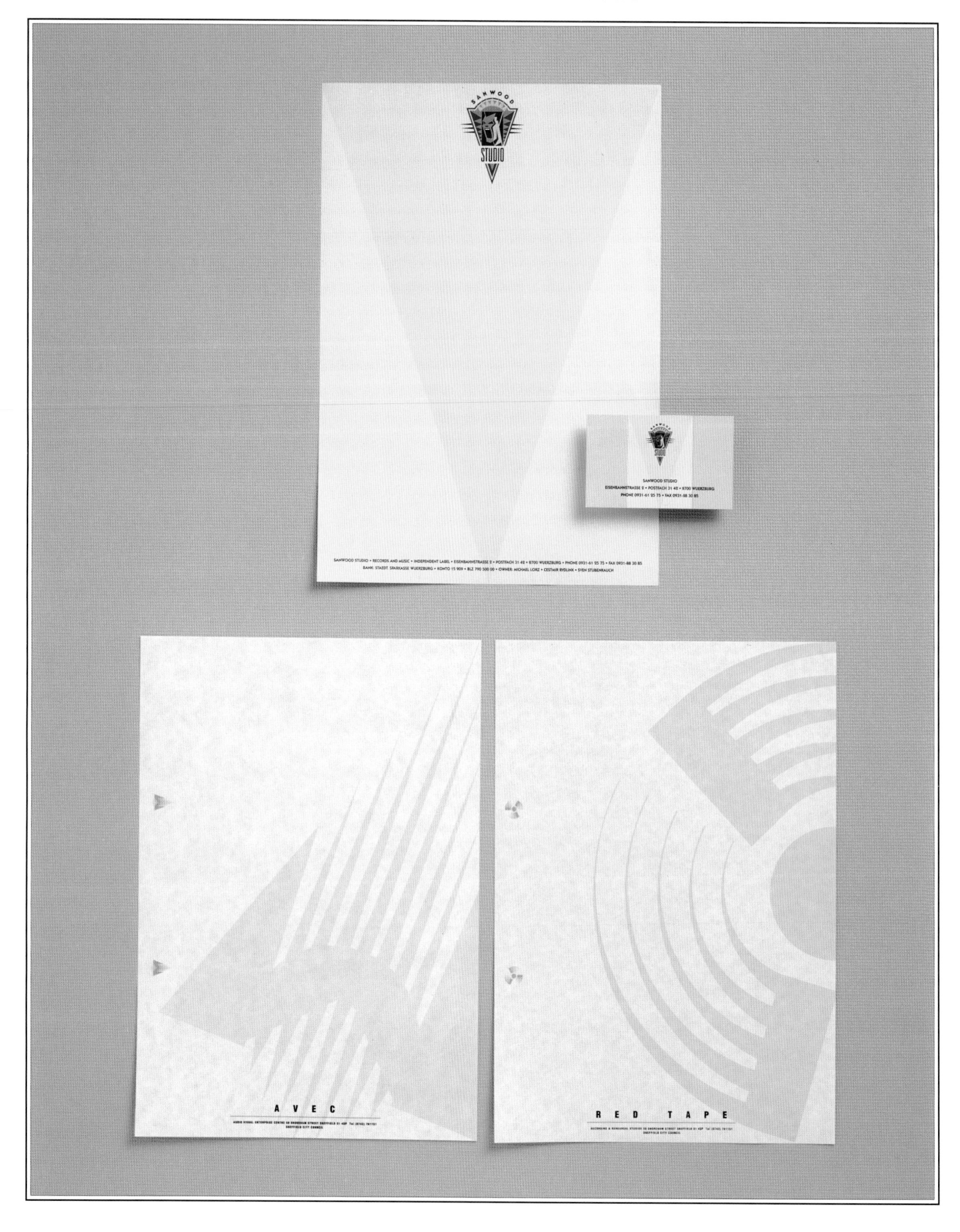

SANWOOD STUDIO Music Studio, Music Publisher and Label ミュージックレーベル、スタジオ、出版 GERMANY 1990 CD: Matthias Simon AD, D, I: Rudiger Gotz DF: Stubenrauch + Simon

AUDIO VISUAL ENTERPRISE CENTRE Center for Cultural Industries 文化産業センター UK 1990 AD, D: The Designers Republic DF: The Designers Republic

SHEFFIELD CITY COUNCIL'S RED TAPE STUDIOS Recording and Rehearsal Studios レコーディング、リハーサルスタジオ UK 1990 AD, D: The Designers Republic DF: The Designers Republic

WARP RECORDS Record Label and Music Shop レコードレーベル、販売 UK 1991 AD, D: The Designers Republic DF: The Designers Republic

JOYCE PUBLISHING Publishing 出版 HONG KONG 1991 AD, D: Alan Chan D: Chen Shun Tsoi DF: Alan Chan Design

MCGUIRE WILHOITE Communications Service 通信サービス USA 1992   CD: Patrick McGuire / Melanie Wilhoite   AD, D: Vittorio Costarella   DF: Modern Dog

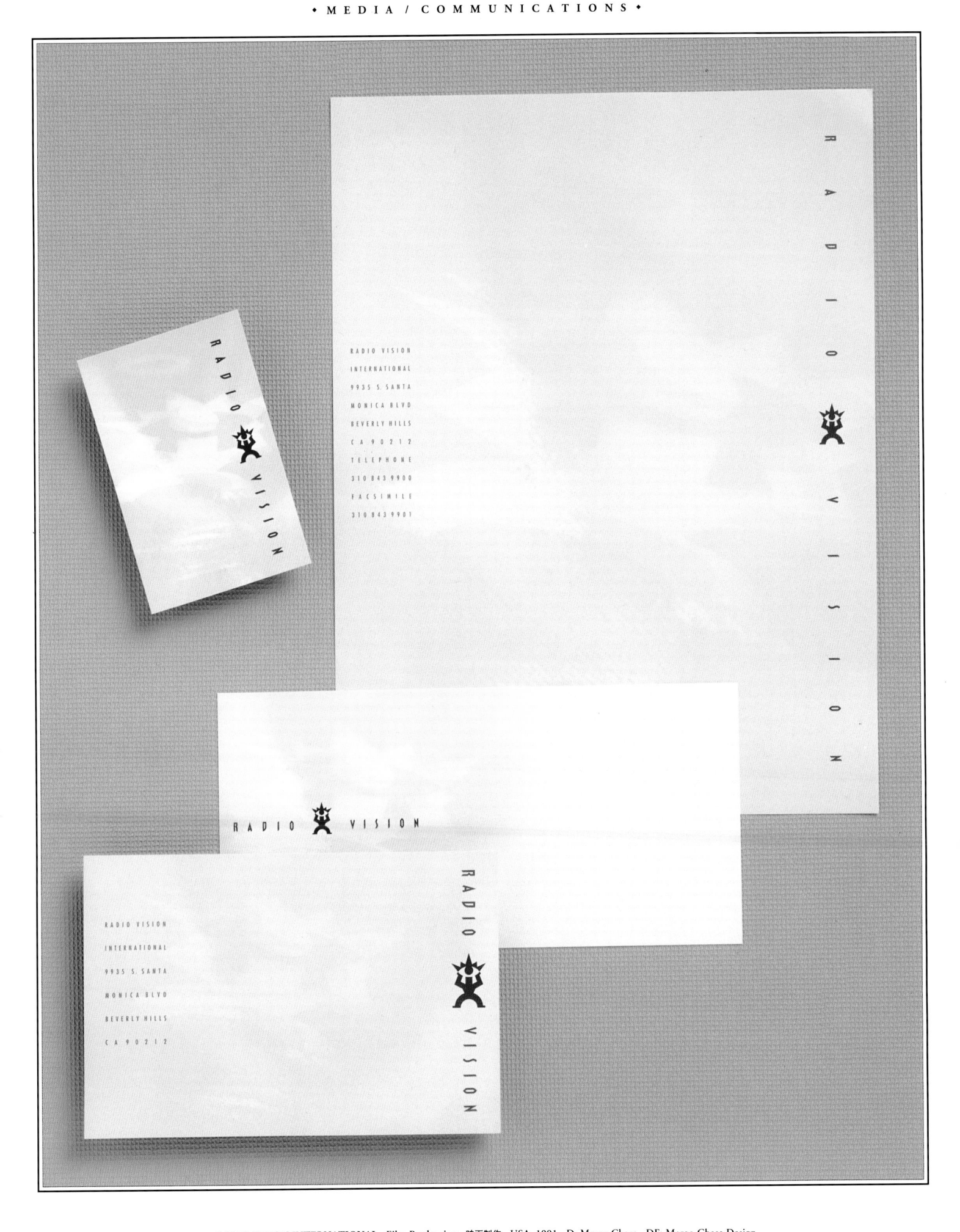

RADIO VISION INTERNATIONAL Film Production 映画制作 USA 1991 D: Margo Chase DF: Margo Chase Design

THE **WATER COMPANY**   Music Publisher   音楽出版   THE NETHERLANDS 1990   AD, D: Anton Vos   DF: Dedato

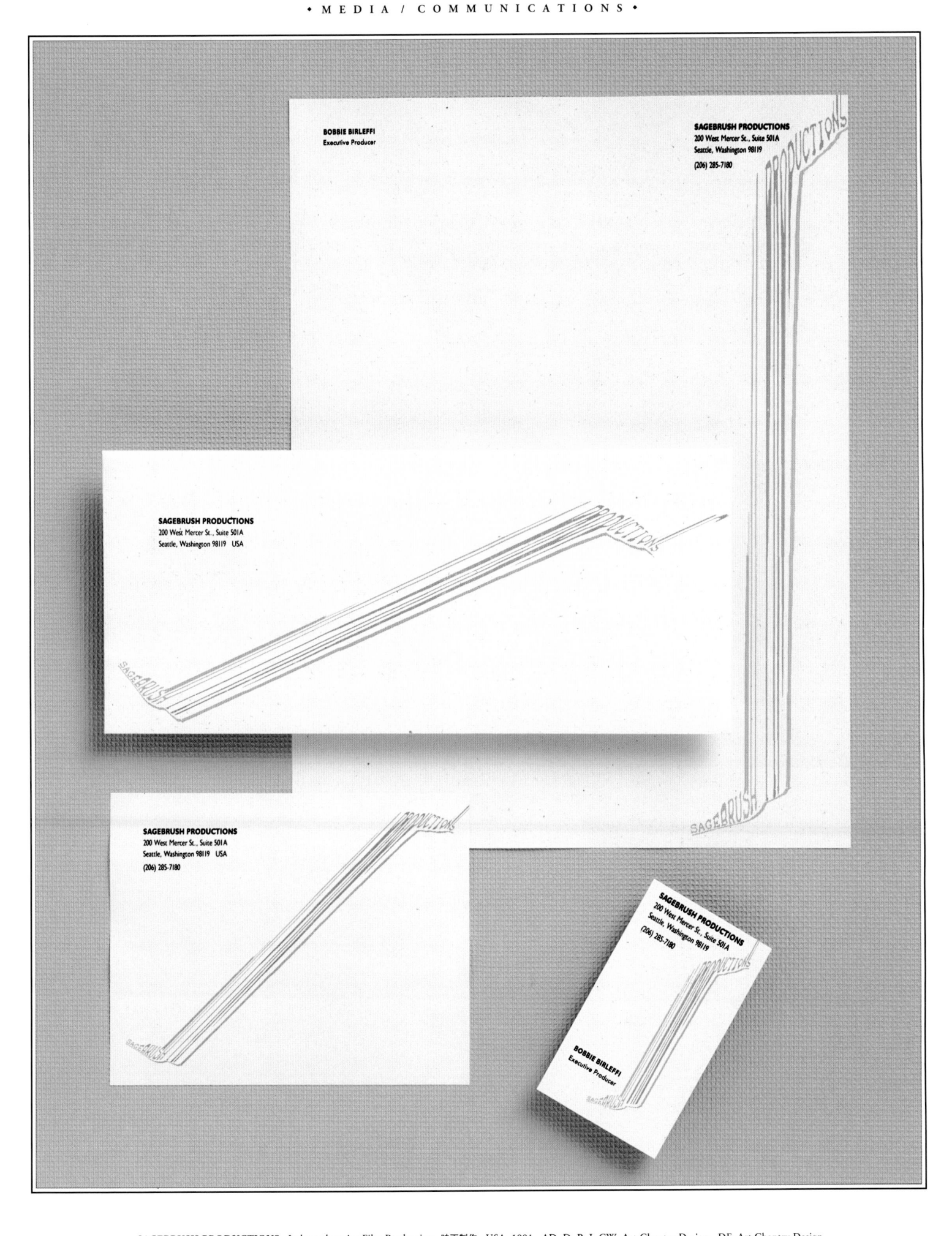

SAGEBRUSH PRODUCTIONS Independent Art Film Production 映画制作 USA 1991 AD, D, P, I, CW: Art Chantry Design DF: Art Chantry Design

THE KENWOOD GROUP Communications (Film, Video, Multimedia, Meetings & Events) メディア、イベント情報通信 USA 1992
AD, D: Hock Wah Yeo   D: Cary Chiao   DF: The Design Office of Wong & Yeo

VELOCITY DEVELOPMENT CORPORATION Computer Software Publishers コンピューターソフトウェア発行 USA 1991
AD, D, I: Hock Wah Yeo D: Cary Chiao DF: The Design Office of Wong & Yeo

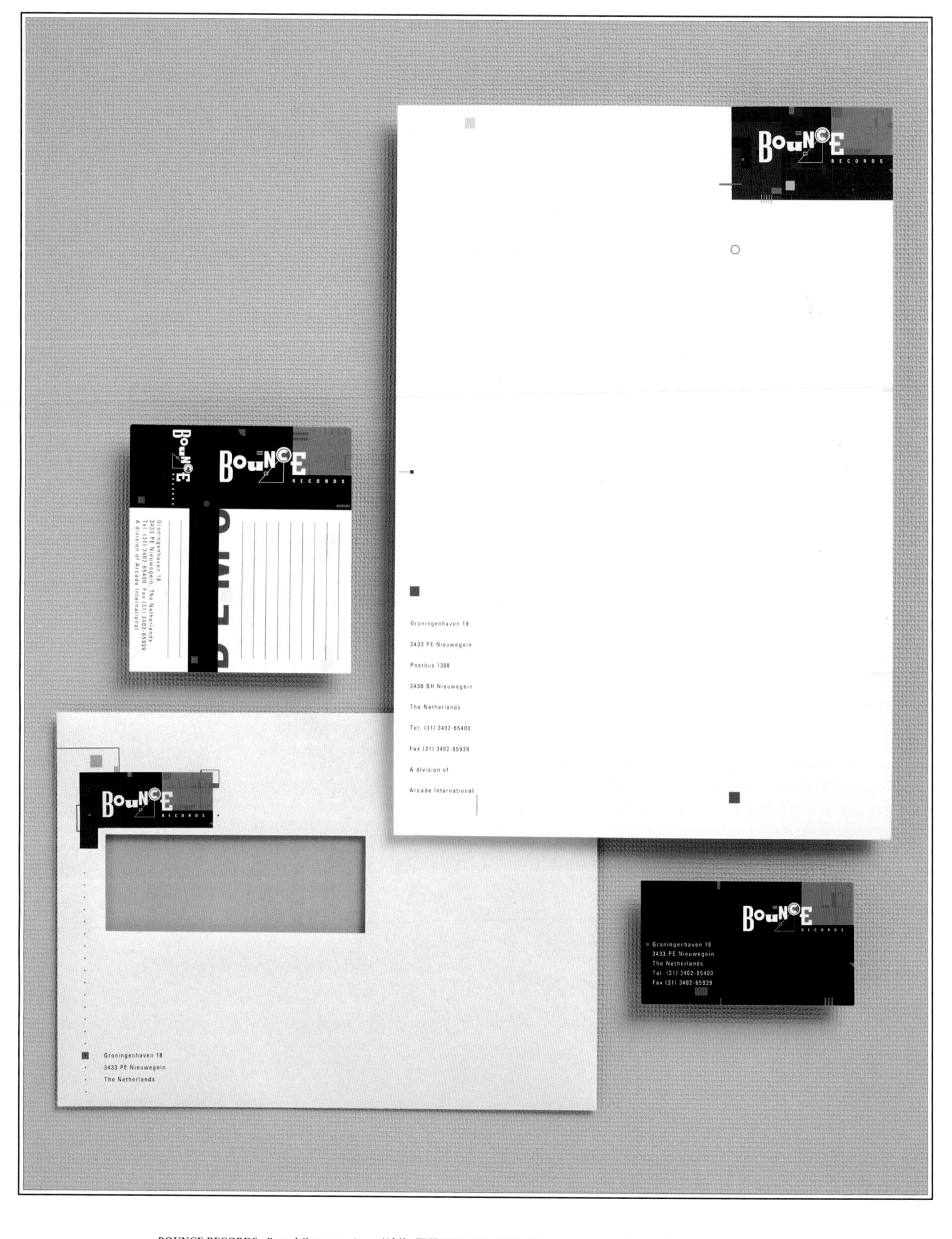

BOUNCE RECORDS Record Company レコード会社 THE NETHERLANDS 1990 AD, D: Anton Vos D: Marute Wigger DF: Dedato

SOFTWARE TOO CORPORATION   Computer Related Service   コンピューター関連ソフト・ハードウェアの輸入、販売、代理業   JAPAN 1991

AD: Naomi Enami   D: Mariko Yamamoto   DF: Propeller Art Works

PRU REX - HASSAN   Film Production   映画制作   UK 1990   AD, D: Teresa Roviras   DF: Teresa Roviras

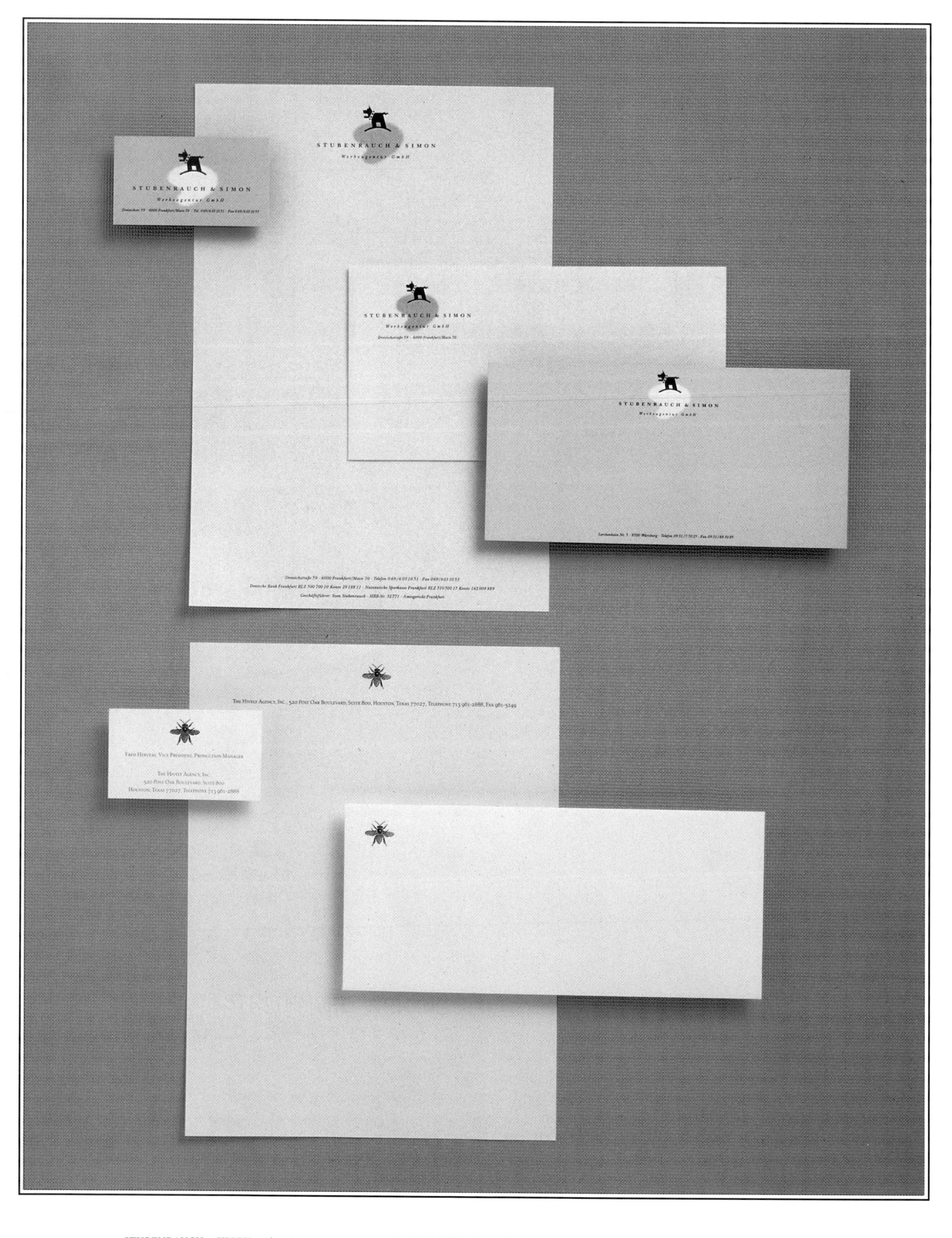

STUBENRAUCH + SIMON   Advertising Agency   広告代理店   GERMANY 1991   CD: Matthias Simon   AD, D, I: Rudiger Gotz   DF: Stubenrauch + Simon

THE HIVELY AGENCY   Advertising Agency   広告代理店   USA 1985   AD, D, CW: Charles Hively   I: Bettman Archives

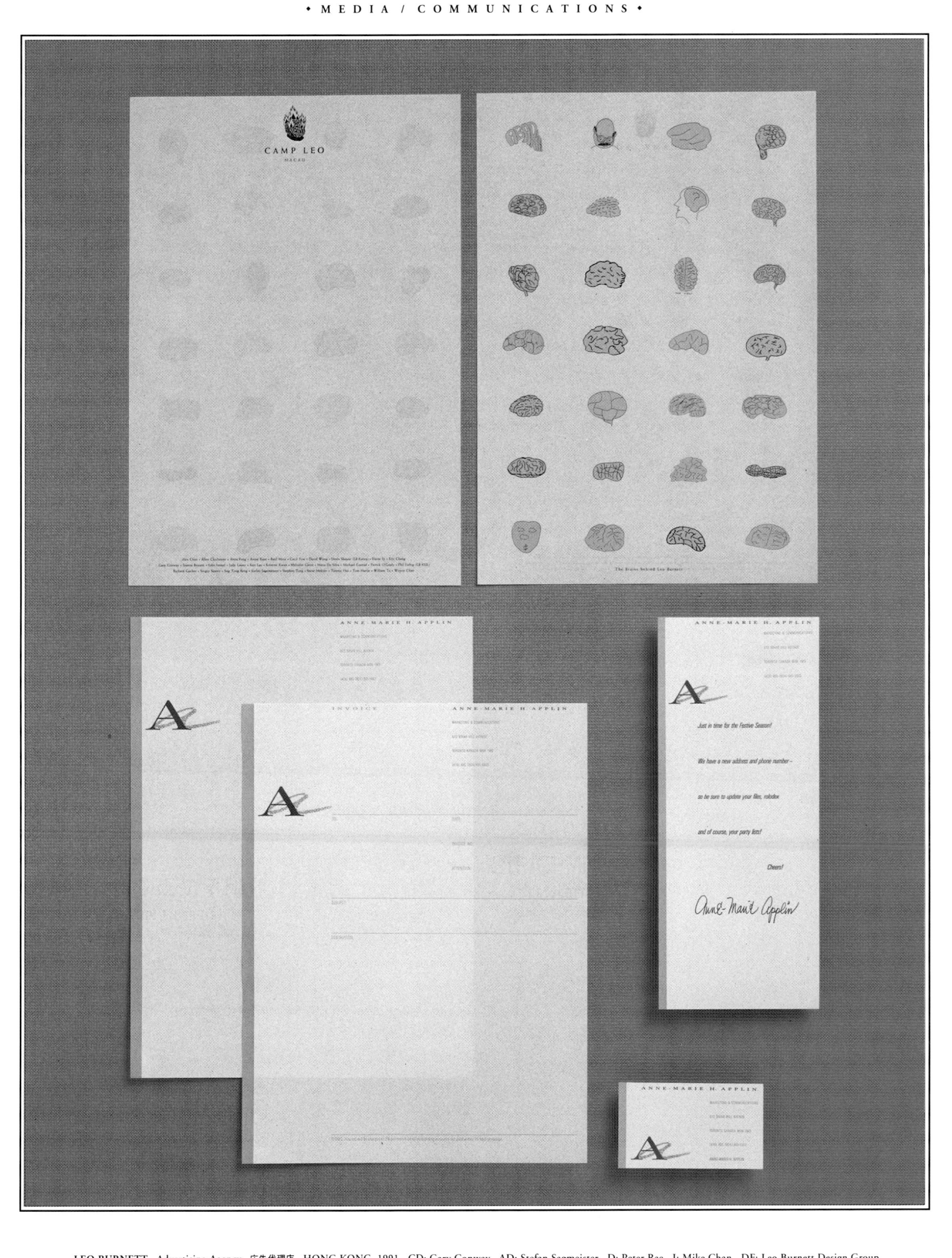

LEO BURNETT Advertising Agency 広告代理店 HONG KONG 1991 CD: Gary Conway AD: Stefan Sagmeister D: Peter Rae I: Mike Chan DF: Leo Burnett Design Group

ANNE-MARIE APPLIN Marketing and Communications マーケティング、通信サービス USA 1989 CD: Paul Browning DF: Taylor & Browning Design Associates

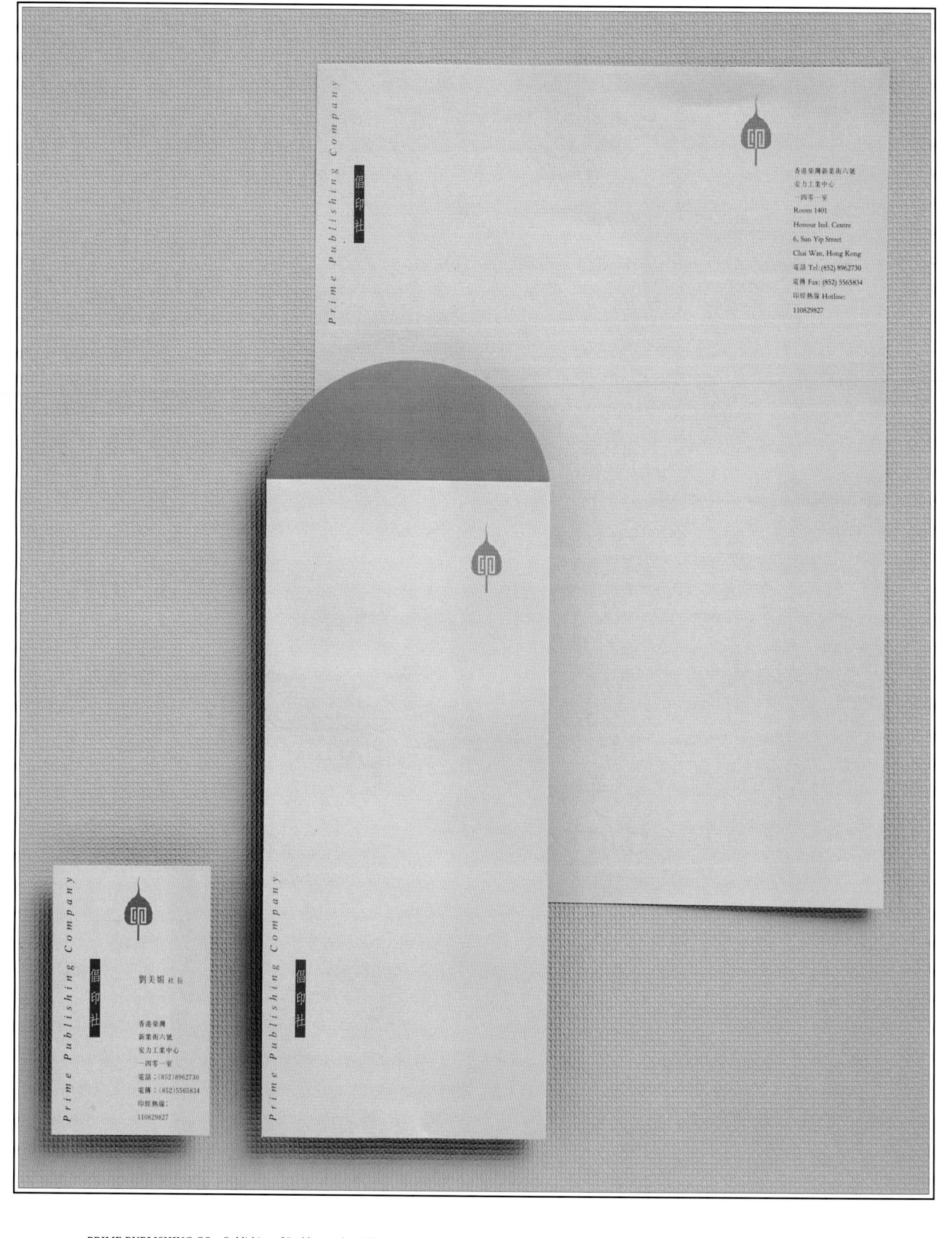

PRIME PUBLISHING CO. Publishing of Buddist Books 仏教本の出版 HONG KONG 1992 AD, D: Freeman Lau Siu Hong DF: Kan Tai-keung Design & Associates

FIELD AND WALL PRODUCTIONS, INC. Television Commercial Productions テレビコマーシャル制作 USA 1989 AD, D: Peter Bradford I: Joyce Rothschild DF: Peter Bradford and Associates

BLIND SPOT, INC. Photography Magazine 写真雑誌 USA 1993 CD: Robert Bergman-ungar D: Liong The

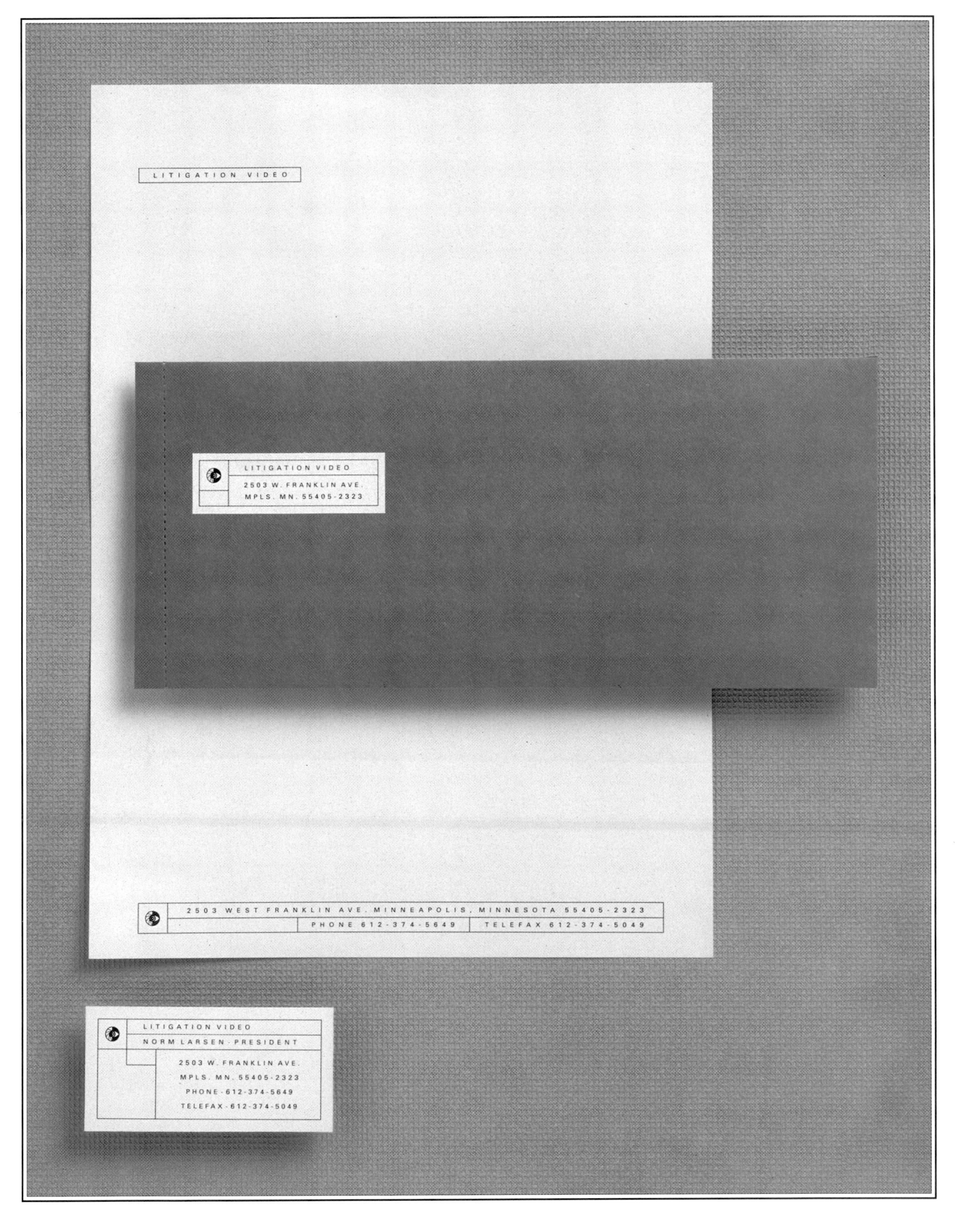

LITIGATION VIDEO (NORM LARSEN, PRES.)   Legal Videos   法定のビデオ会社   USA 1992 AD, D: Todd Hauswirth   AD: Daniel Olson   DF: Charles S. Anderson Design

MOMENTUM FILMS Commercial and Film Production Company コマーシャル、映画制作 USA 1988

CD: Forrest Richardson   CD, AD: Varerie Richardson   D: Jim Bolek   DF: Richardson or Richardson

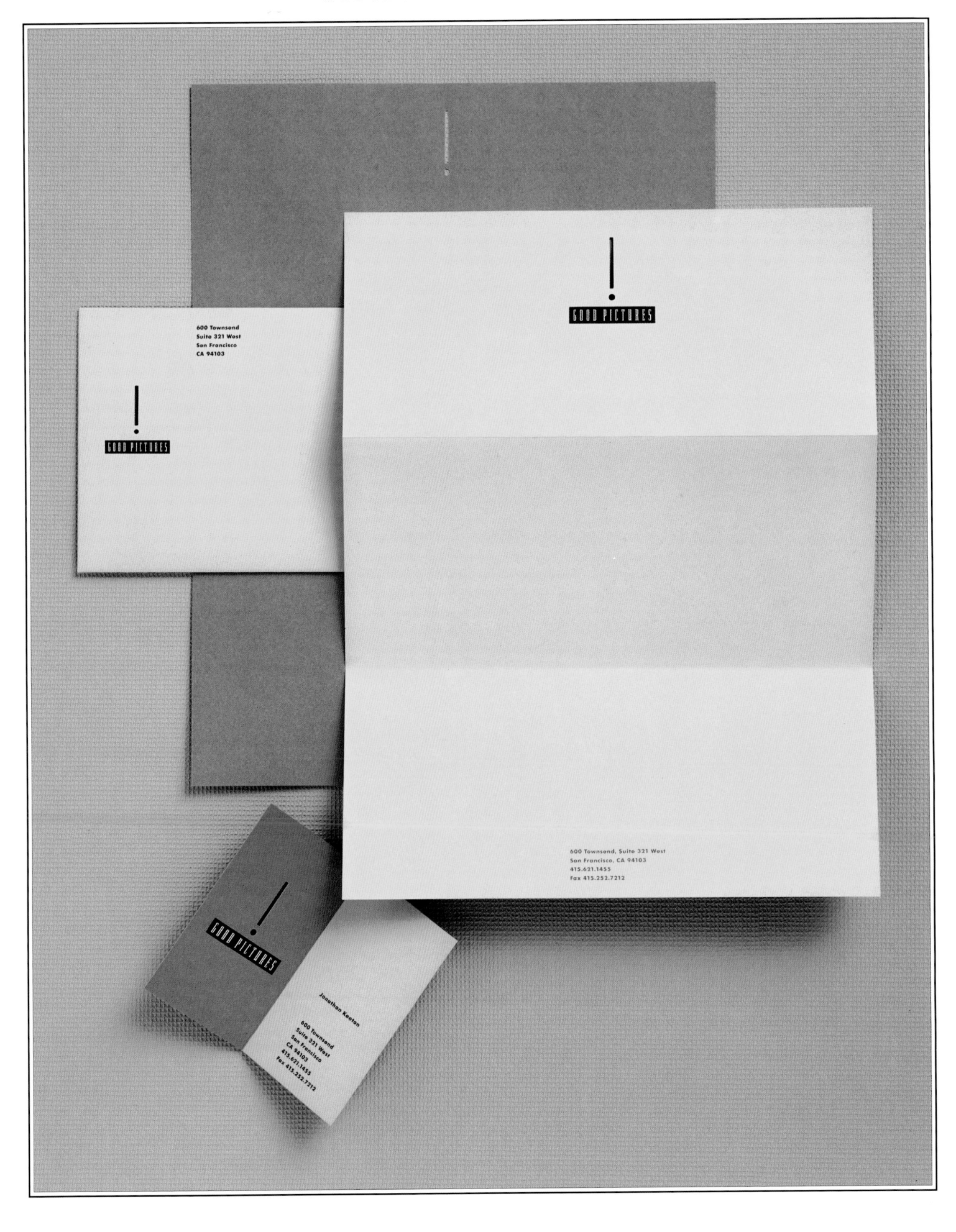

GOOD PICTURES Video Production Facility ビデオ制作 USA 1991 AD, D: Jennifer Morla D: Sharrie Brooks

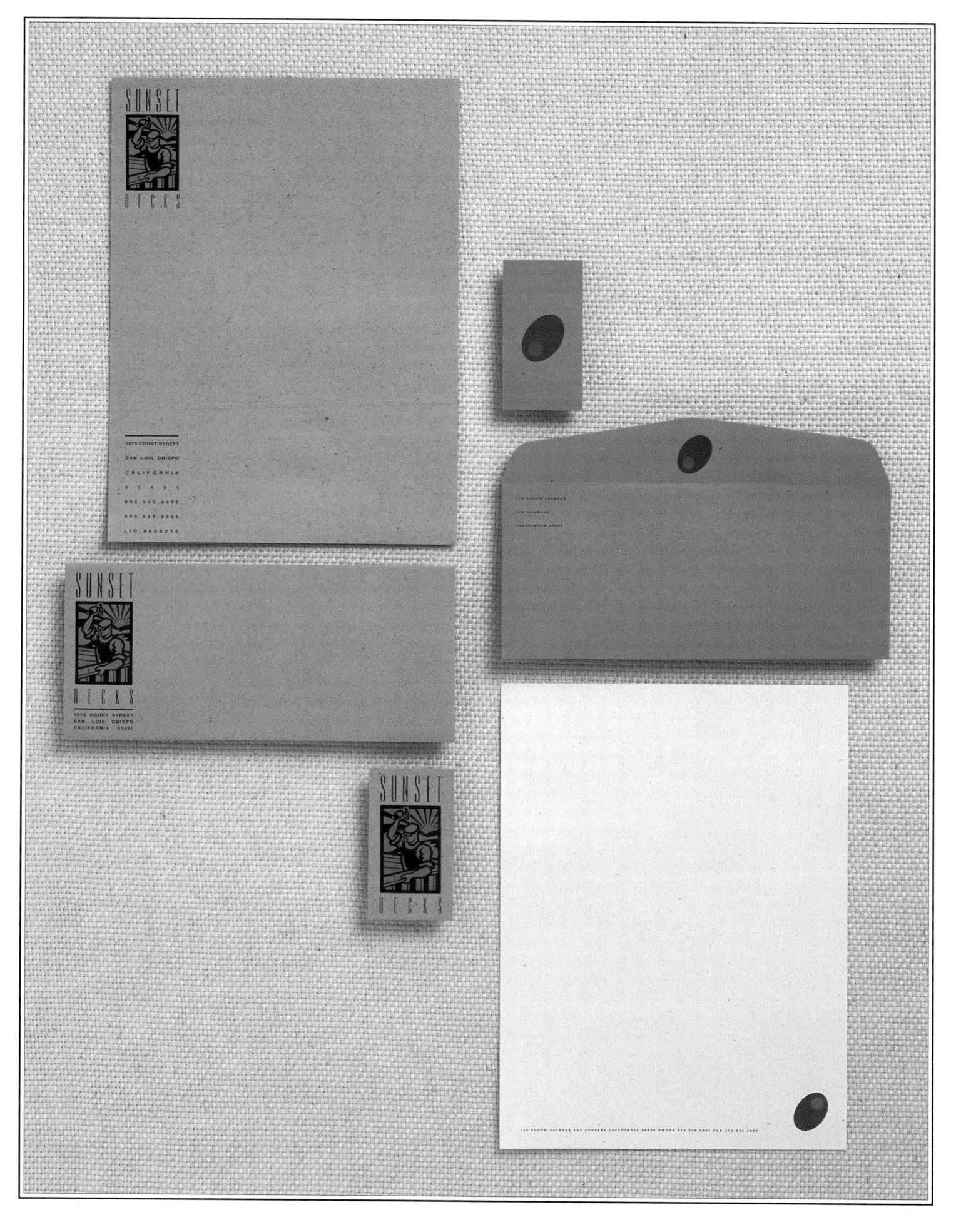

SUNSET DECKS Custom Design and Crafts 受注デザイン、手工芸 USA 1991 AD: Stephen Kowalski D: Janél Apple I: Camille Sauvé DF: Kowalski Design Works

THE OLIVE Restaurant レストラン USA 1990 CD: Richard Seireeni D: Romane Cameron DF: Studio Seireeni

RITA'S CATERING   Catering   料理調達   USA 1990   AD, D: Mark Oldach   DF: Mark Oldach Design

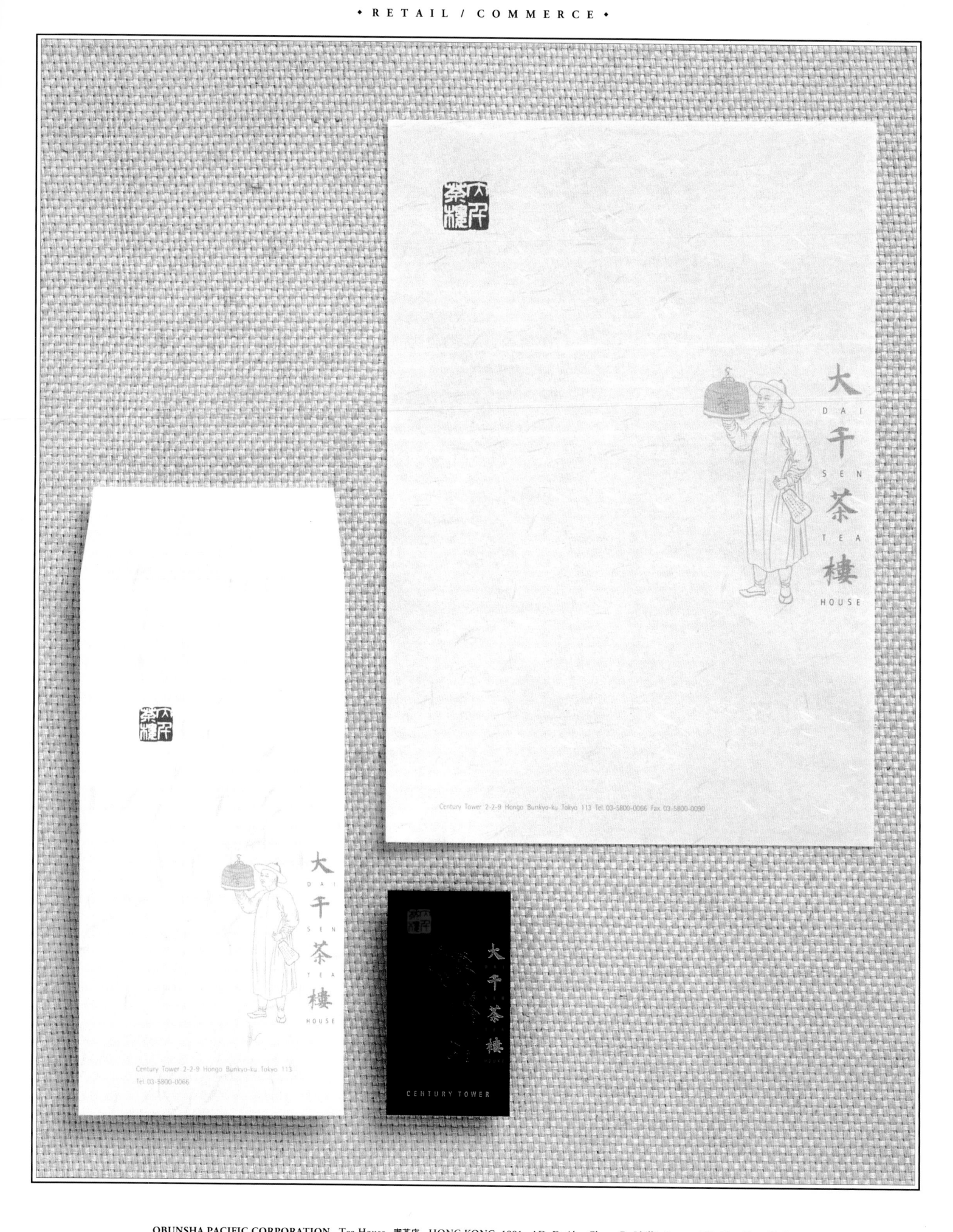

OBUNSHA PACIFIC CORPORATION Tea House 喫茶店 HONG KONG 1991 AD, D: Alan Chan D: Phillip Leung DF: Alan Chan Design

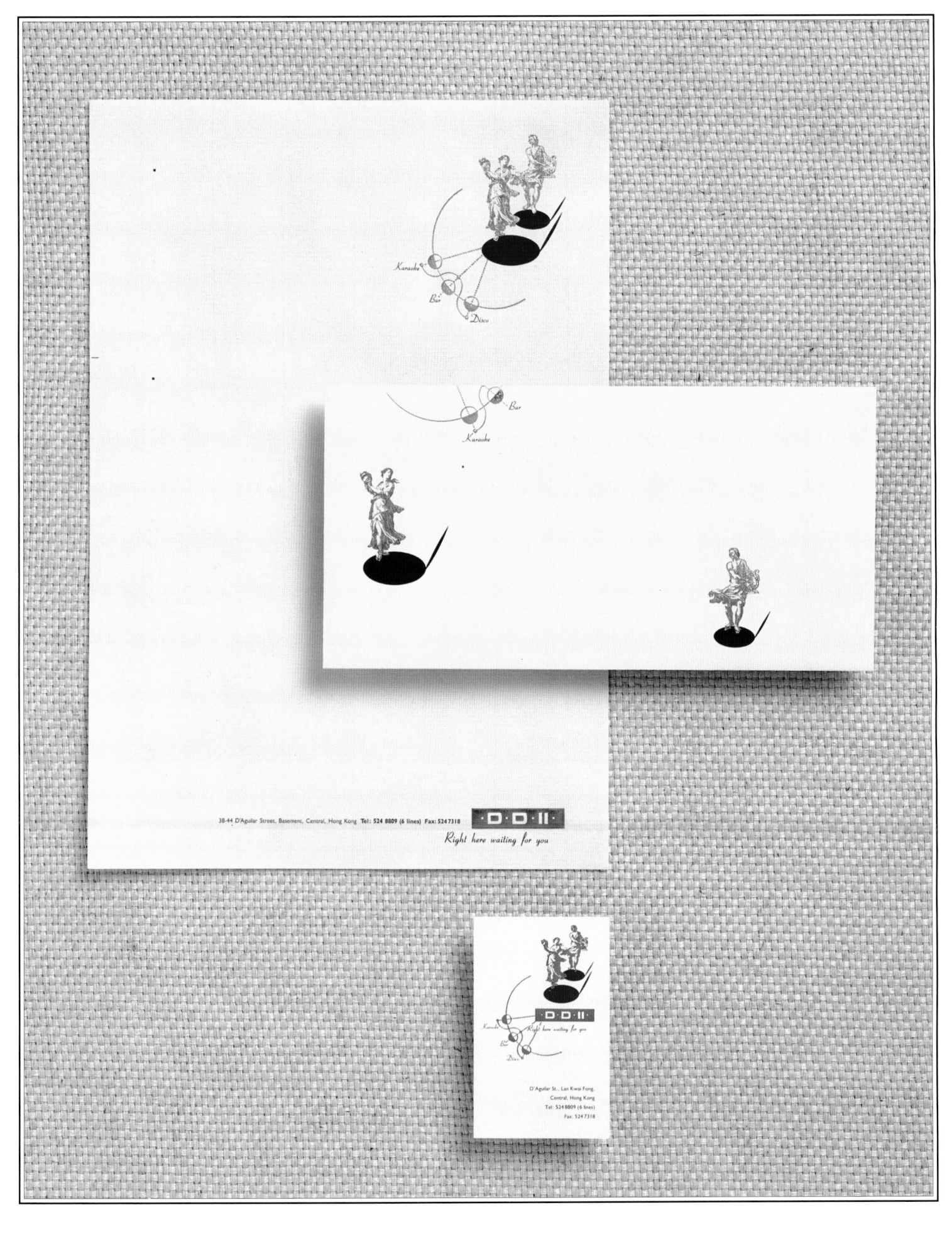

D. D. Ⅱ **KARAOKE** Karaoke Lounge カラオケラウンジ HONG KONG 1990 AD, D: Alan Chan D: Alvin Chan DF: Alan Chan Design
Special Effects: Metallic inks has been used for the logo and illustration. ロゴとイラストにメタリック・インクを使用。

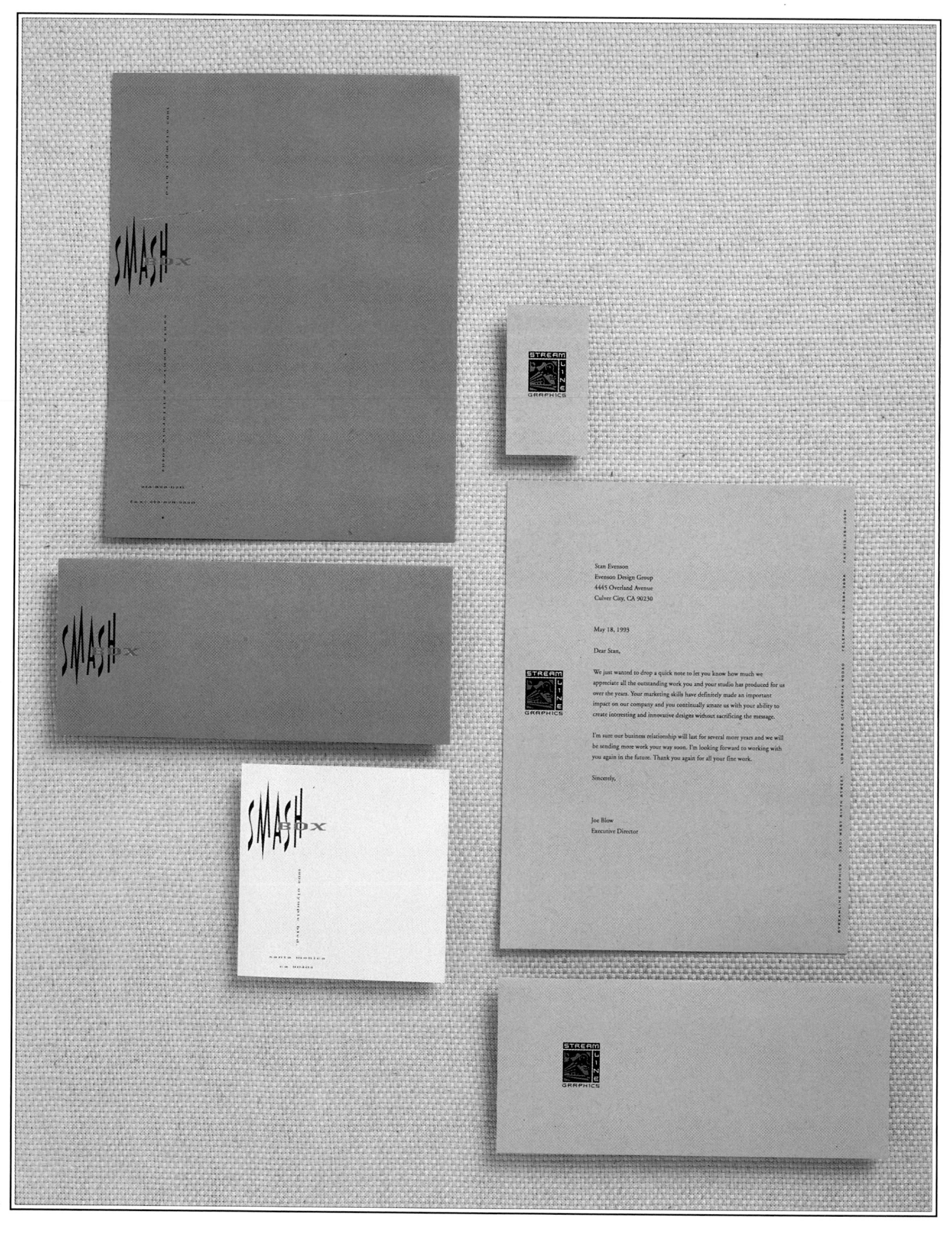

SMASH BOX   Rental Photo Studio   貸撮影室   USA 1990   D: Margo Chase   DF: Margo Chase Design

STREAMLINE GRAPHICS   Pre-press Service Bureau   予約サービス所   USA 1991   AD: Stan Evenson   D: Glenn Sakamoto

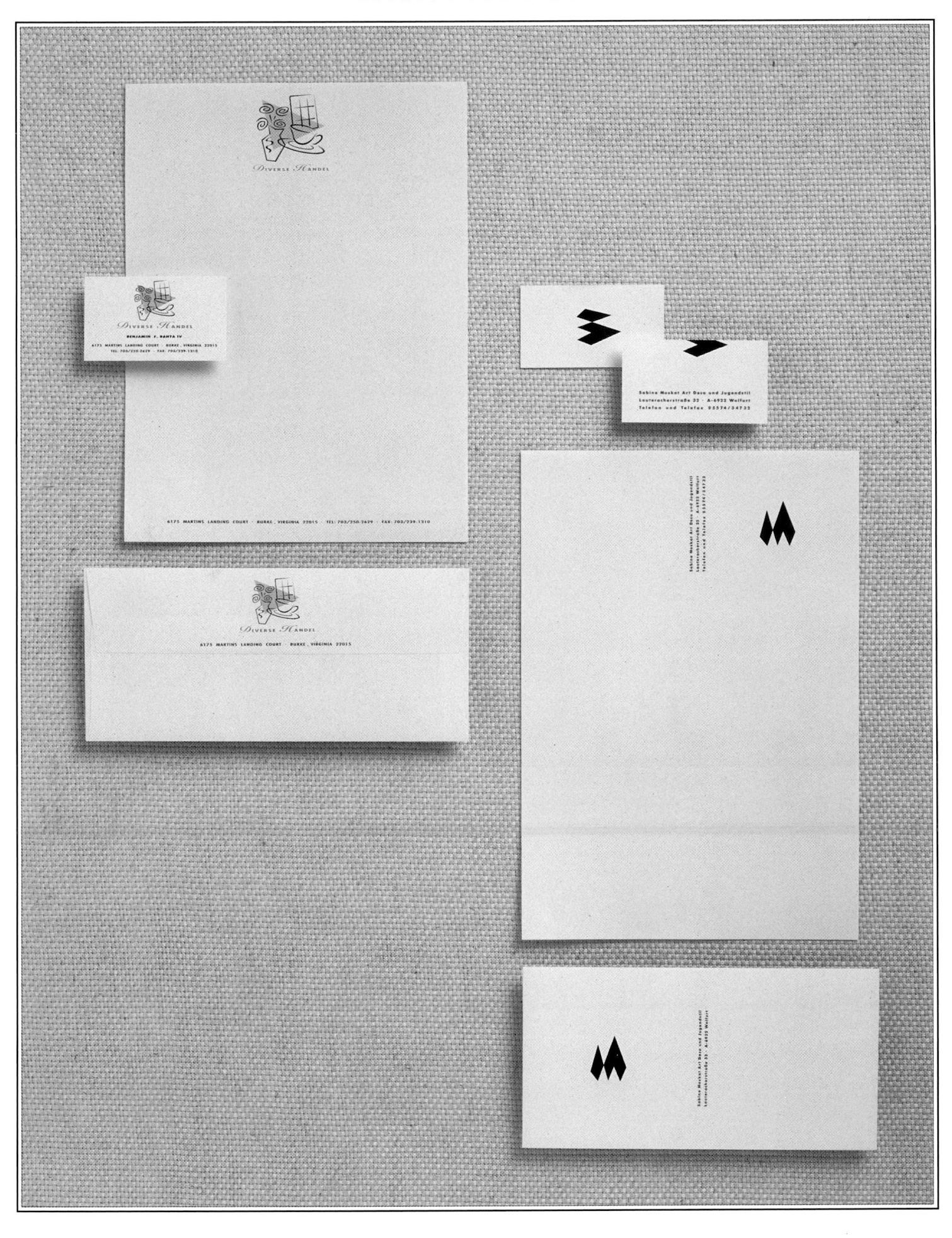

DIVERSE HANDEL   Swedish Gift Shop   スウェーデンのギフトショップ   USA 1993   AD: Supon Phornirunlit   D, I: Richard Lee Heffner   DF: Supon Design Group

SABINE MOSKAT   Art Deco Antique Furniture and Art   アールデコの家具、調度品   AUSTRIA 1991   D: Kurt Dornig   DF: Dornig Grafik Design

VIANSA WINERY Winery ワイン醸造所 USA 1992 AD, D: Patti Britton CALLIGRAPHER: Georgia Deaver DF: Britton Design

STREAMLINE CORPORATE PLANNERS Travel Consultants 旅行相談所 USA 1991 AD: Michael Dunlavey D: Heidi Tomlinson DF: The Dunlavey Studio

JASPER CONRAN Clothing Design ファッションデザイン UK 1990 D: Stephanie Nash / Anthony Michael DF: Michael Nash Associates

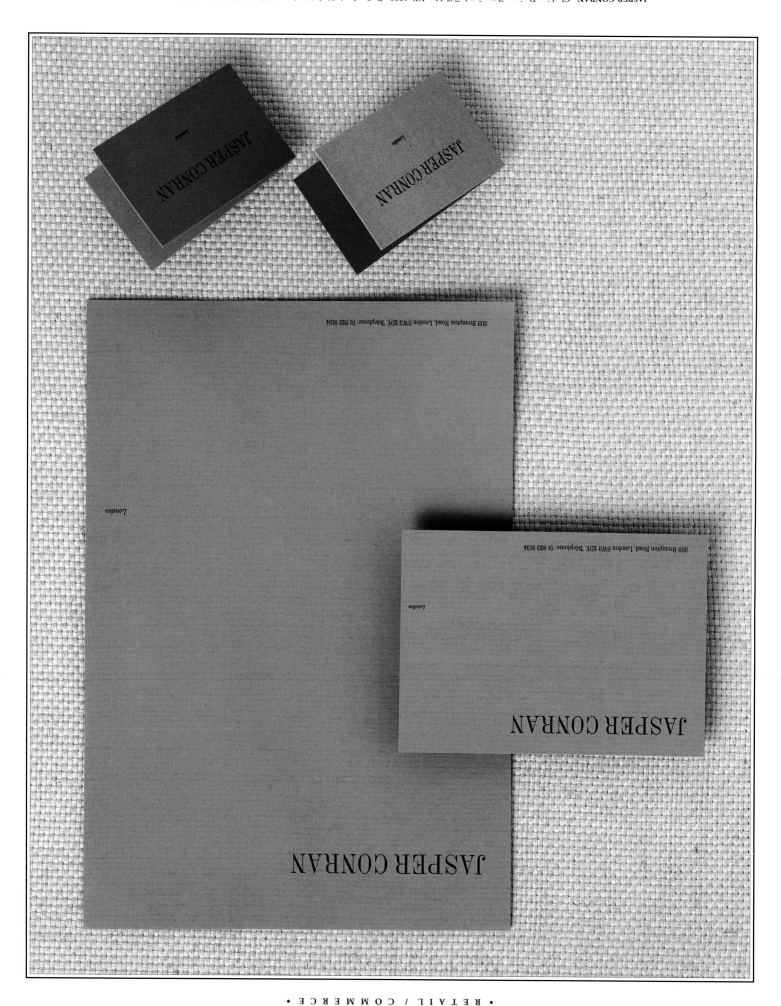

VIÑA VALORIA CELLAR   Traditional Wine Cellar ワインセラー   SPAIN 1991   D: Carmen Peña   DF: Carmen Peña / Provenio Design Studio

FACTORY Fashion Shop ファッションショップ GERMANY 1989 CD: Thomas Feicht AD, D, I: Peter Hinz CW: Ralf Merboth DF: Trust Corporate Culture

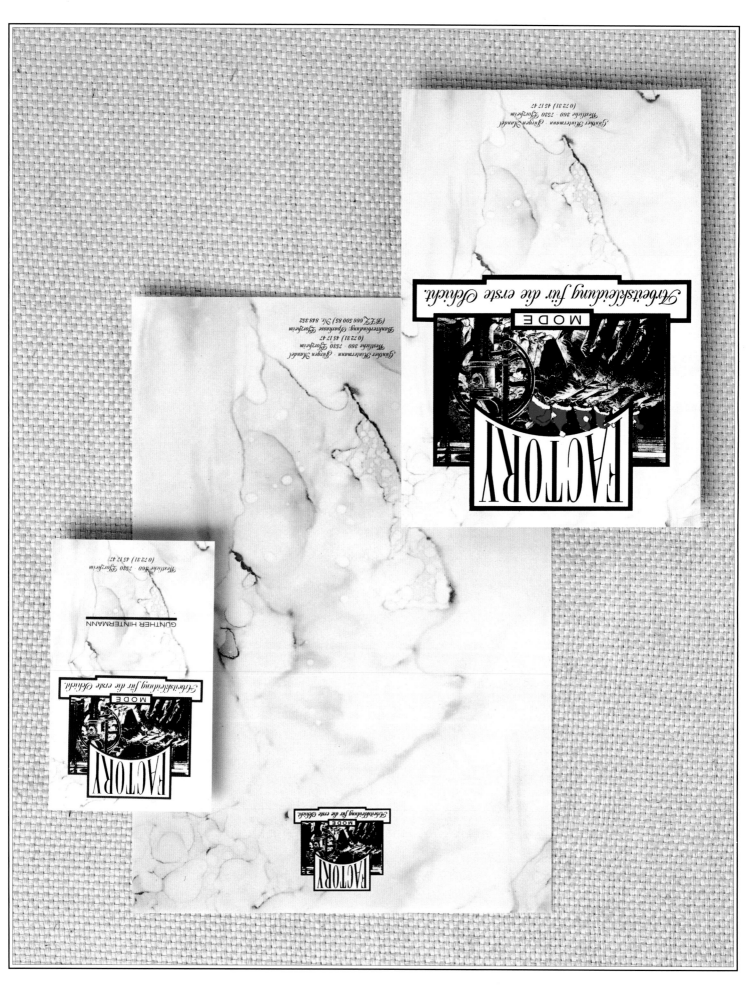

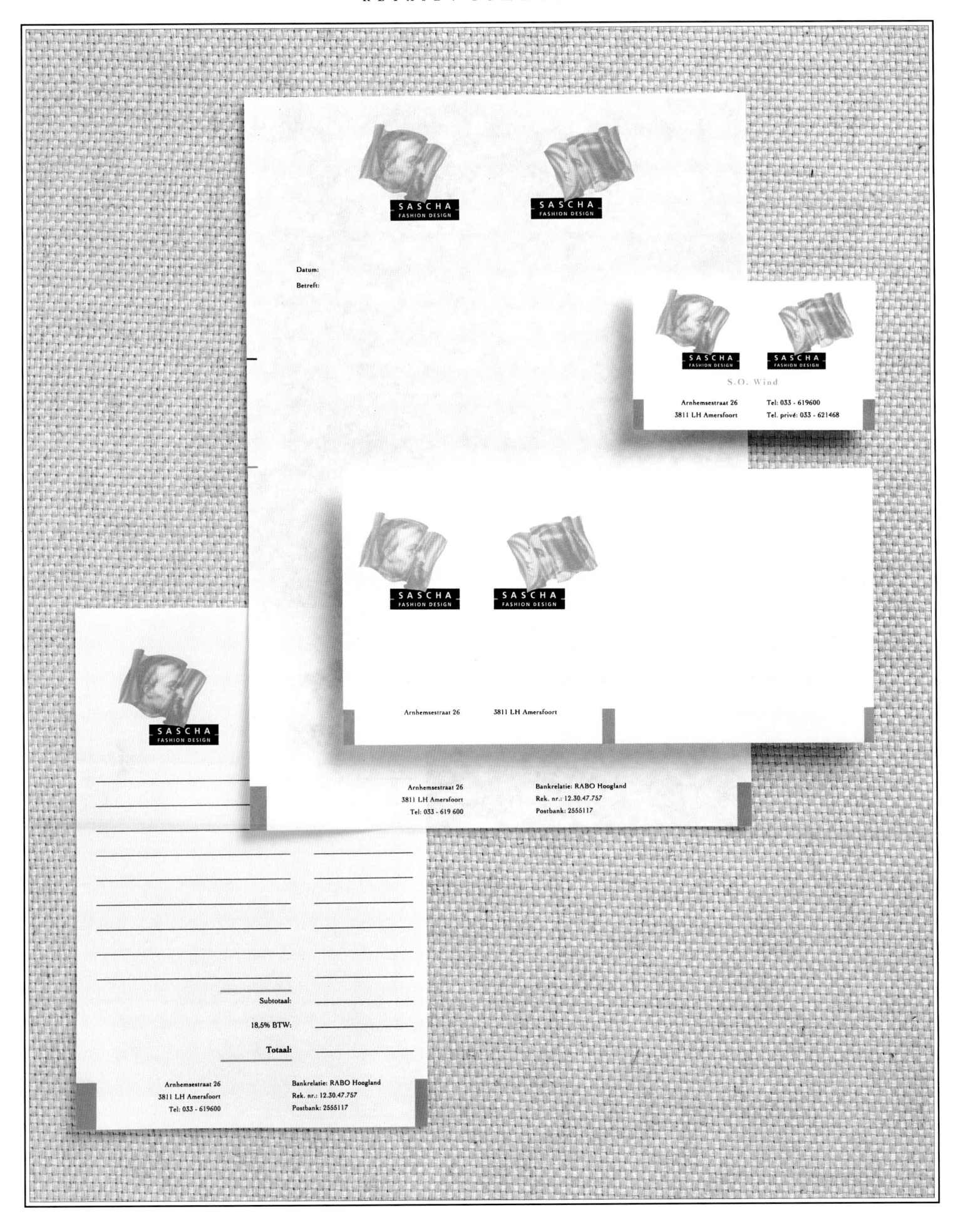

SASCHA FASHION DESIGN　Fashion for Men & Women, Italian & French Collection　イタリア、フランスの紳士、婦人服　THE NETHERLANDS　1992　D, I: Luc Reefman Bno　DF: KBO & R Design

MIKI CO, LTD.   Jewelry Shop   宝石店   JAPAN 1991   AD: Douglas Dollittle

KIMURA KOHKI CO., LTD.   Imported Bag Shop   輸入バッグ販売   JAPAN 1992   CD: Nio Kimura   AD, D: Masayuki Shimuzu   DF: Heter-O-Doxy Proprast

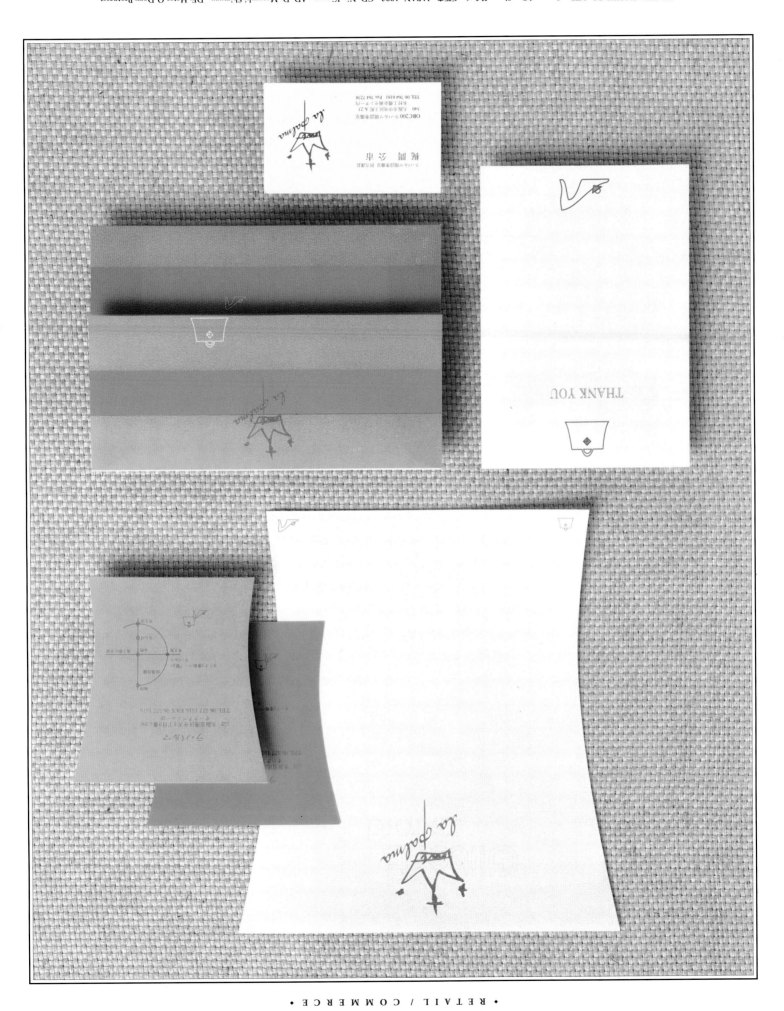

LILO OPERA Fashion Shop ファッションショップ GERMANY 1990 CD: Thomas Feicht AD, D, I: Regina Reiling CW: Ralf Merboth DF: Trust Corporate

GERY ROEKENS / HET BURGER MEESTERS HUYS Belgian Restaurant ベルギー料理レストラン THE NETHERLANDS 1993

D: Luc Reefman Bno / Klaas Jan Woudsma Bno   P: Mariolein Van Den Bos   DF: KBO & R Design

STIL + BLÜTE, SILVIA RIEMANN + UTE REUSSENZEHN Flower Shop 花屋 GERMANY 1990 CD: Thomas Feicht AD, D, I: Sudith Heinz DF: Trust Corporate Culture

POWDER Apparel Maker and Shop 綿人種衣装、帽子 JAPAN 1989-1993 D: Hideki Shimosako

VAZARA Hair & Make up ヘア＆メイク JAPAN 1991 AD, D: Yoshiro Kajitani D: Michiko Arakawa P: Hitoshi Iwakiri DF: Kajitani Design Room

CHEZ LAHLOU   French, Italian Restaurant   フランス、イタリア料理レストラン   UK 1992   AD, D, I: The Designers Republic   DF: The Designers Republic

ZONK, INC.   Screen Printed Activewear   スクリーンプリントの活動服販売   USA 1990   CD: Greg Sabin   D, I: Tracy Sabin   DF: Sabin Design

HONG KONG SEIBU ENTERPRISE CO., LTD. Department Store 百貨店 HONG KONG 1991 AD, D: Alan Chan D: Phillip Leung I: Gary Cheung DF: Alan Chan Design

TAKEO CO., LTD. Paper Wholesaler 洋紙卸売業 JAPAN 1991 CD: Tsuyokatsu Kudo AD, D: Yuriko Tomita D: Design Laboratory DF: Design Laboratory

JOYCE BOUTIQUE LIMITED Fashion Boutique ファッションブティック HONG KONG 1990 AD, D: Alan Chan D: Phillip Leung DF: Alan Chan Design

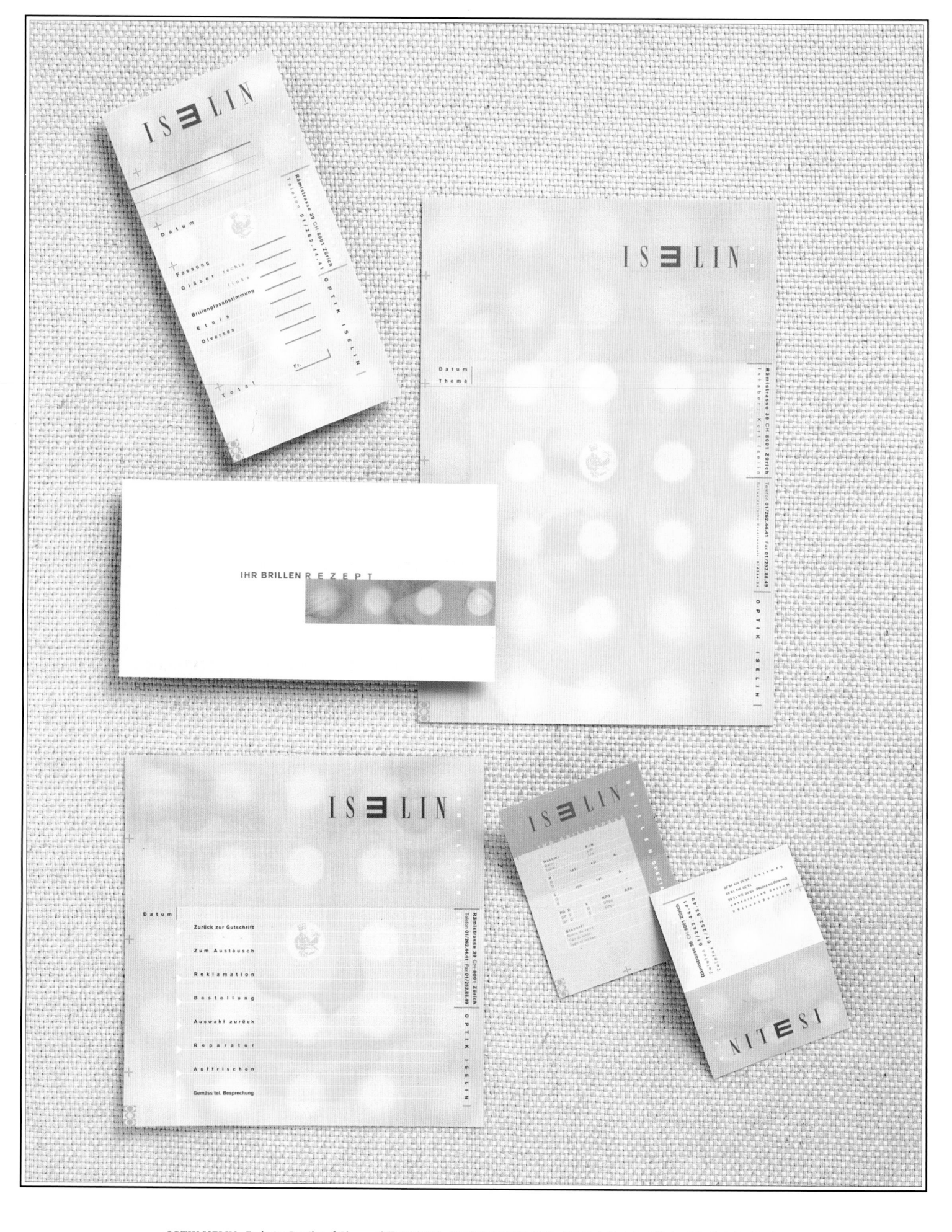

OPTIK ISELIN   Exclusive Retailer of Glasses   高級メガネ販売   SWITZERLAND   1991   AD, D, I: Christian Hügin   DF: Christian Hügin

TAKEO CO., LTD.   Paper Wholesaler   洋紙卸売業   JAPAN 1991   CD: Tsuyokatsu Kudo   AD: Nobuyoshi Kikuchi   D: Design Laboratory   DF: Design Laboratory

BOWHAUS   Rental Photo Studio   貸撮影室   USA 1992   D: Margo Chase / Alan Disparte   DF: Margo Chase Design

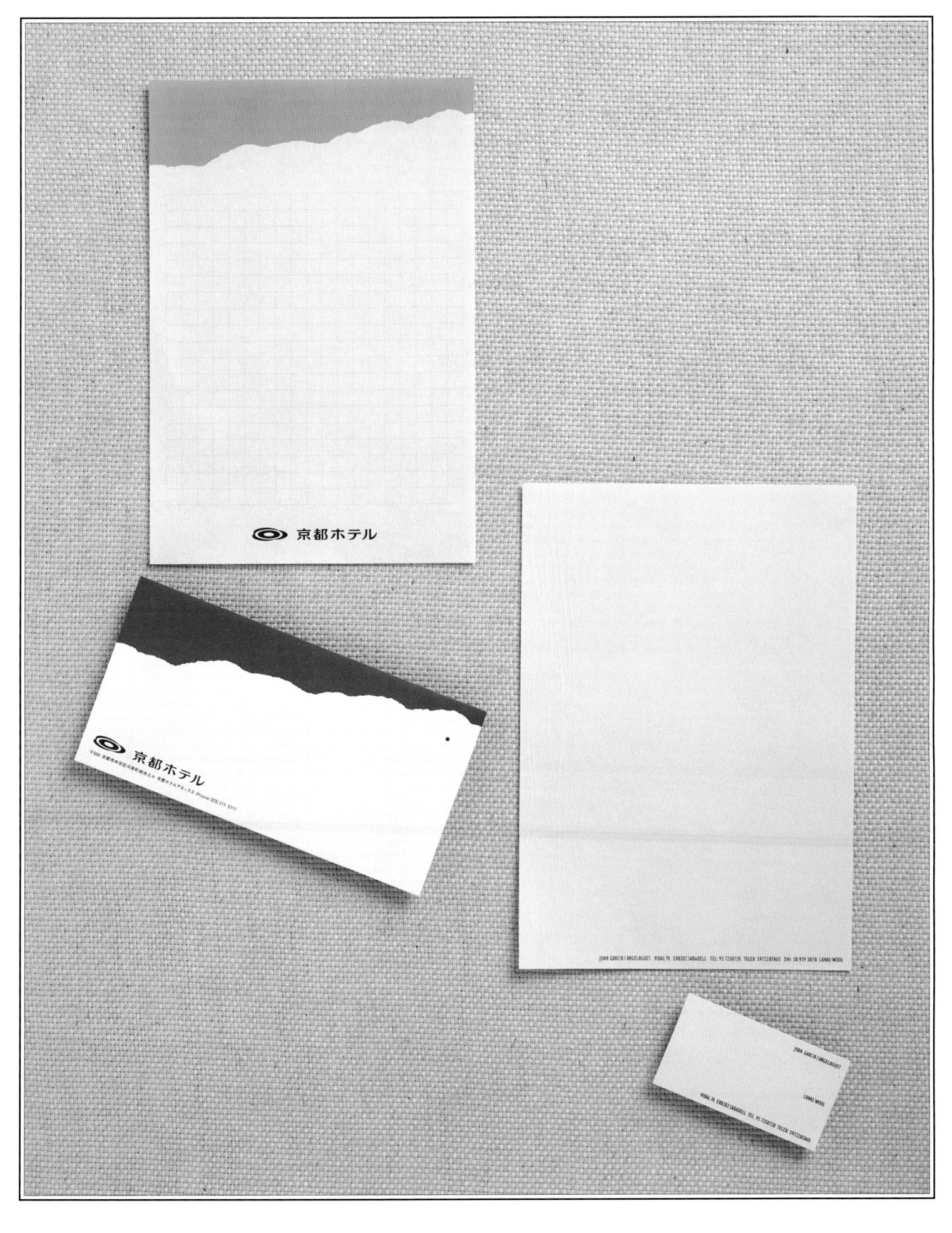

THE KYOTO HOTEL LTD. Hotel ホテル JAPAN 1993 AD: GK Kyoto / Daisuke Nakatsuka   D: Yasuhiko Matsumoto / Masami Ishibashi   DF: Nakatsuka Daisuke

JOAN GARCIA ARGELAGUET Wool Buyer 羊毛仕入れ業 UK 1989 AD, D: Teresa Roviras   DF: Teresa Roviras

COLLEGE POSTERS + PRINTS   Poster and Art Print Merchandisers   ポスター、アートプリント商品取扱い   UK 1990   AD, D: The Designers Republic   DF: The Designers Republic

801 STEAK AND CHOP HOUSE Restaurant レストラン USA 1993 AD, D, I: John Sayles DF: Sayles Graphic Design

I. A. BEDFORD   Textile Manufacturer   テキスタイル製造   USA 1992   AD, D, I: John Sayles   CW: Wendy Lyons   DF: Sayles Graphic Design

ROSS SUTHERLAND Farm 農場 USA 1992 CD: James M. Skiles AD: Kathryn Klein D: Tim McGrath

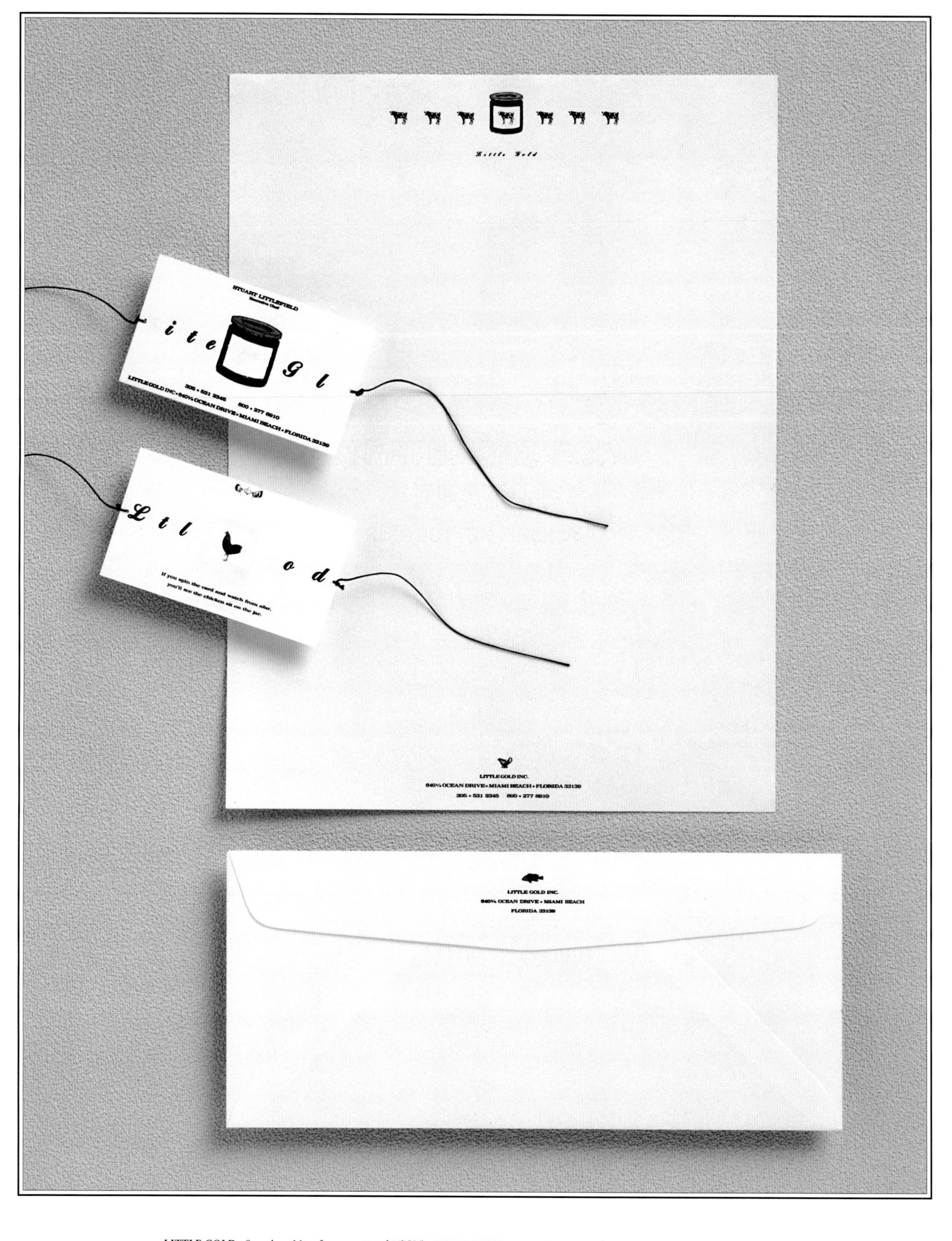

LITTLE GOLD   Soup-base Manufacturer   スープの素製造   HONG KONG 1989   AD, D, I: Stefan Sagmeister   DF: Sagmeister Graphics

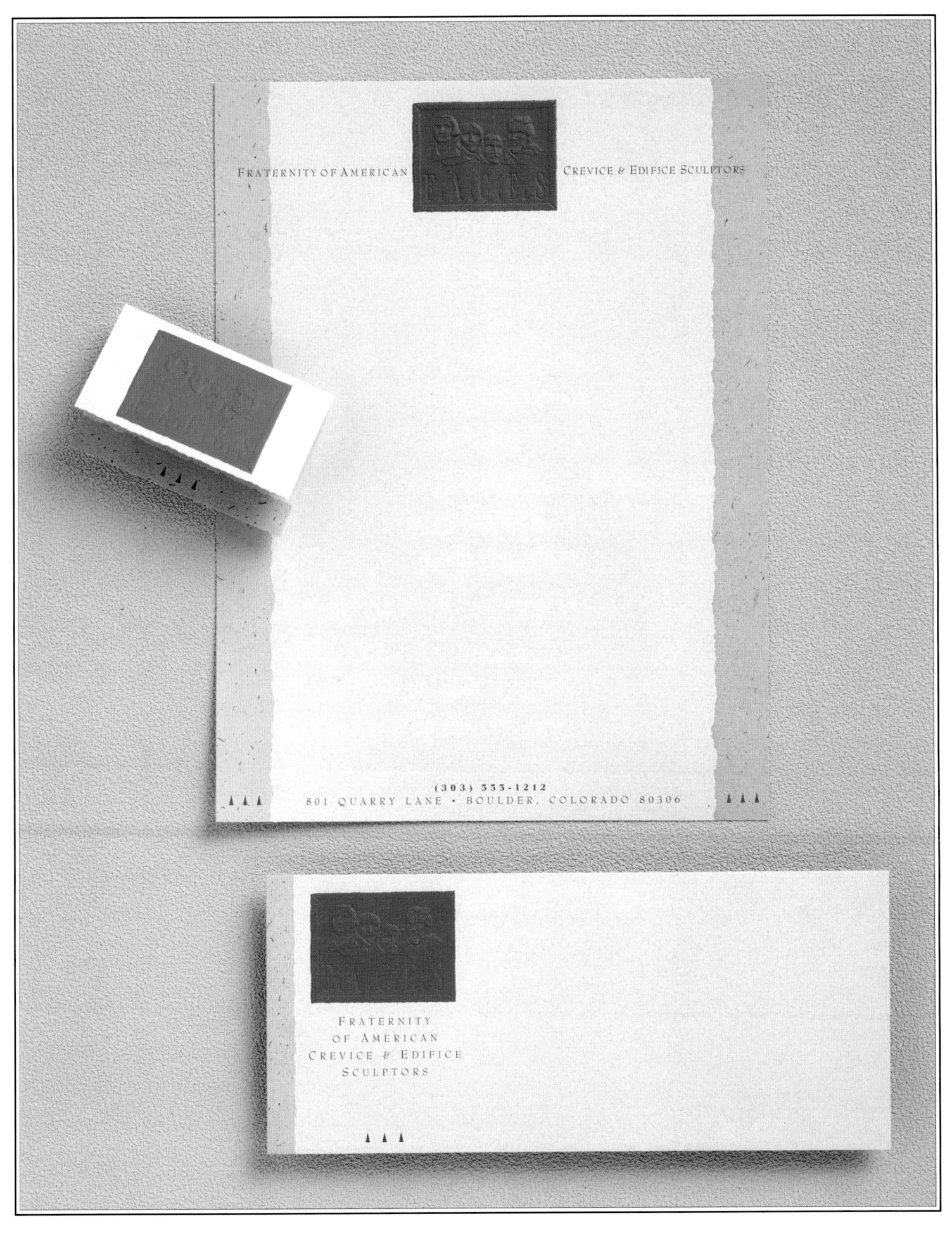

THE BECKETY PAPER COMPANY Paper Manufacturer 紙製造 USA 1989 AD, D: Eric Rickabaugh DF: Rickabaugh Graphics
Special Effects: Trademark has been embossed. マークが型押しされている。

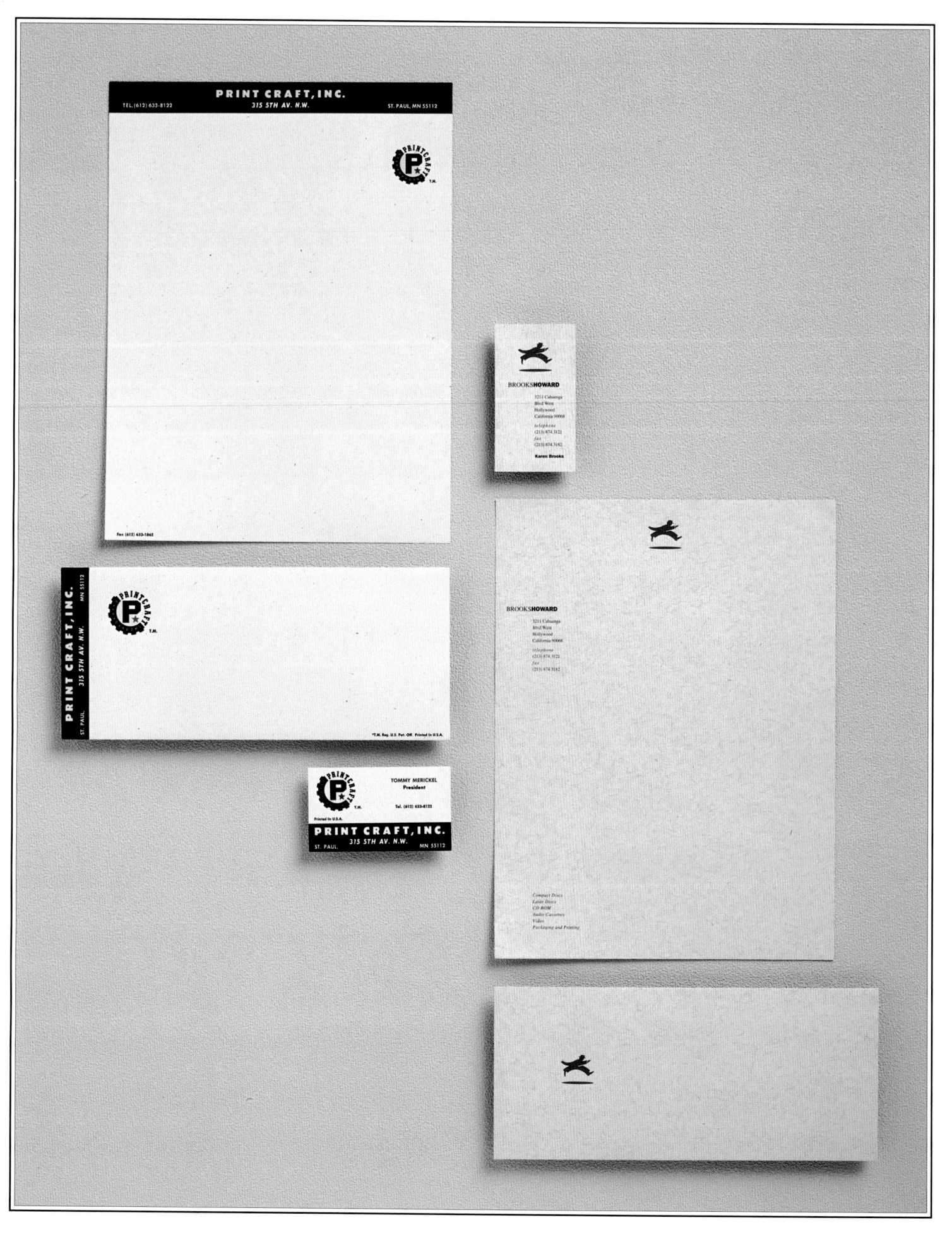

PRINT CRAFT, INC. Printer 印刷業 USA 1989 AD, D: Charles Spencer Anderson D: Daniel Olson DF: Charles S. Anderson Design

BROOKS HOWARD Duplicator 複製業 USA 1991 AD, D: Stan Evenson D: Glenn Sakamoto

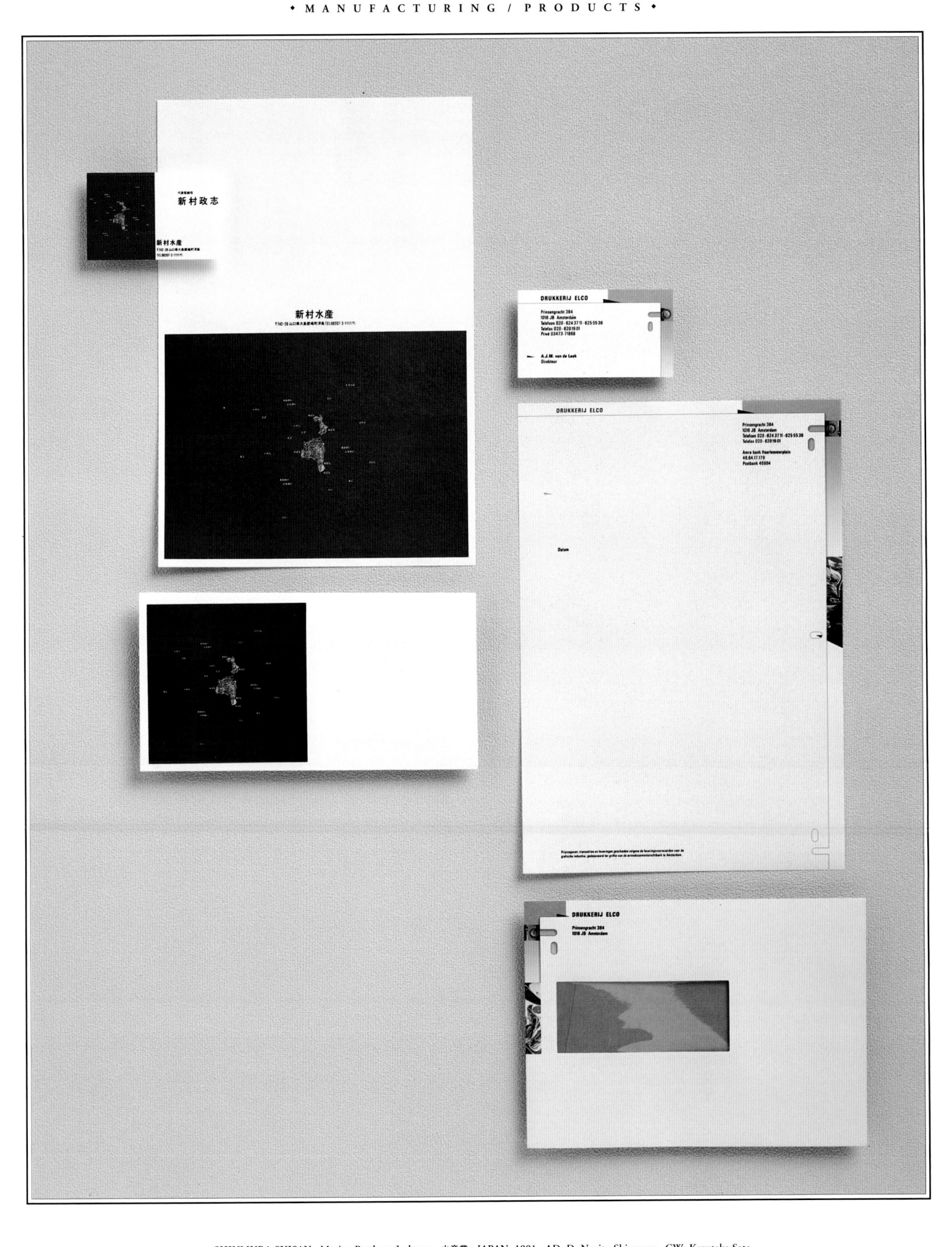

SHINMURA SUISAN Marine Products Industry 水産業 JAPAN 1991 AD, D: Norito Shinmura CW: Kazutaka Sato

DRUKKERIJ ELCO Printer 印刷業 THE NETHERLANDS 1991 AD, D: Anton Vos DF: Dedato

JAQUET PARQUET AG Exclusive Parquet Firm 高級寄せ木細工 SWITZERLAND 1990 AD, D: Christian Hügin P: Felix Strfuli CW: Roland Mùllek Muller DF: Christian Hügin

CURRAN ART GLASS Maker of Fine Glass　ファインガラス製造　USA　1991　CD: Mark Oldach　AD, D: Don Emery　P: Bob Huff　DF: Mark Oldach Design

DATUM

GWEN MACLAINE PONT ARCHITEKTE HBO BNI	
ATELIER: SPUI 165	RABOBANK
2511BM 's-GRAVENHAGE	REK. NR. 35.76.88.716
TELEFOON 070.3605350	POSTBANK 715310

GWEN MACLAINE PONT ARCHITEKTE HBO BNI

GWEN MACLAINE PONT ARCHITEKTE HBO BNI

GWEN MACLAINE PONT ARCHITEKTE HBO BNI	
ATELIER: SPUI 165	
2511BM 's-GRAVENHAGE	

GWEN MACLAINE PONT ARCHITEKTE HBO BNI
ATELIER: SPUI 165
2511BM 's-GRAVENHAGE
TELEFOON 070.3605350

GWEN MACLAINE PONT   Architect   建築家   THE NETHERLANDS 1990 AD, D: Anton Vos   DF: Anton Vos

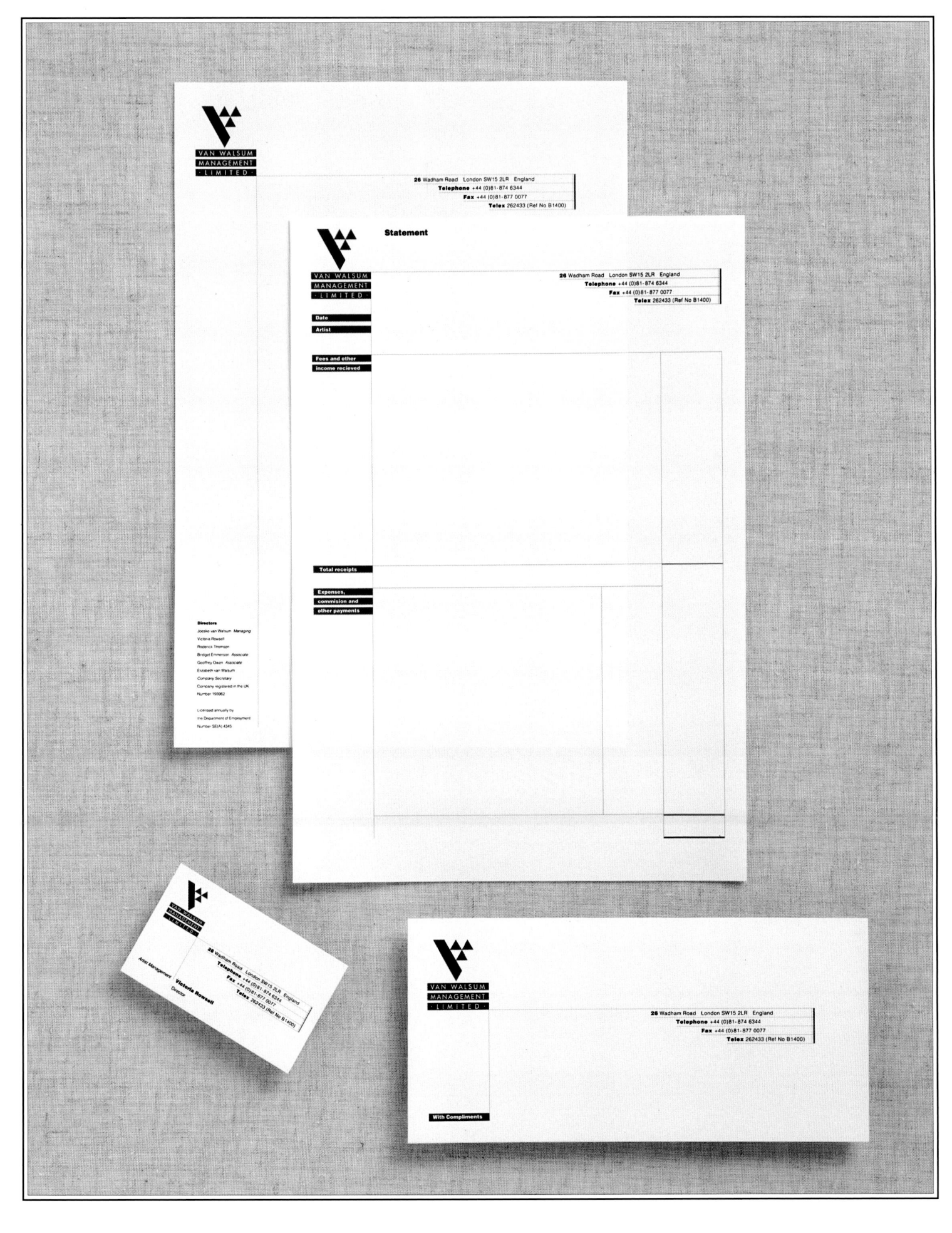

VAN WALSUM MANAGEMENT   Musical Artist Agents, Management and Promotion   ミュージシャンの管理、促進   UK 1992   D: Richard Ward   DF: The Team

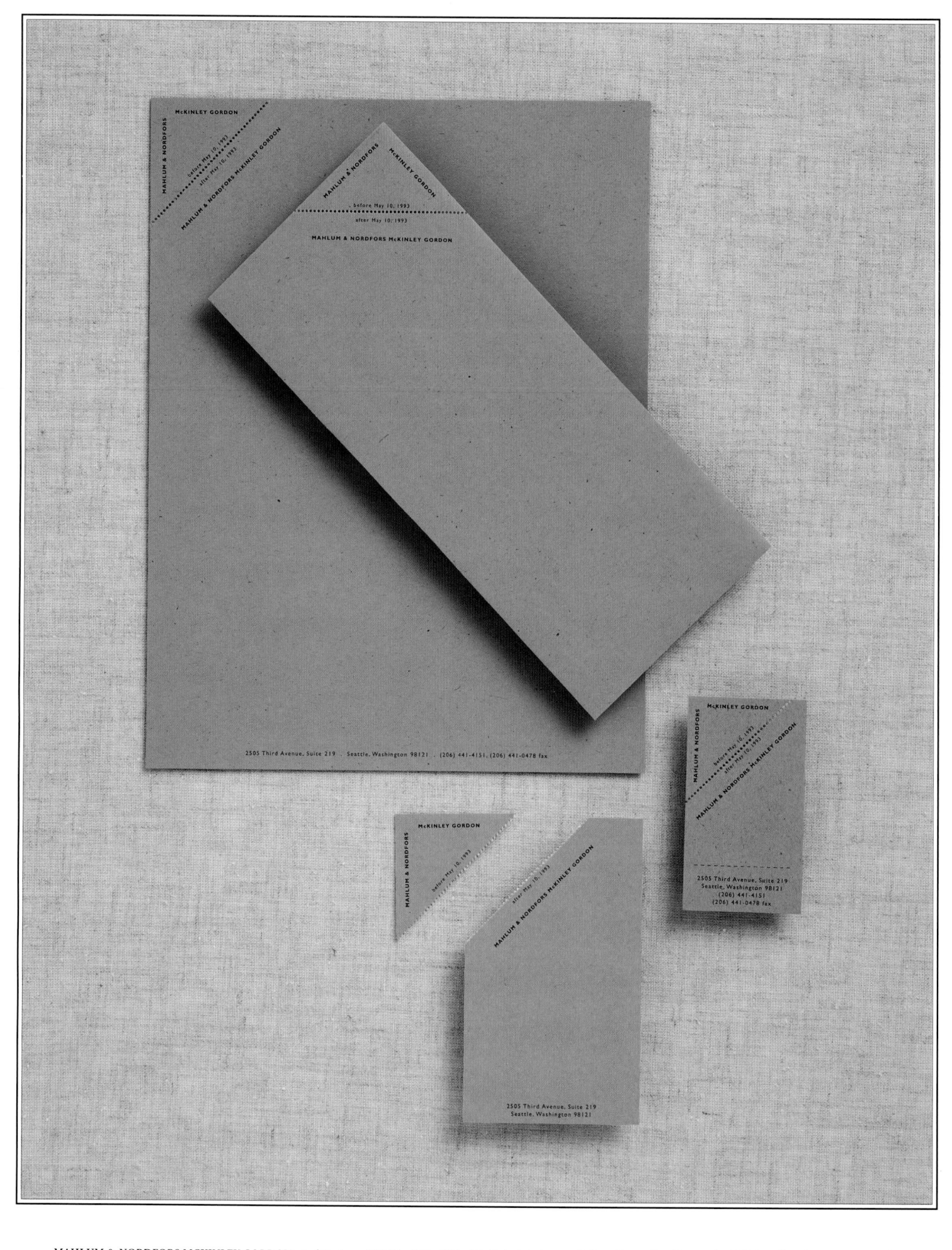

MAHLUM & NORDFORS MCKINLEY GORDON Architecture 建築設計 USA 1993 AD, D: Jack Anderson D: Scott Eggers / Leo Raymundo DF: Hornall Anderson Design Works

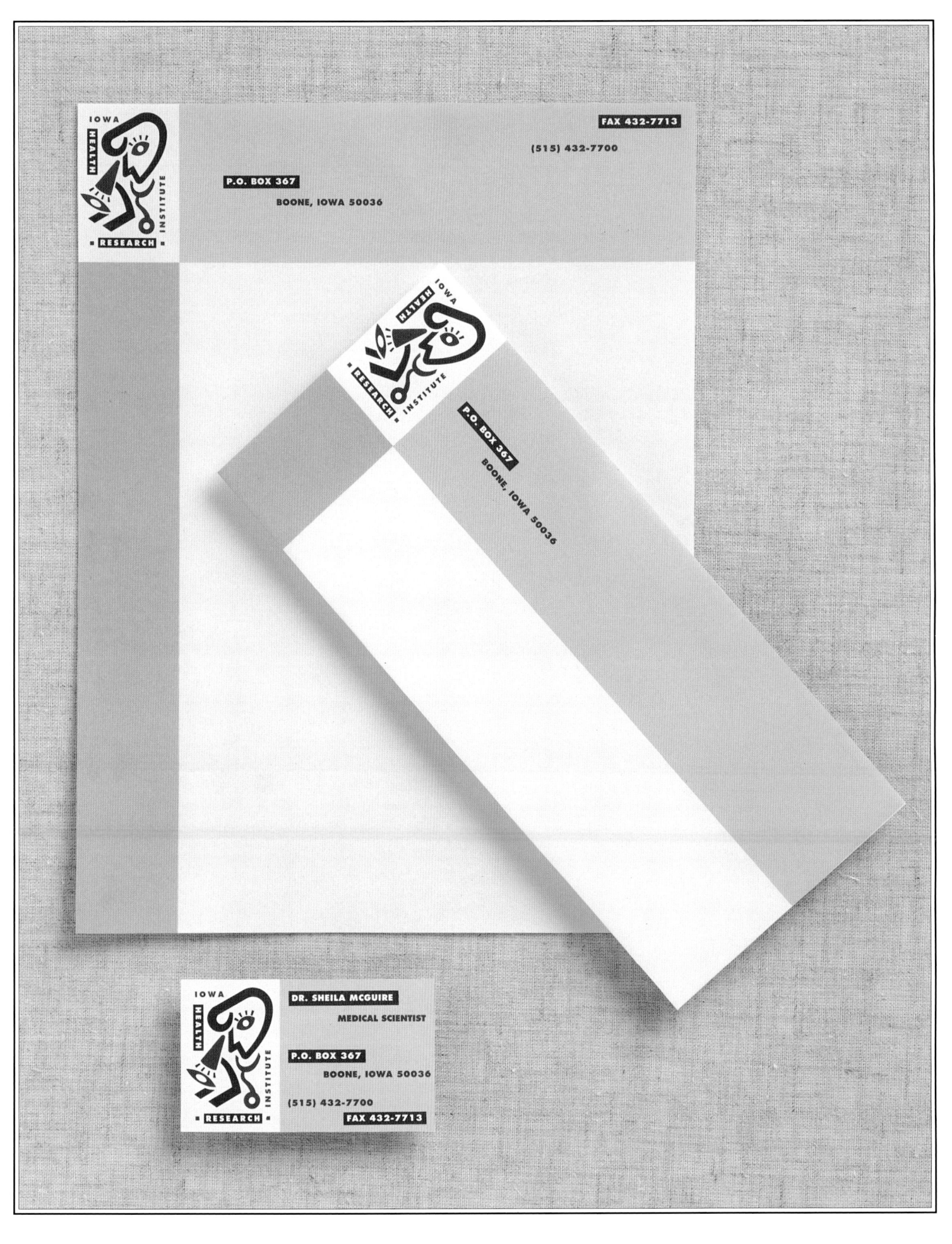

IOWA HEALTH RESEARCH INSTITUTE Medical Scientific Research Organization 医療科学研究協会 USA 1992 AD, D, I: John Sayles DF: Sayles Graphic Design

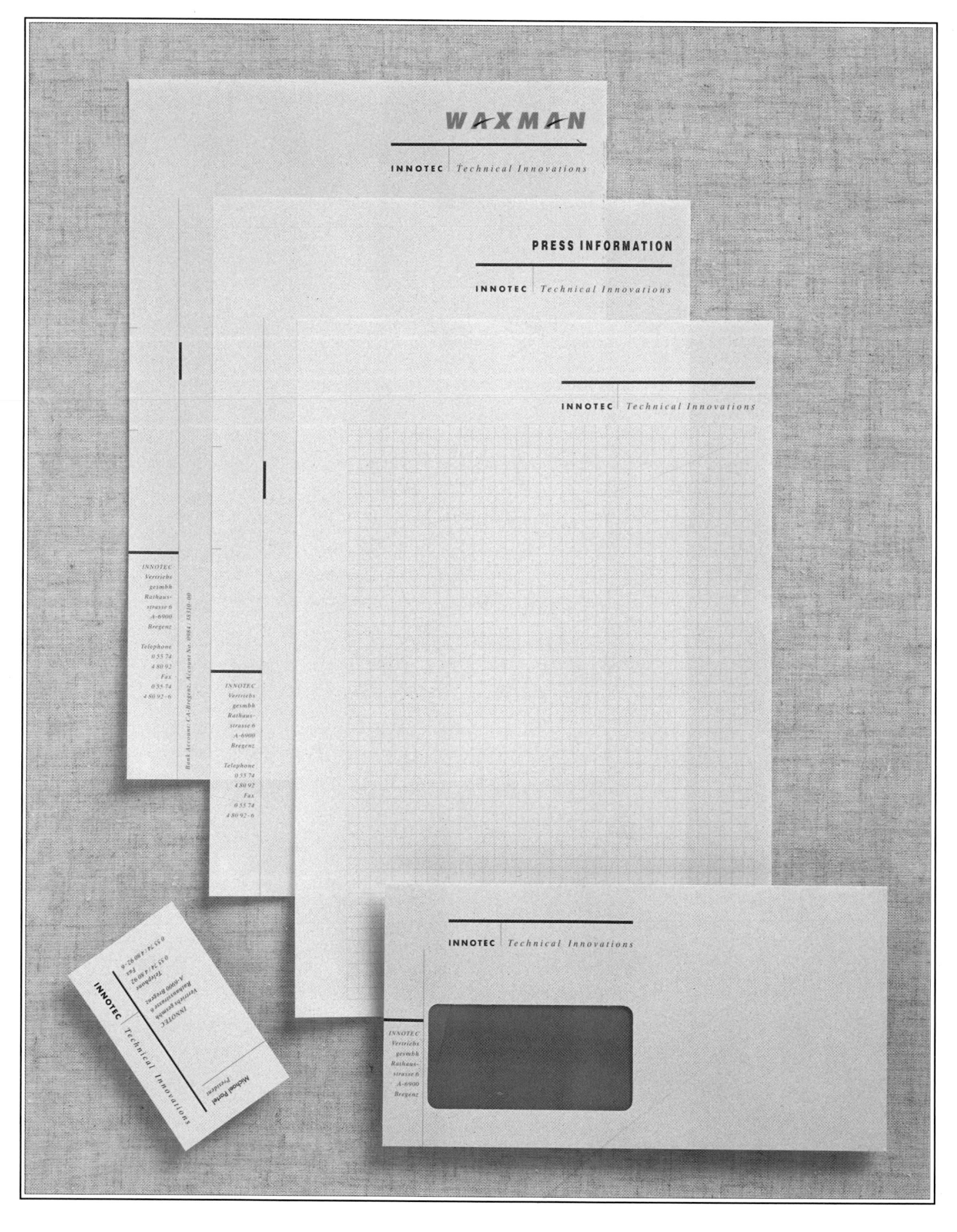

INNOTEC GMBH Technical Innovations 技術革新業 AUSTRIA 1992 D: Kurt Dornig DF: Dornig Grafik Design

BARTHOLOMÄUS MOOSBRUGGER Architect 建築家 AUSTRIA 1992 AD, D, I: Sigi Ramoser DF: Sigi Ramoser

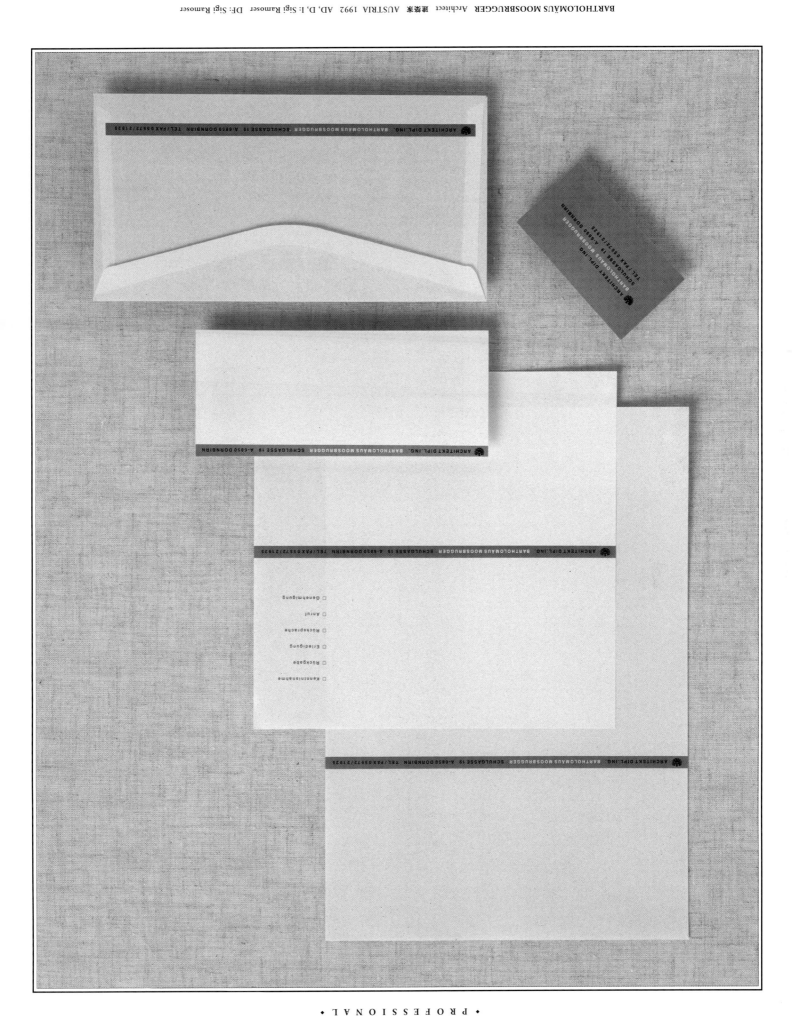

GRZELAK & BRYANT Architecture and Landscape Architects 建築景觀、庭園設計 AUSTRALIA 1992 AD, D: Graham Rendoth CW: Grzelak & Bryant DF: Reno Design Group

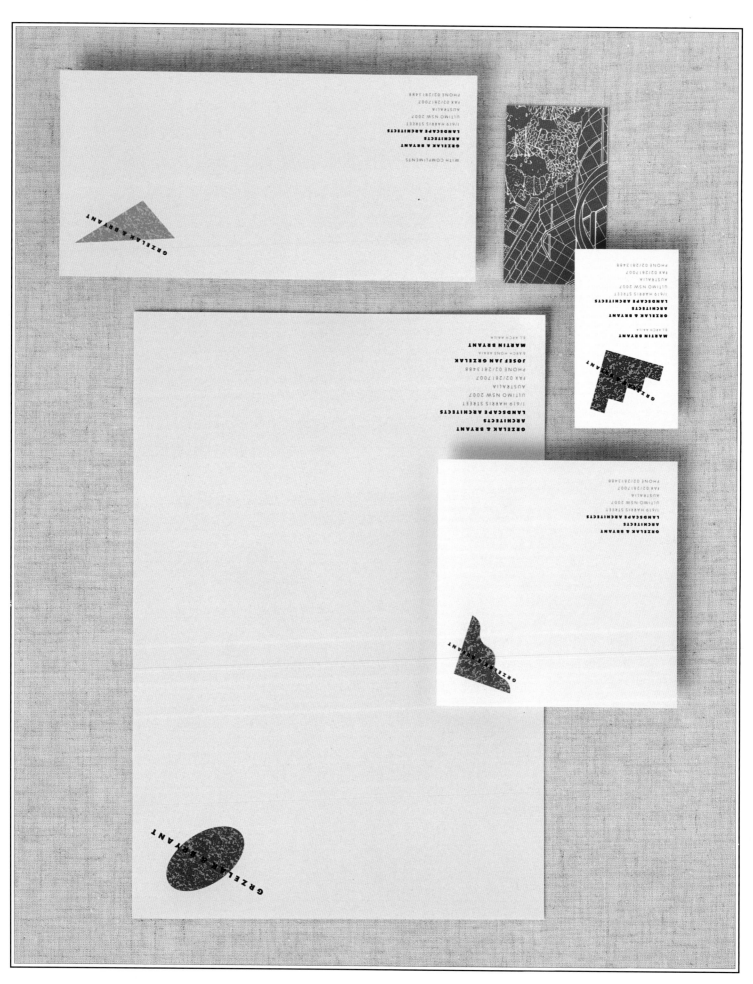

SPARE, TENGLER, KAPLAN & BISCHEL Investment Company 投資会社 USA 1990 AD: Bill Cahan D: Stuart Flake DF: Cahan & Assoc.

RETAIL PORTFOLIO GROUP Leasing Company 借地経営会社 CANADA 1991 AD: Del Terrelonge DF: Terrelonge Design

ARCHITECTO Architectural Engineering 建築設計工学 USA 1989 AD, D, I, CW: Charles Hively

MISTER FIX - IT General Repairs Contractor 一般修理業、工事兼業 USA 1991 AD, D: Kristin Sommese AD, I: Canny Sommese DF: Sommese Design

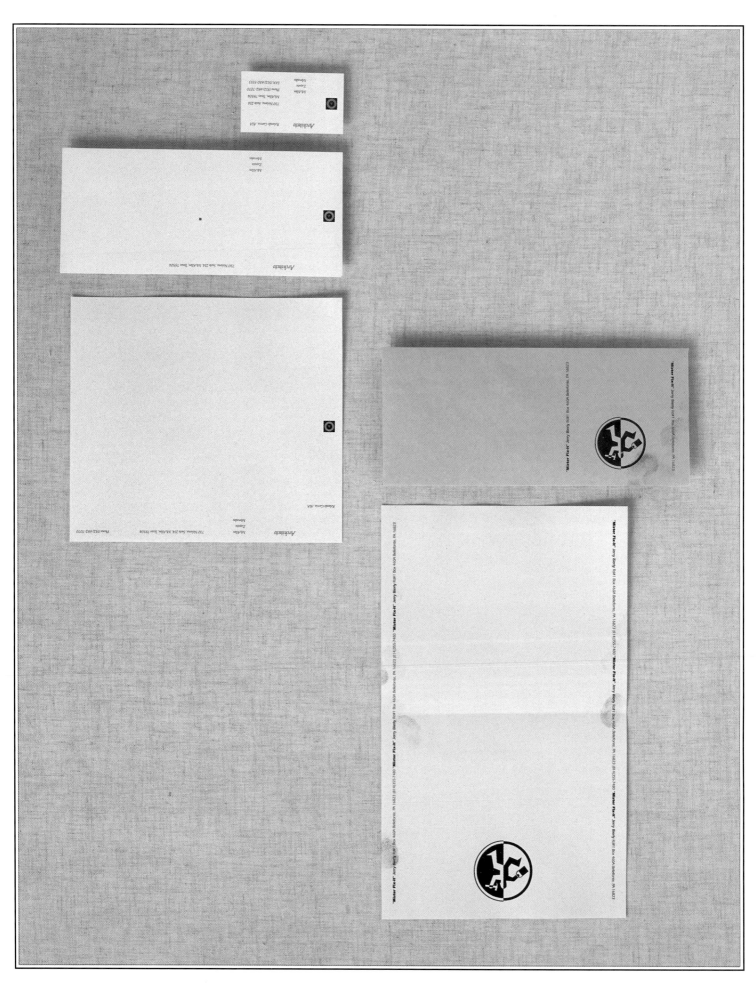

NBBJ Architecture, Design and Planning. 建築意匠設計、デザイン、プランニング CD: Doug Keyes / Stefanie Choi / Margo Sepanski / Susan Dewey. D: Doug Keyes DF: NBBJ - Graphic Design
CHAMELEON INVESTIGATIONS, INC. Private Investigations and Corporate Security. 個人調査、企業保護サービス USA 1992 AD, I: Peter Bradford DF: Peter Bradford and Associates

BECKLEY IMPORTS, INC.　Car Repair Service　車輛整備サービス　USA 1993　AD, D, I: John Sayles　DF: Sayles Graphic Design

DOUGLAS K. LARSON, D. D. S　Dentist　歯科医　USA 1986　D: Lauren Smith　DF: Lauren Smith Design

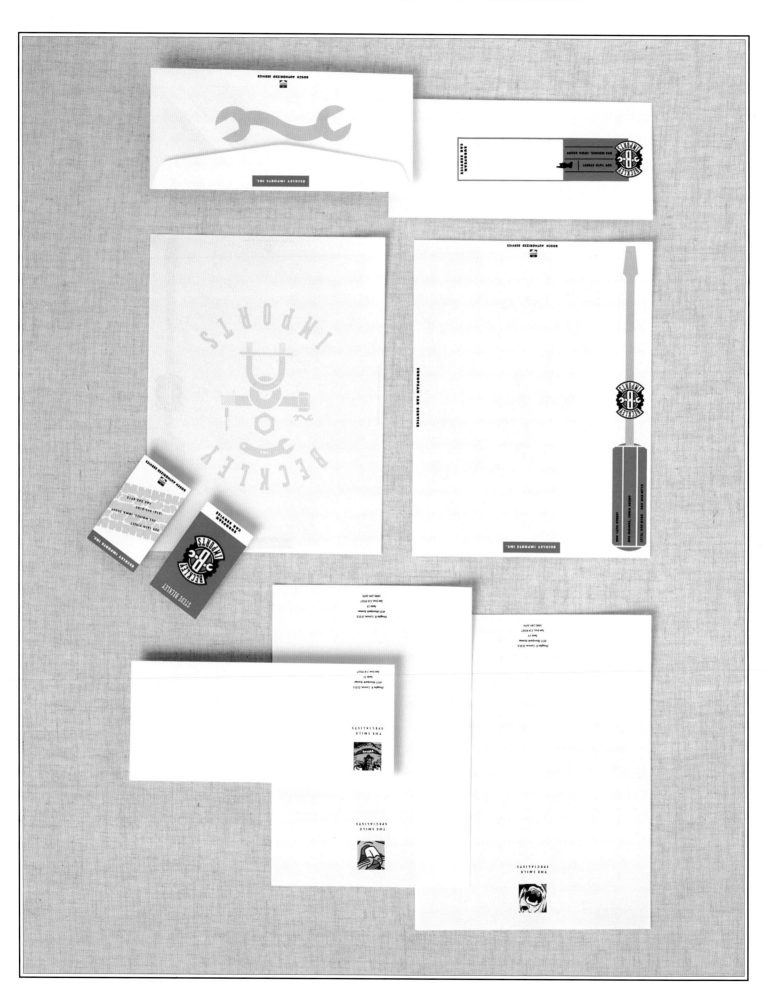

HOOGSTRATEN PARTNERS Consultancy Organization コンサルタント協会 THE NETHERLANDS 1991 D: Luc Reefman Bno DF: KBO & R Design

V. FRANK, AIA　Architect　建築家　USA 1993　AD, D: Iva Frank　DF: Iva Frank Graphic Design

AHA-JACEK BRETSZNAJDER　Architecture　建築設計　POLAND 1990　AD, D: Tadeusz Piechura　DF: Atelier Tadeusz Piechura

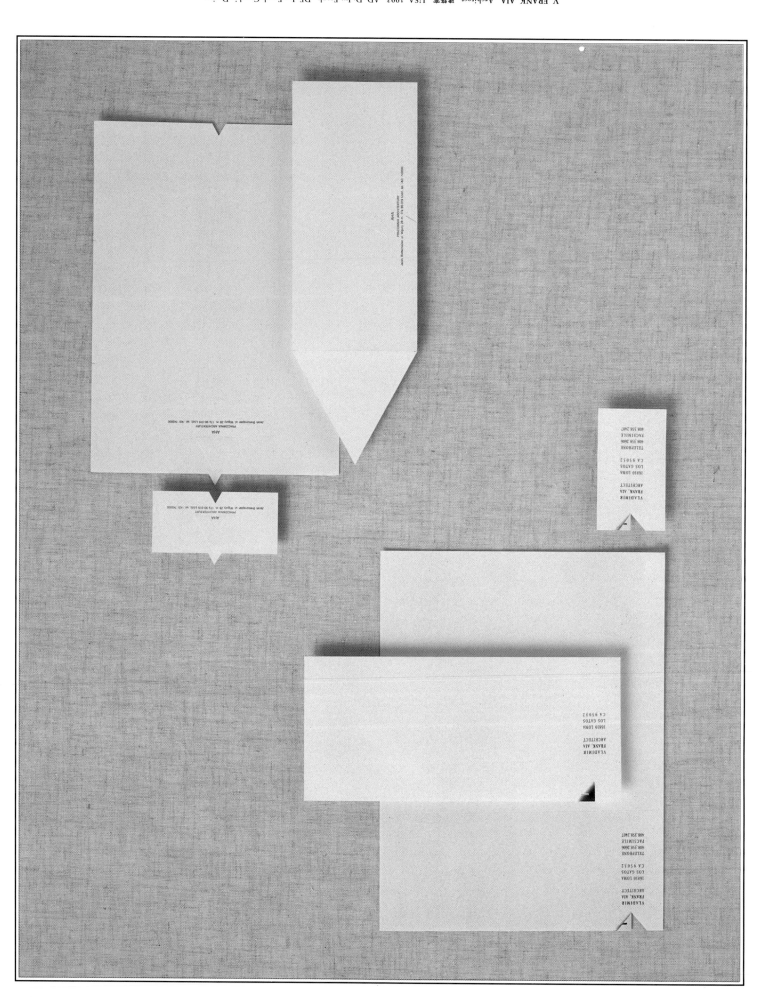

PARADIGM HEALTH CORP. Health Care バリメアアア USA 1991 AD, D: Neal Zimmermann DF: Zimmermann Crowe Design

JOHN F. KILEY III CPA Certified Public Accountants 公認会計士 USA 1991 AD, D: Teddie Barnhart DF: Barnstorming Designs

ROMY SIEBER (MRS.), ZÜRICH   Career Management for Women   女性の職業管理   SWITZERLAND 1991   AD, I, CW: Michael Baviera   D: Siegrun Nuber   DF: BBV

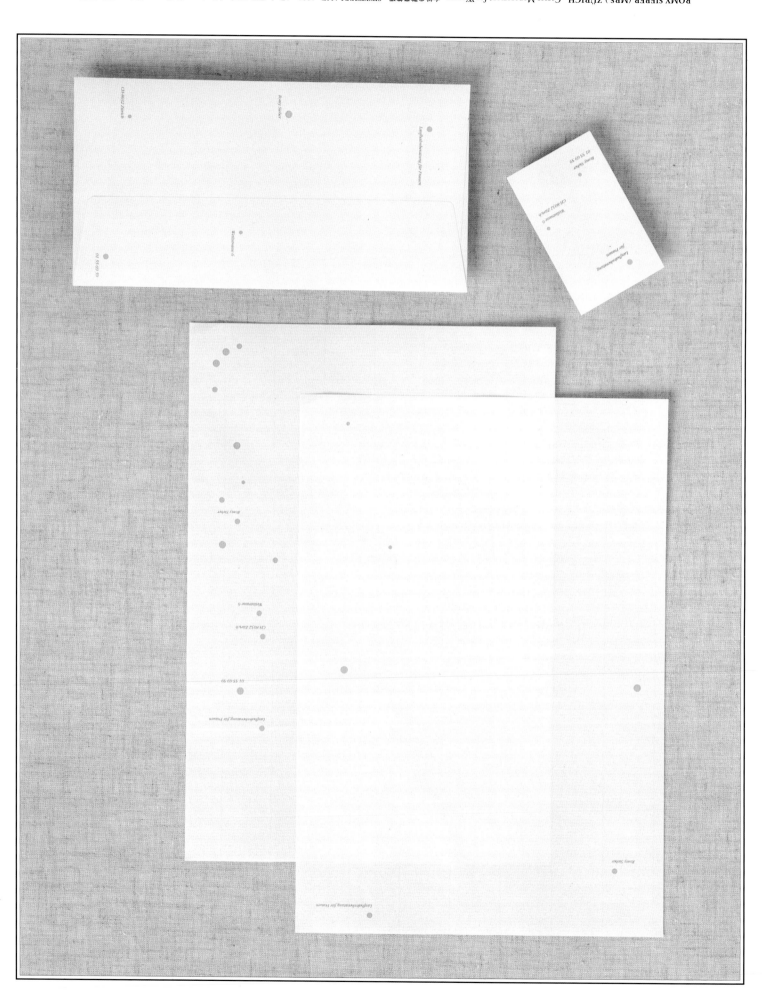

BECKER - KORREKTUREN 校正業 Proofreader GERMANY 1989 CD: Thomas Feicht AD, D: Willie Demel P: Bernd Mayer DF: Trust Corporate Culture

DALE F. STEELE Fashion Consultant ファッション・コンサルタント USA 1990 AD, D: Iva Frank DF: Iva Frank Graphic Design

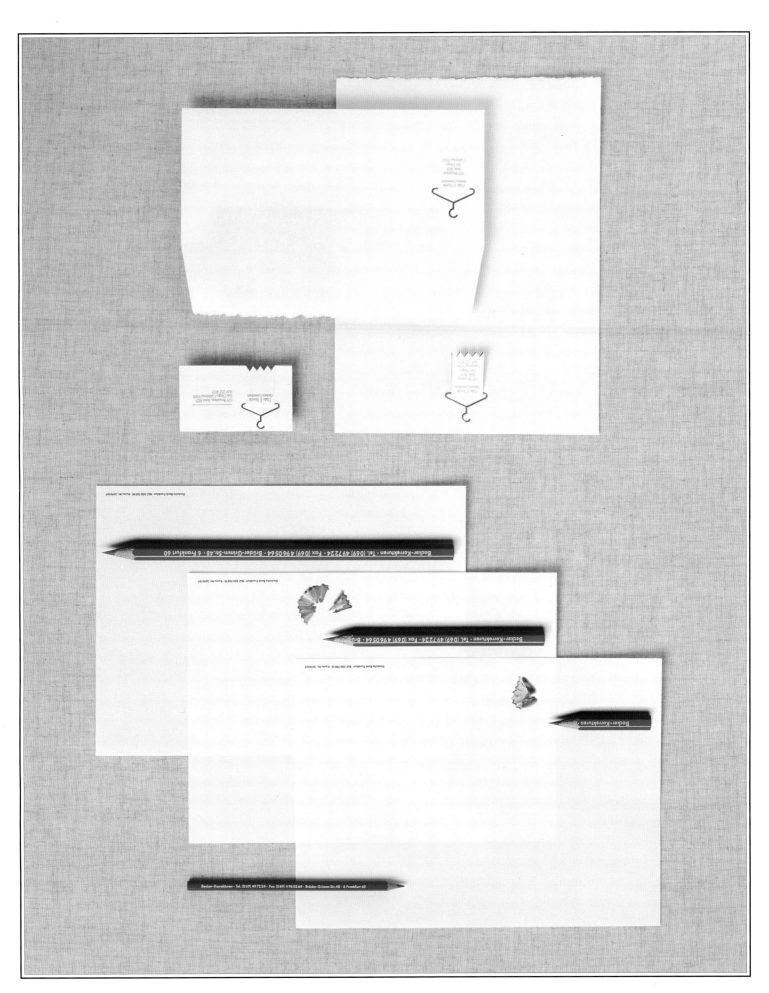

KOKI KOGEI INC. Display Business ディスプレイ施工 AD, D: Eiichi Sakota D: Toshio Kawakami DF: Rec 2nd

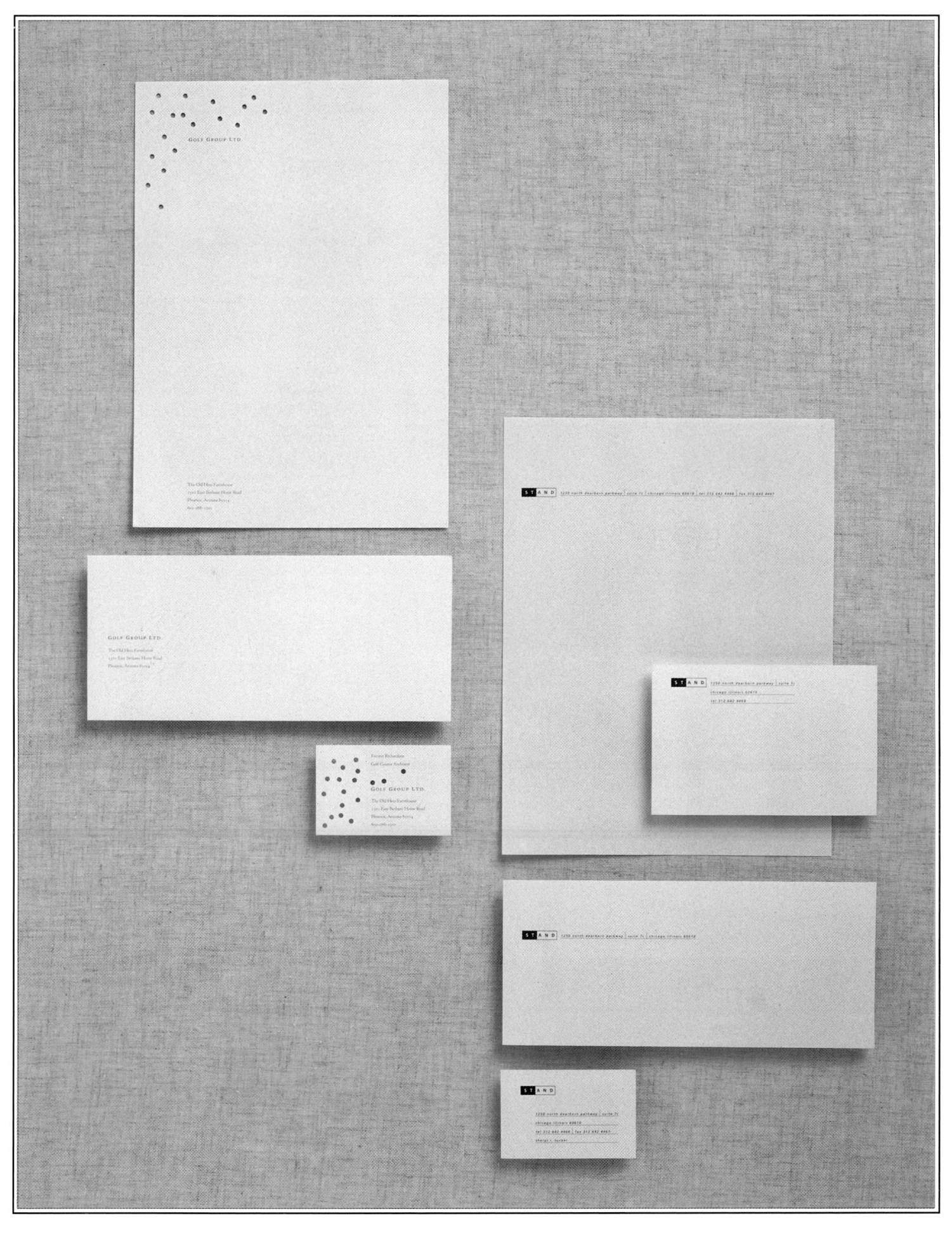

GOLF GROUP LTD. Golf Course Architects ゴルフコース設計 USA 1988 AD, D: Forrest Richardson DF: Richardson or Richardson

STAND Entrepreneur with Several Businesses 数種職業の仲介 USA 1992 D: Jilly Simons DF: Concrete, Chicago

ARMIN SCHNEIDER   Badminton Trainer   バドミントンコーチ   HONG KONG 1990   CD, D, I: Stefan Sagmeister   DF: Sagmeister Graphics

PAUL BARGEHR Massage Parlour マッサージ新療院 AUSTRIA 1992 AD, D: Sigi Ramoser DF: Sigi Ramoser

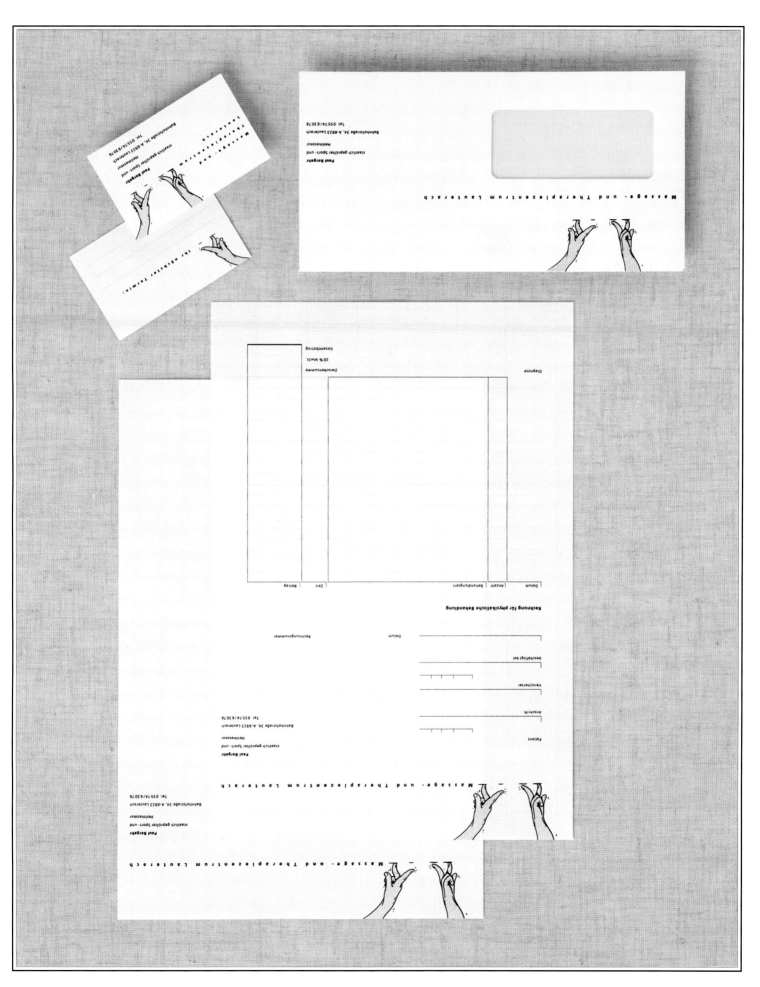

CD: Forrest Richardson   AD, D: Debi Young Mees   I: Jim Bolek   DF: Richardson or Richardson

GOLF MANAGEMENT INTERNATIONAL   Golf Development and Management   ゴルフの開発・経営   USA 1990

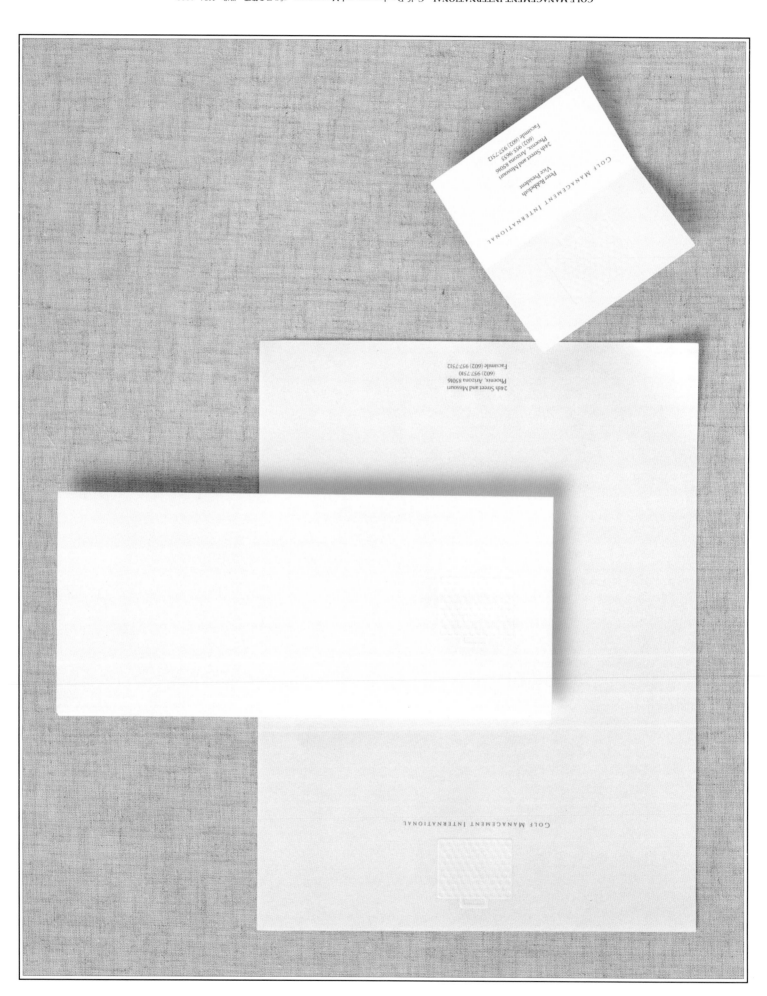

DAVID WARREN DESIGN Graphic Design グラフィックデザイン USA AD, D: David Warren P: Jim Havey DF: David Warren Design

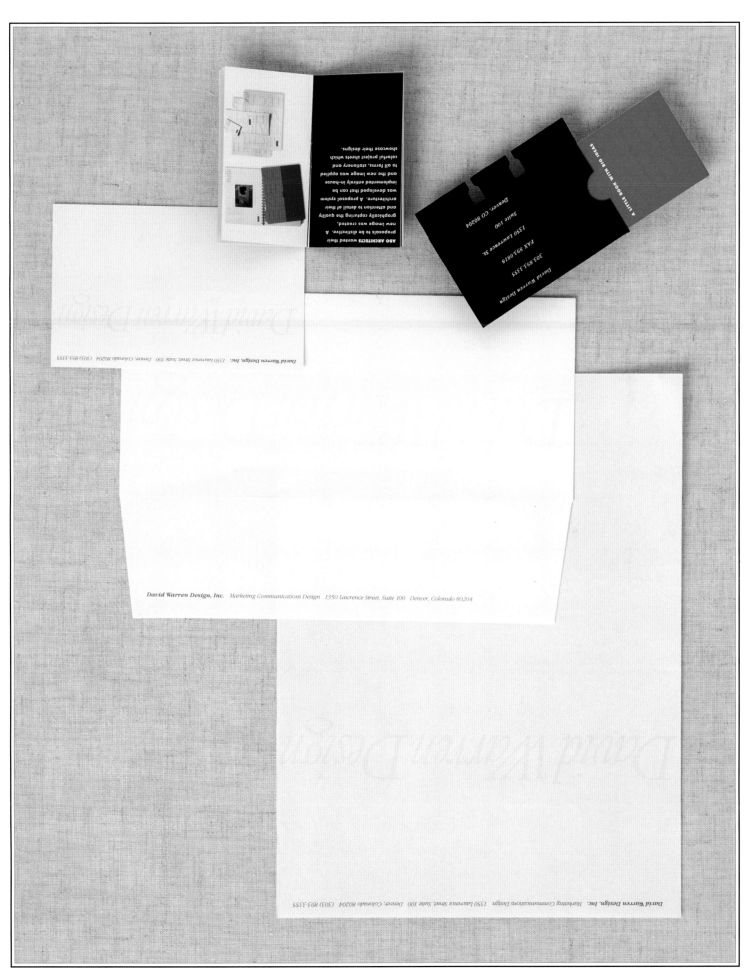

IDEAPAJA　Model Making　モデルメイキング　FINLAND 1988　D, I: Viktor Kaltala　DF: Viktorno Design

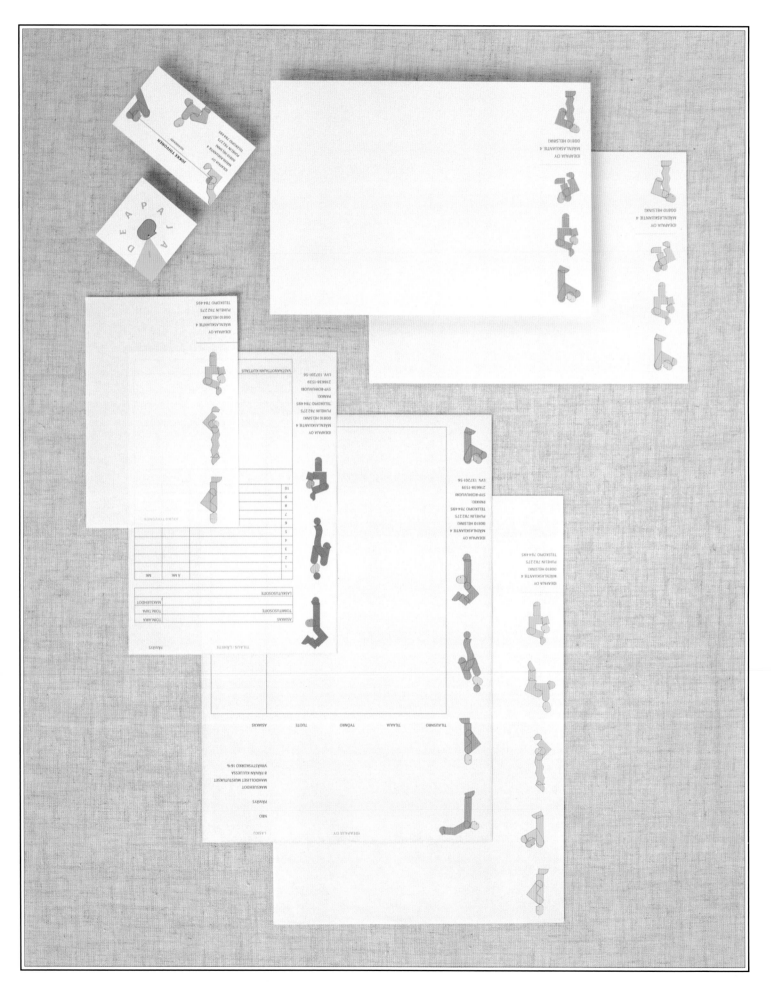

Univ. Med. Dr. Günter Ludescher · Facharzt für Zahn-, Mund- und Kieferheilkunde · A-6850 Dornbirn · Marktstraße 21 · Tel. 0 5572 / 68817

Univ. Med. Dr. Günter Ludescher · Facharzt für Zahn-, Mund- und Kieferheilkunde · A-6850 Dornbirn · Marktstraße 21 · Tel. 0 5572 / 68817

HONORAR-NOTE

Herrn/Frau/Frl. _____   Dornbirn, am _____

Zahl	Behandlung von _____ bis _____	Honorar

Summe	
plus 20% MwSt.	
Gesamthonorar	
Anzahlung	
Restbetrag	

R   L

8 7 6 5 4 3 2 1 1 2 3 4 5 6 7 8

Dr. Günter Ludescher
Facharzt f. Zahn-, Mund-
u. Kieferheilkunde
6850 Dornbirn · Marktstr. 21
Tel. 0 5572 / 68817

NÄCHSTER TERMIN

Tag	Datum	Zeit

Bitte diese Karte jedesmal mitzubringen. Bei Nicht-
einhaltung der Stunden wird höflichst ersucht, dies
mindestens 24 Stunden vorher bekannt zu geben.

Univ. Med. Dr. Günter Ludescher · Facharzt für Zahn-, Mund- und Kieferheilkunde · A-6850 Dornbirn · Marktstraße 21 · Tel. 0 5572 / 68817

DR. GÜNTER LUDESCHER Dentist 歯科医 AUSTRIA 1991 D: Kurt Dornig DF: Dornig Grafik Design

COLOR CONTROL Color Separation and Prepress 印刷前の色分解 USA 1992 AD, D: Rick Eiber DF: Rick Eiber Design (Red)

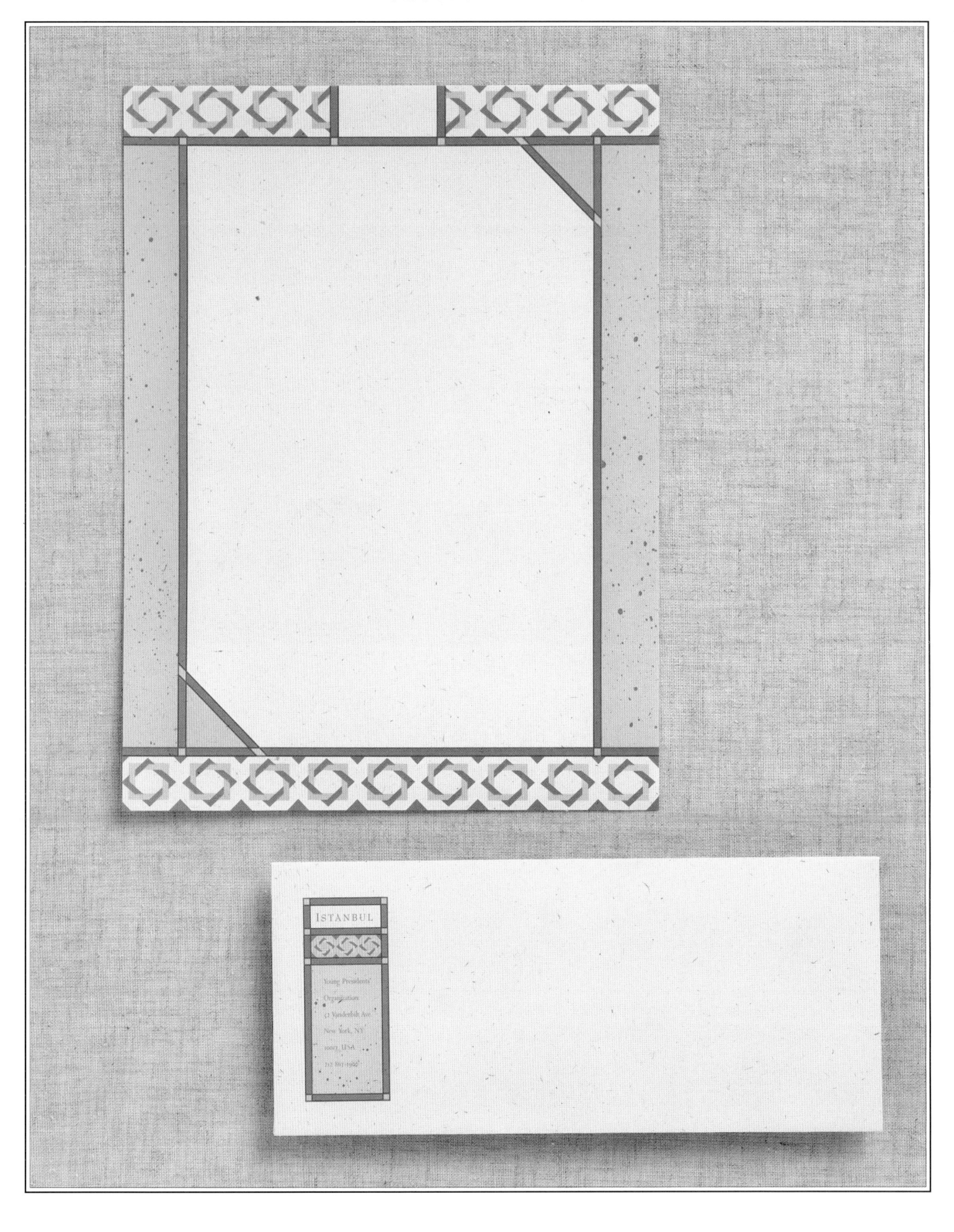

YOUNG PRESIDENT'S ORGANIZATION Association of Corporate Presidents　企業主協会　USA

AD: John Waters　D: Margaret Riegal　CW: Young President's Organization　DF: Waters Design Associates

KINETIC ART AND BUSINESS AMERICA, INC. 111 4TH AVENUE 11K NEW YORK 10003

KINETIC ART AND BUSINESS AMERICA, INC. 111 4TH AVENUE 11K NEW YORK 10003 TEL. 212.254.1112 FAX 212.254.1113

KAB, INC. (RYUICHI SAKAMOTO) Promotion and Management アーティストの管理、促進 USA 1993 CD: Robert Bergman‑Ungar D: Liong The

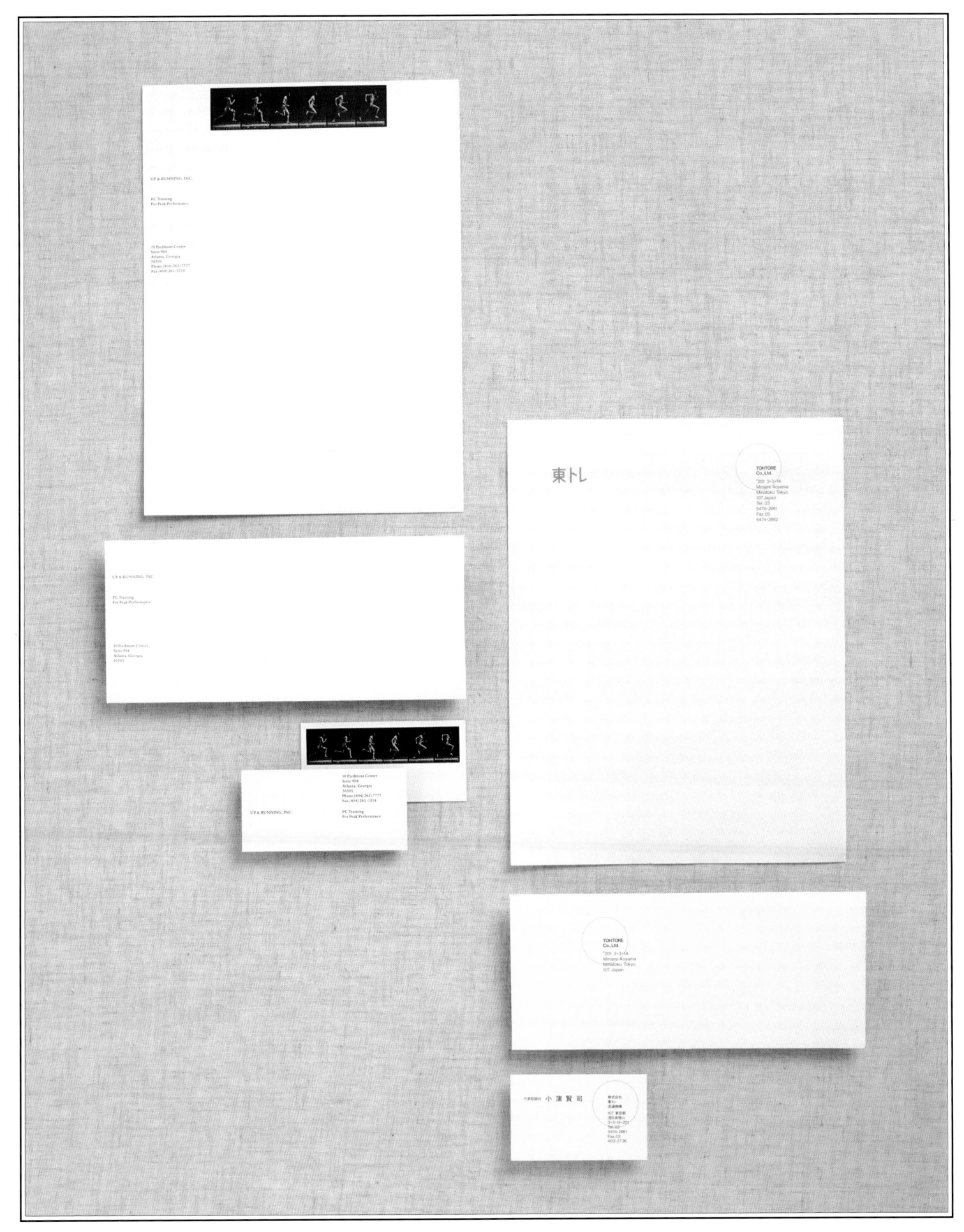

UP & RUNNING, INC. Computer Based Fitness Service　コンピュータ処理のフィットネスサービス　USA　1989　CD: Kim Youngblood　P: Eadweard Muybridge　DF: Youngblood, Sweat & Tears

TOHTORE CO., LTD. Produce　プロデュース　JAPAN　1990　AD, D: Keisuke Unosawa　DF: Keisuke Unosawa Design

EAGLE LAKE ON ORCAS ISLAND Island Development 島開発 USA 1992 AD, D, I: Julia LaPine D, LETTERER: Denise Weir DF: Hornall Anderson Design Works

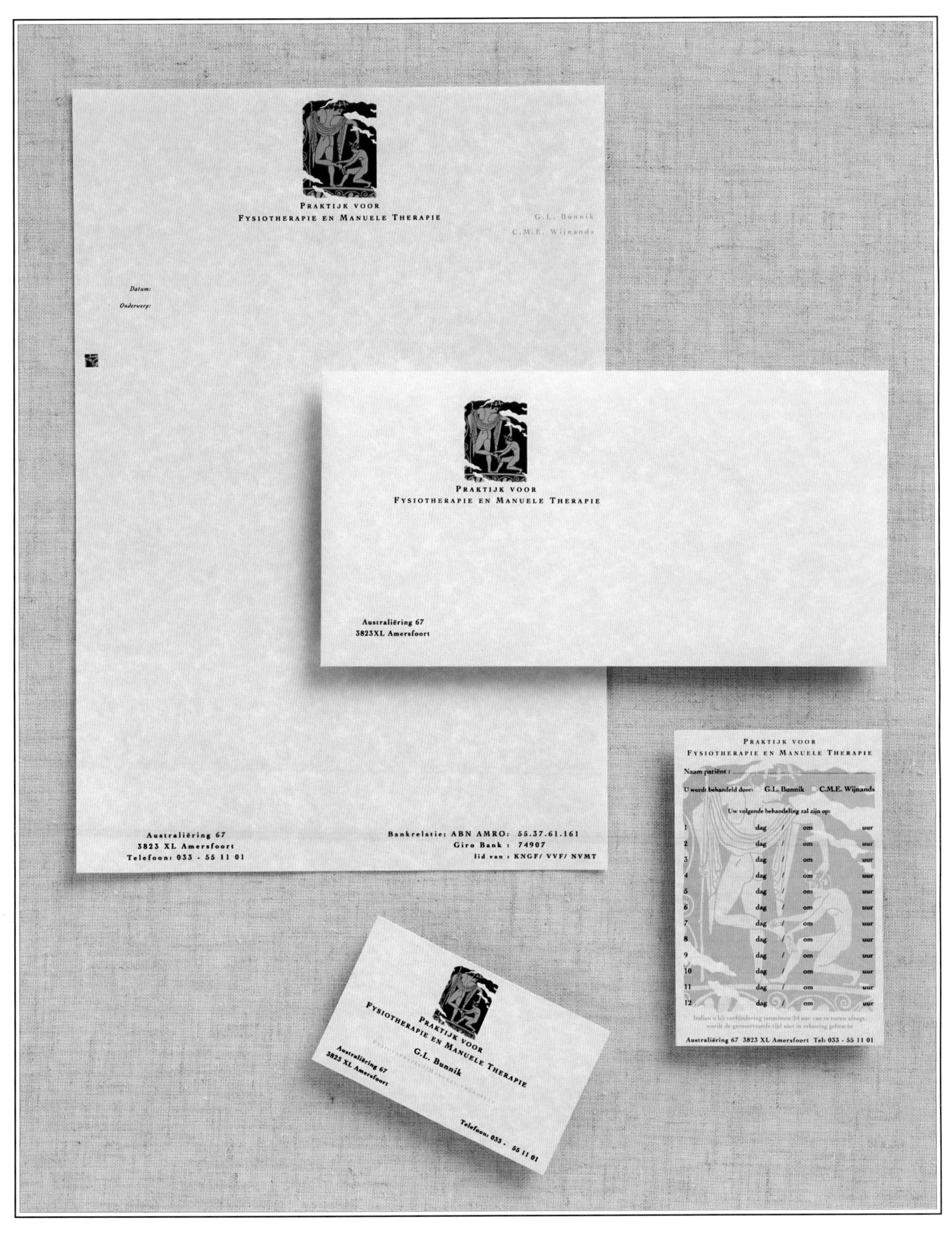

ERWIN WIJNANDS & LEX BUNNIK Physiotherapy and Manual Therapy 物理療法、手動療法 THE NETHERLANDS 1992 D, I: Luc Reefman Bno DF: KBO & R Design

BARNEY TABACH, AVID Golfer (personal) ゴルファー USA 1992 AD, D, I: John Sayles DF: Sayles Graphic Design

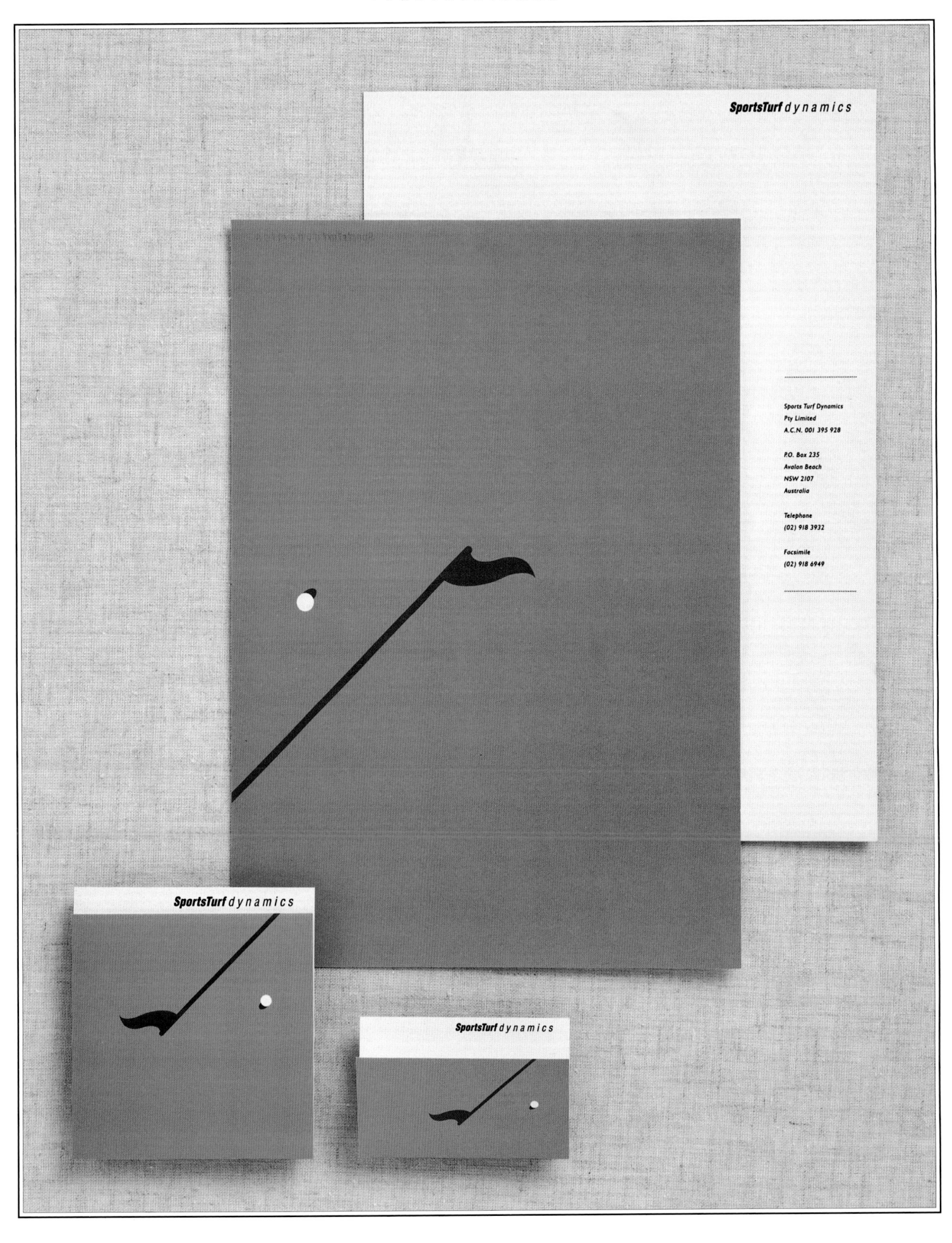

SPORTS TURF DYNAMICS Designers and Installers of Turf Management Systems 芝生管理装置のデザイン、設計 AUSTRALIA 1991 D, I: David Roffey DF: David Roffey Design

b³ BLUMENTHAL Office Communication オフィス通信サービス GERMANY 1992 AD, D: Detlef Behr DF: Detlef Behr, Graphik-design

CURATOR OFFICE INC.　Curator　キュレーター　JAPAN　1992　AD, D: Tatsuaki Yasuno　DF: T. Y. D.

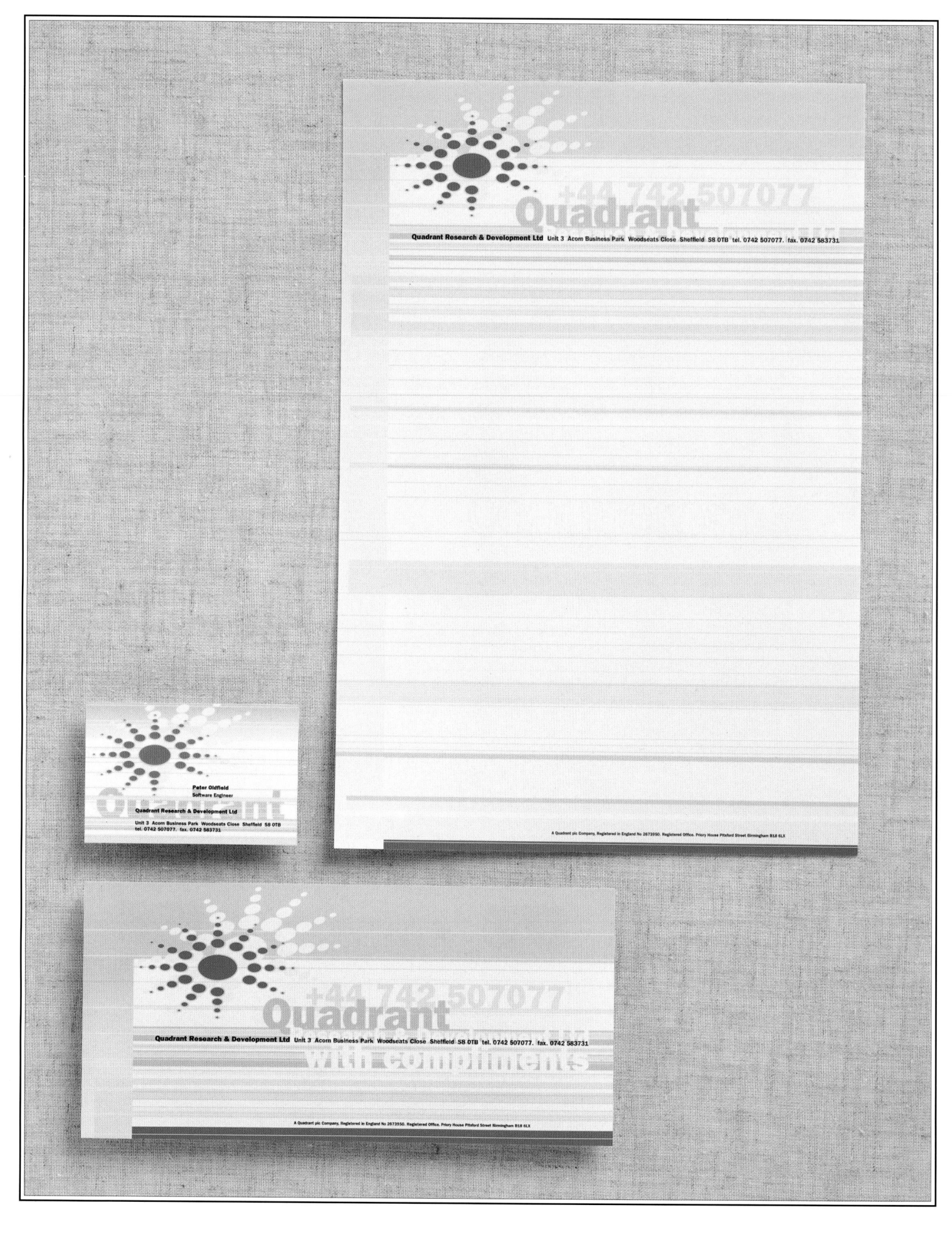

QUADRANT RESEARCH & DEVELOPMENT LTD   Systems Software Research and Development   システムソフトウェアの研究開発   UK 1993

AD, D: The Designers Republic   DF: The Designers Republic

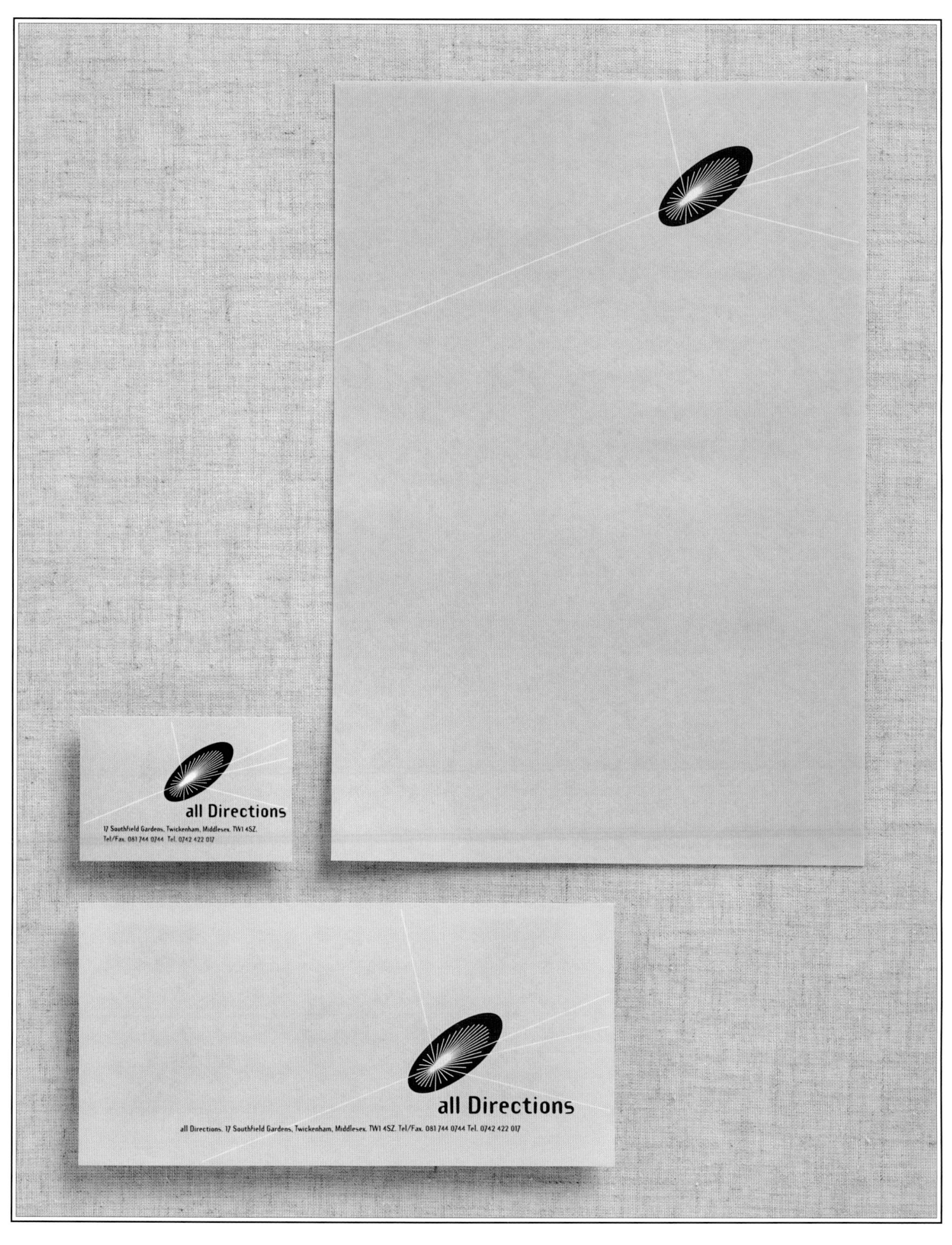

ALL DIRECTIONS Theatrical Agents and Artist Management 劇団取次、アーティスト管理 UK 1992 AD, D: The Designers Republic DF: The Designers Republic

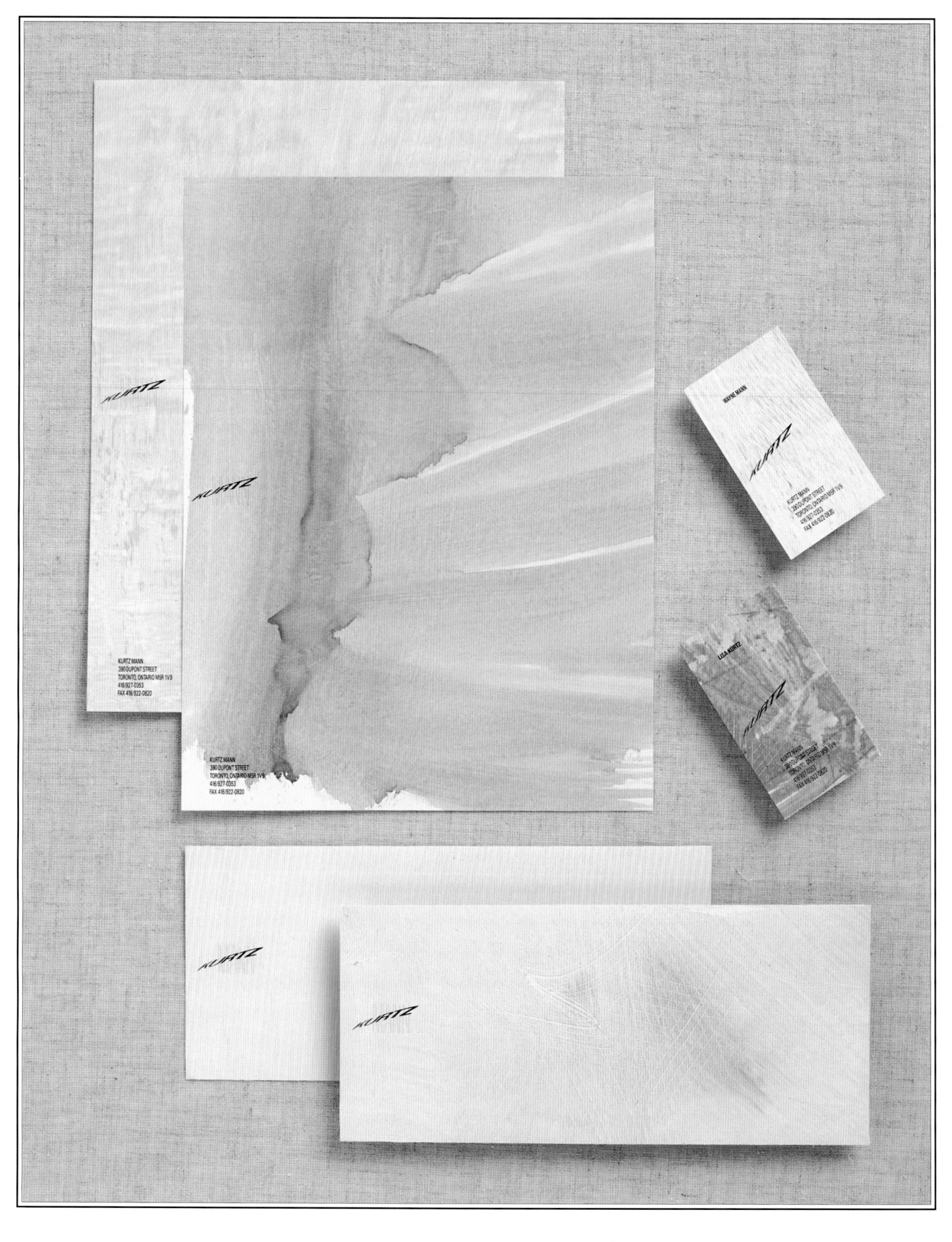

KURTZ MANN   Mural Painters and Wall Decorators   壁のペイント、壁面装飾   CANADA   1991   AD, D: Del Terrelonge   I: Kurtz Mann studio   DF: Terrelonge Design
Special Effects: Black and varniched lettering have been overlaid on a patterned background.   地模様の入った紙に黒文字とニス状の文字を重ねている。

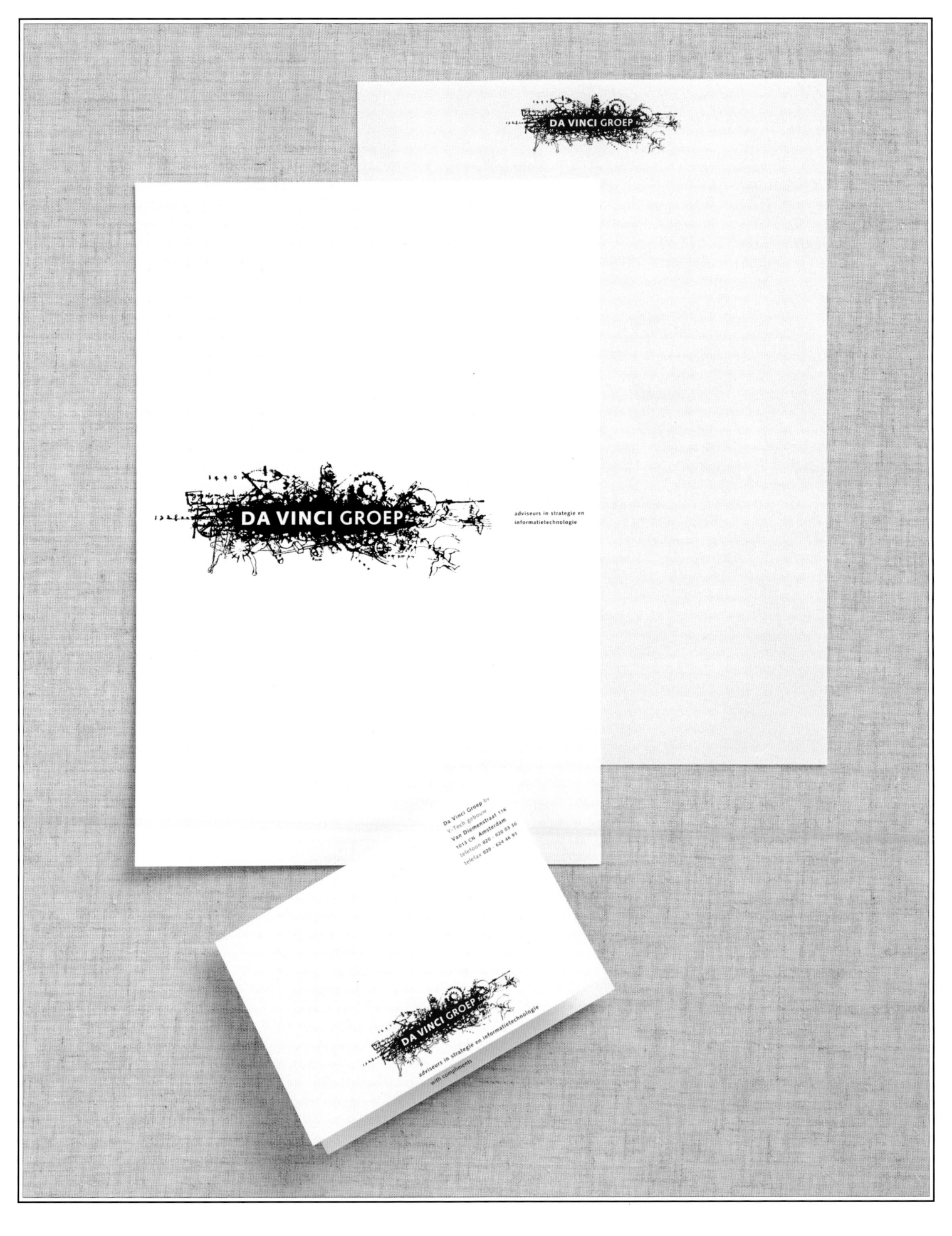

DA VINCI GROEP Consultancy in Information Technology 情報技術コンサルタント THE NETHERLANDS 1991
CD: André Toet AD, D: Hans Meiboom I: Leonardo da Vinch DF: Samenwerkende Ontwerpers

EUROPEAN MARKETING DISTRIBUTION Finance Organisation 金融協会 AUSTRIA 1991 D: Kurt Dornig DF: Dornig Grafik Design

CORPORATE WORLD RELOCATION　Relocation Services　引越専門会社　USA 1993　AD, D, I: Stefanie Choi　DF: Stefanie Choi

AD, D: Jack Anderson D: Brian O'Neill / Lian Ng I: John Fretz DF: Hornall Anderson Design Works
CENTER FOR ORAL AND MAXILLOFACIAL SURGERY Dentistry-Oral and Maxillofacial Surgery 口腔外科医院 USA 1991
KATRIN FUCHS Logopaedics 言語医学 AUSTRIA 1992 AD, D, I: Hubert Egartner DF: Egartner Grafik Design Gda

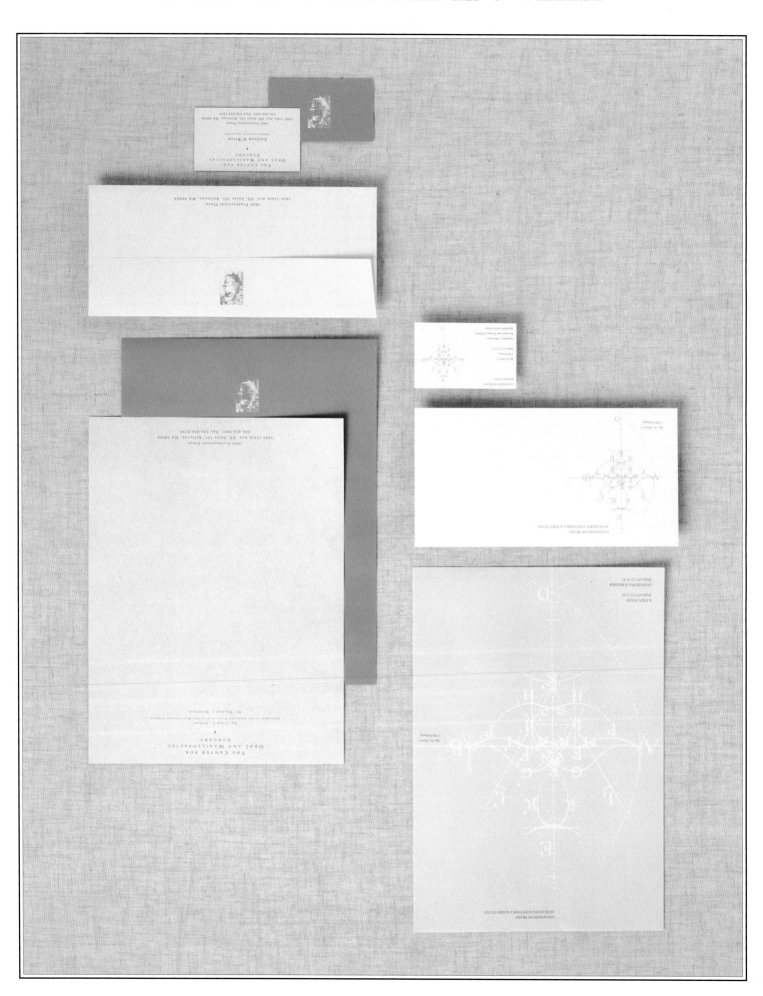

INTEGRUS ARCHITECTURE Architecture 建築設計業 USA 1991 AD, D: John Hornall D: Paula Cox / Brian O'Neill / Lian Ng DF: Hornall Anderson Design Works

BERGMANN WASMER & ASSOCIATES Builders and Developers of Environmental Homes 住宅建造の発展、開発 USA 1991 AD, D: David Warren I: Diego Ruiz DF: David Warren Design

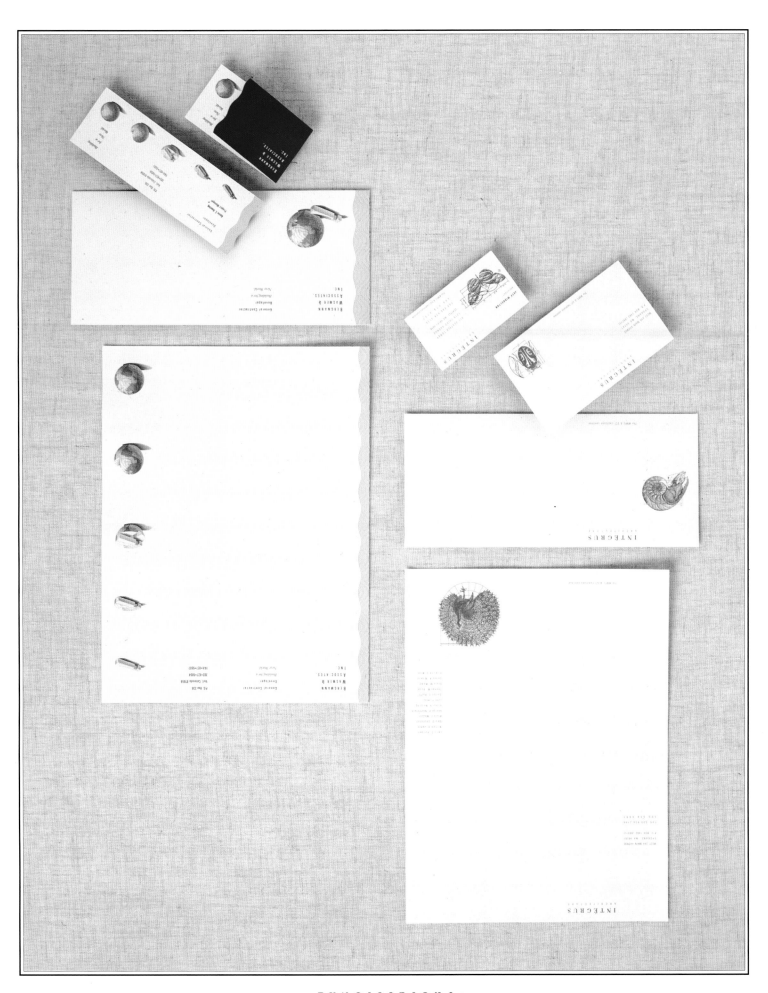

AD, D: Rebeca Méndez   D: Kevin Downey   P: Steven A. Heller   PRINTER: Typecraft, Pasadena, California

ART CENTER ANNUAL FUND, ART CENTER COLLEGE OF DESIGN   Art College   美術専門学校   USA 1991

art center annual fund

Art Center College of Design 1700 Lida Street. Post Office Box 7197, Pasadena, California, Zip Code 91109-7197 Phone 818 584 5105 Fax 818 405 9104

1991
Annual Fund
Committee

National Fund Chair
Gordon Bruce 1972
New Milford, CT

Advertising
Roy A. Keener 1970
Evanston, IL

Environmental Design
Carter W. Lee 1985
Newport Beach, CA

Film
Valerie Gordon 1978
New York, NY

Fine Art
Fred Fehlau 1979
Los Angeles, CA

Graphic and
Packaging Design
Ramone Muñoz 1977
Los Angeles, CA

Illustration
Bart Forbes 1963
Dallas, TX

Photography
Rick Amex 1986
San Francisco, CA

Product Design
Barbara R. Lewis 1972
Sunnyvale, CA

Transportation Design
Mark Jordan 1978
Laguna Niguel, CA

art center annual fund

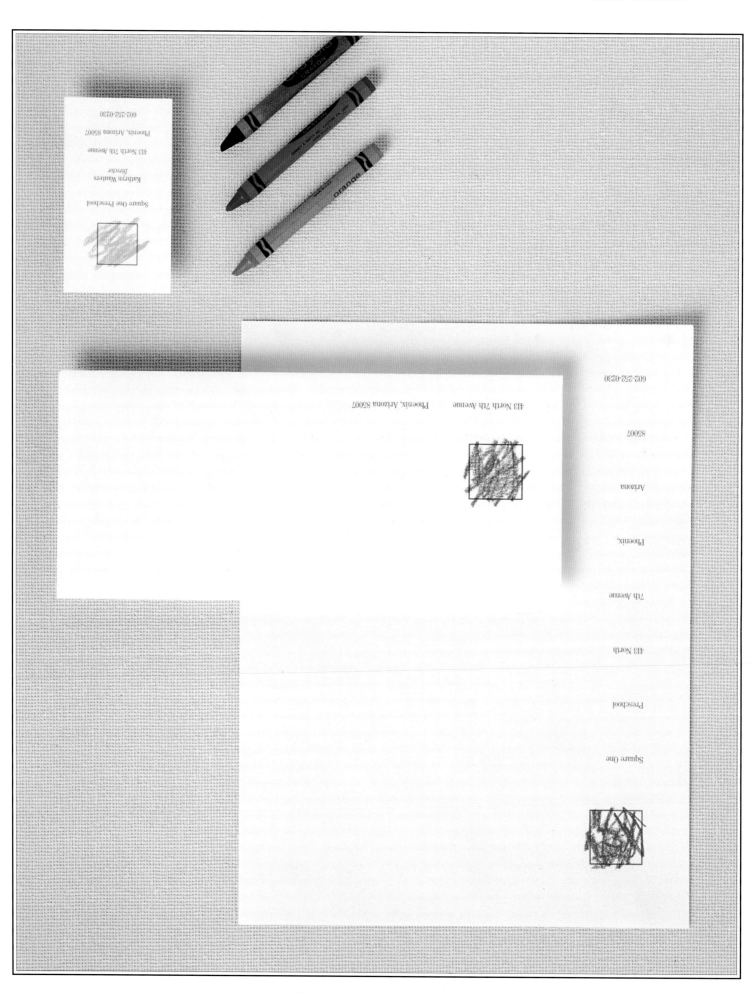

ONE REEL / SEATTLE ARTS COMMISSION Events Promoter イベント促進 USA 1993 CD: Kerry Burg AD, D: Susan Dewey DF: NBBJ-Graphic Design

AD, D, I, CW: Sigi Ramoser   DF: Atelier Gassner / Schlins-Austria

MOBILER HAUSHILFEDIENST FELDKIRCH   Social Programme Union (helping old and sick people stay home)   社会福祉共同組合（老人や病人の外出を助ける）   AUSTRIA 1991

AMM.NE PROVINCIALE DI FERRARA   Administration management provinces   地方行政管理   ITALY   AD, D, I, CW: Nedda Bonini

WESTERN REGIONAL GREEK CONFERENCE   Association of Fraternities and Sororities   冊子、女子学生クラブの略称   USA 1991 AD, D, I: John Sayles DF: Sayles Graphic Design

UNIVERSITEIT UTRECHT 大学 University THE NETHERLANDS 1992 AD, D: Aad van Dommelen CW: Elsvan Klinken DF: Proforma Rotterdam bNO Association for Design & Consultancy

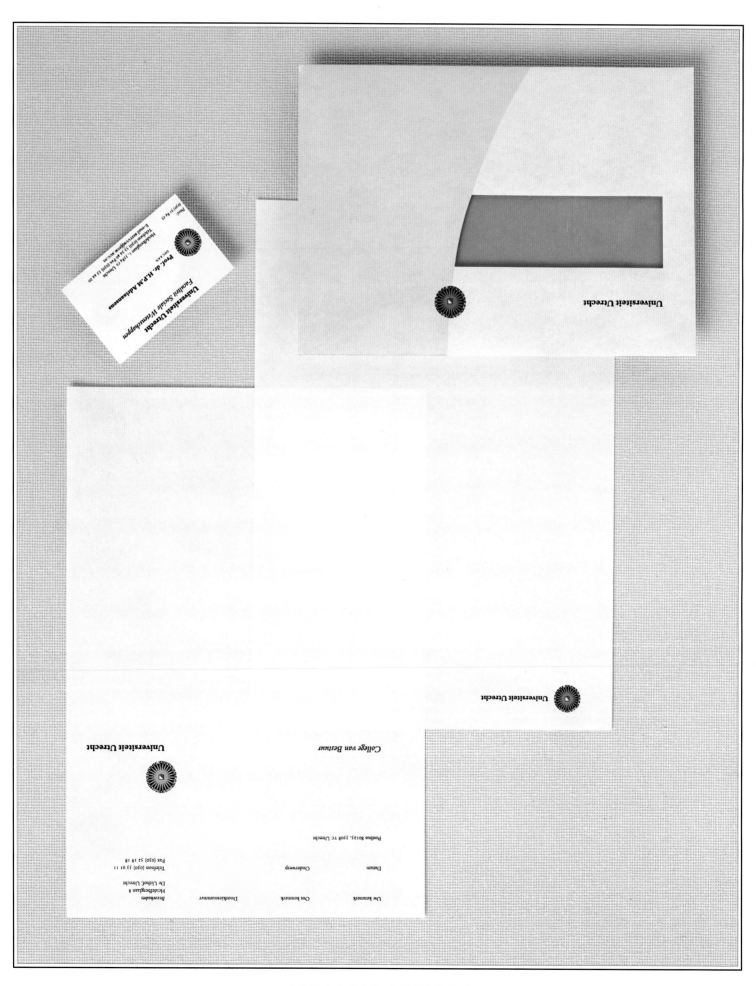

THE CENTER FOR FAMILIES AND CHILDREN   Non-profit Social Service Organization   非营利社会事业机构   USA 1993   AD, D: Gail Rigelhaupt   DF: Rigelhaupt Design, NYC

WEIDEMAFONDS Foundation 財团 THE NETHERLANDS 1992 CD: André Toet AD: Simon Davies CW: Alwin van Steijn DF: Samenwerkende Ontwerpers

ARTS COUNCIL OF GREAT BRITAIN Arts Funding Body アート産業団協体 UK 1989 AD: The Designers Republic D: Patrick Glower DF: The Designers Republic

LE BATEAU FEU Cultural Center カルチャー・センター FRANCE 1991 AD, D: Jean-Jacques Tachdjian DF: I Comme Image

OHIO ARTS COUNCIL State Council on The Arts 芸術協議会 USA AD, D: John Waters D, I: Bob Kellerman CW: Peter Maloney DF: Waters Design Associates

GREENMILL DANCE PROJECT. Performing Arts and Dance Project 舞蹈企劃 AUSTRALIA 1993 AD, D: Richard Henderson P: Tat-Mingh Yu DF: FHA Design Australia

BARRY MACKAY SPORTS Tennis Tournament テニストーナメント USA 1990 AD: Bill Cahan D: Stuart Flake / Talin Gureghian DF: Cahan & Assoc.

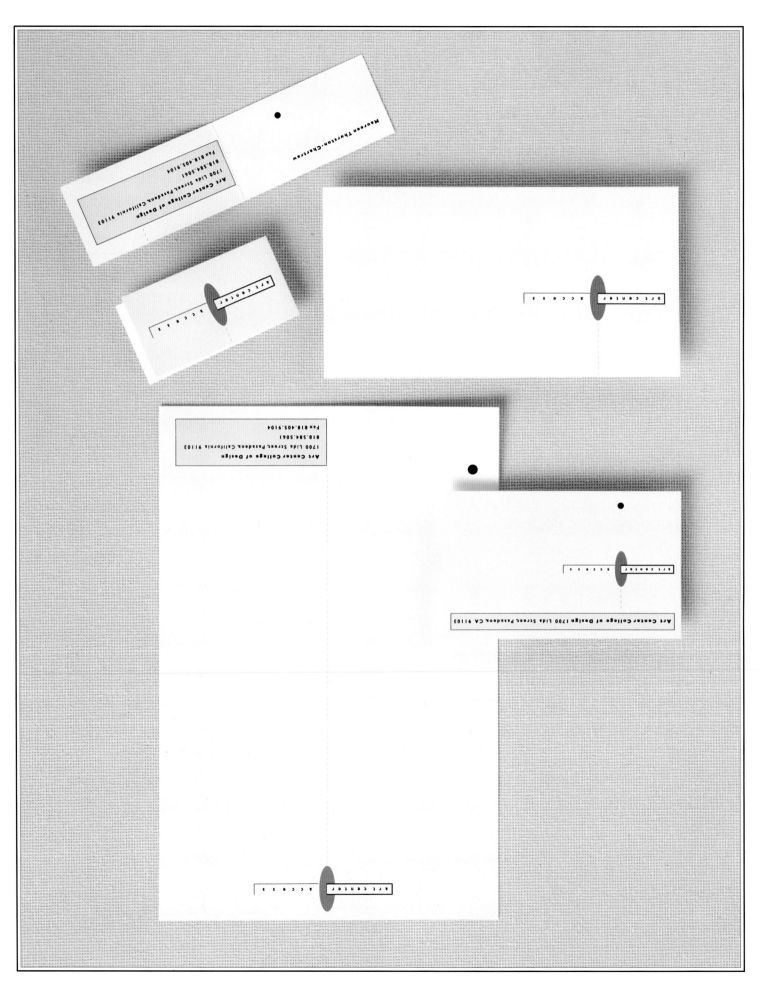

ART CENTER ACCESS, ART CENTER COLLEGE OF DESIGN　Art College　美術專門學校　USA 1992　AD, D: Rebeca Méndez　PRINTER: Star Printing, Los Angeles, California

ART CENTER COLLEGE OF DESIGN   Art College   美術専門学校   USA 1990   AD, D: Rebeca Méndez   PRINTER: Typecraft., Pasadena, California

IZU 21 KAIGI   Regional Planning   伊豆半島を伊豆の未来を考える会   JAPAN 1992   CD: Kenji Hanaue / Hiroshi Hasegawa   AD, D: Yoshiro Kajitani   D: Michiko Arakawa   DF: Kajitani Design Room

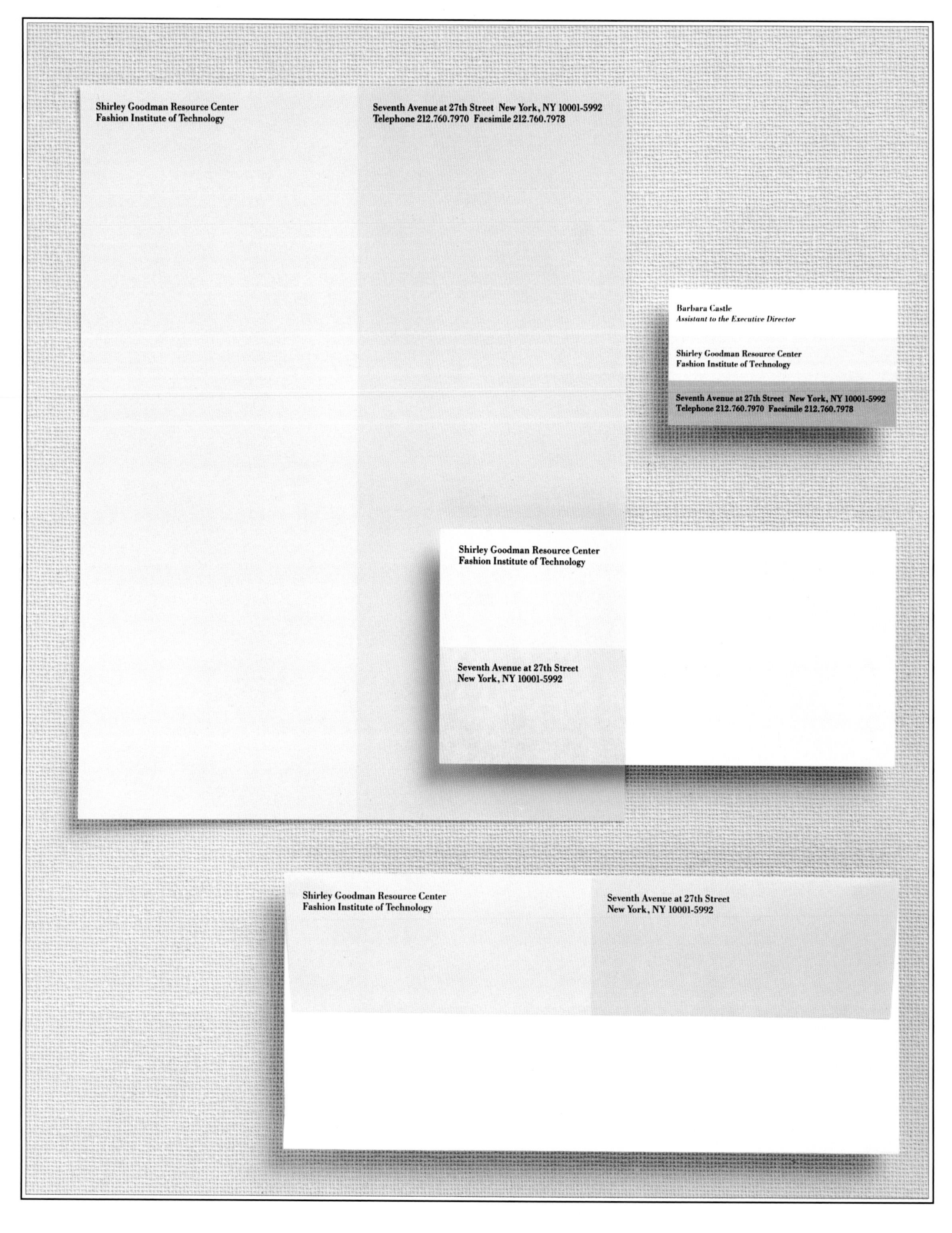

Shirley Goodman Resource Center
Fashion Institute of Technology

Seventh Avenue at 27th Street New York, NY 10001-5992
Telephone 212.760.7970 Facsimile 212.760.7978

Barbara Castle
Assistant to the Executive Director

Shirley Goodman Resource Center
Fashion Institute of Technology

Seventh Avenue at 27th Street New York, NY 10001-5992
Telephone 212.760.7970 Facsimile 212.760.7978

Shirley Goodman Resource Center
Fashion Institute of Technology

Seventh Avenue at 27th Street
New York, NY 10001-5992

Shirley Goodman Resource Center
Fashion Institute of Technology

Seventh Avenue at 27th Street
New York, NY 10001-5992

SHIRLEY GOODMAN RESOURCE CENTER Fashion Institute of Technology 科学技術のファッション専門学校 USA 1990
AD, D: Takaaki Matsumoto AD: Michael McGinn D: Mikio Sakai DF: M Plus M

◆ SPECIAL PROGRAM (Fax headers) ◆

KINEMA MOON DESIGNING Graphic Design フラフィックデザイン JAPAN 1993 AD: Yuichi Nakagawa D: Sachiko Kitani DF: Kinema Moon Designing

AD, D: The Designers Republic

QUADRANT RESEARCH & DEVELOPMENT LTD Systems Software Research and Development システムソフトウエアの研究開発 UK 1993

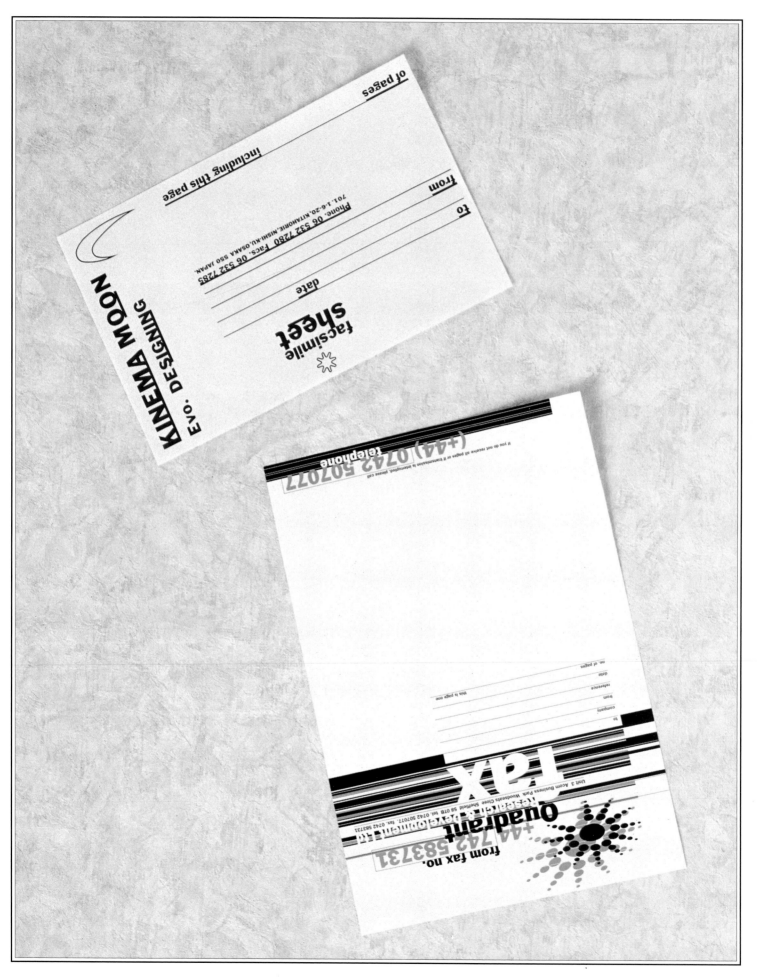

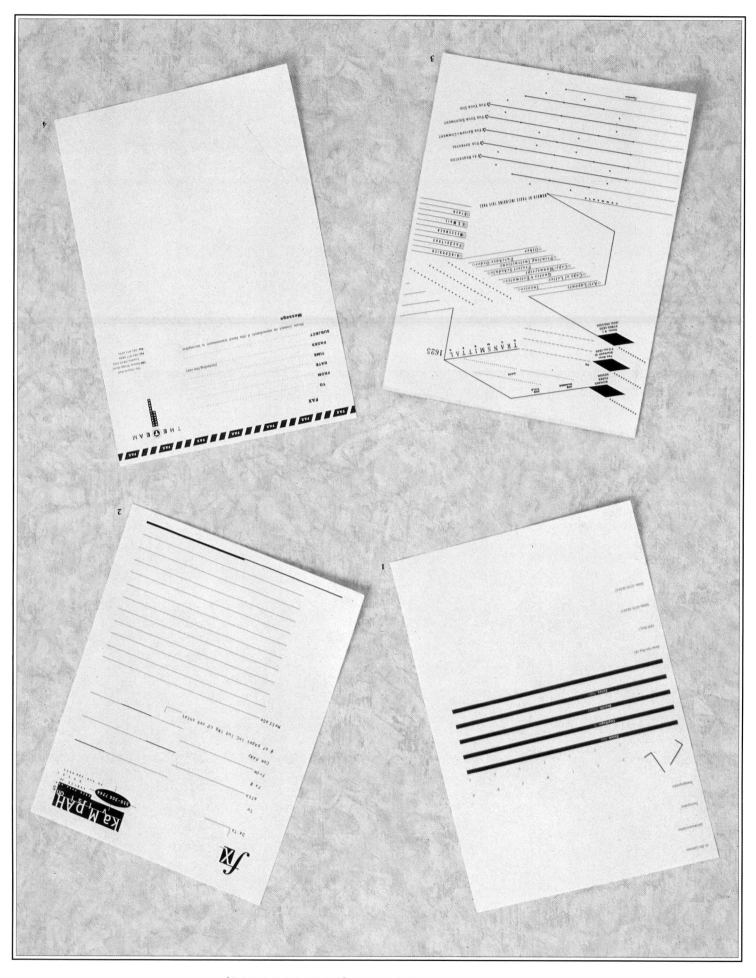

1. DR. ELKE LUDEMANN Sports-Science 運動科学研究 GERMANY 1991 AD, D: Detlef Behr DF: Detlef Behr, Graphik-Design
2. KAMPAH VISIONS Broadcast Design 放送局デザイン USA 1993 AD, D: Flavio Kampah DF: Kampah Visions
3. RICHARD PUDER DESIGN Visual Communication Design 視覚伝達デザイン USA 1989 CD: Richard Puder D: Lee Grabarczyk DF: Richard Puder Design
4. THE TEAM Graphic Design グラフィックデザイン UK 1990 CD, D: Richard Ward DF: The Team

1. RENO DESIGN GROUP   Graphic Design and Consultancy   グラフィックデザイン、コンサルタント   AUSTRALIA 1990   AD, D: Graham Rendoth   CW: Reno Design Group   DF: Reno Design Group
2. CONCEPT 1 / SAKAMOTO   Jewelry Manufacturer   宝石製造販売   USA 1993   AD, D: Cindy Luck   DF: Luck Design
3. TASTE INC.   Graphic Design   グラフィックデザイン   JAPAN 1992   AD, D: Toshiyasu Nanbu
4. OPTIK ISELIN   Exclusive Retailer of Glasses   眼鏡メガネ販売店   SWITZERLAND 1991   AD, D, I: Christian Hügin   DF: Christian Hügin

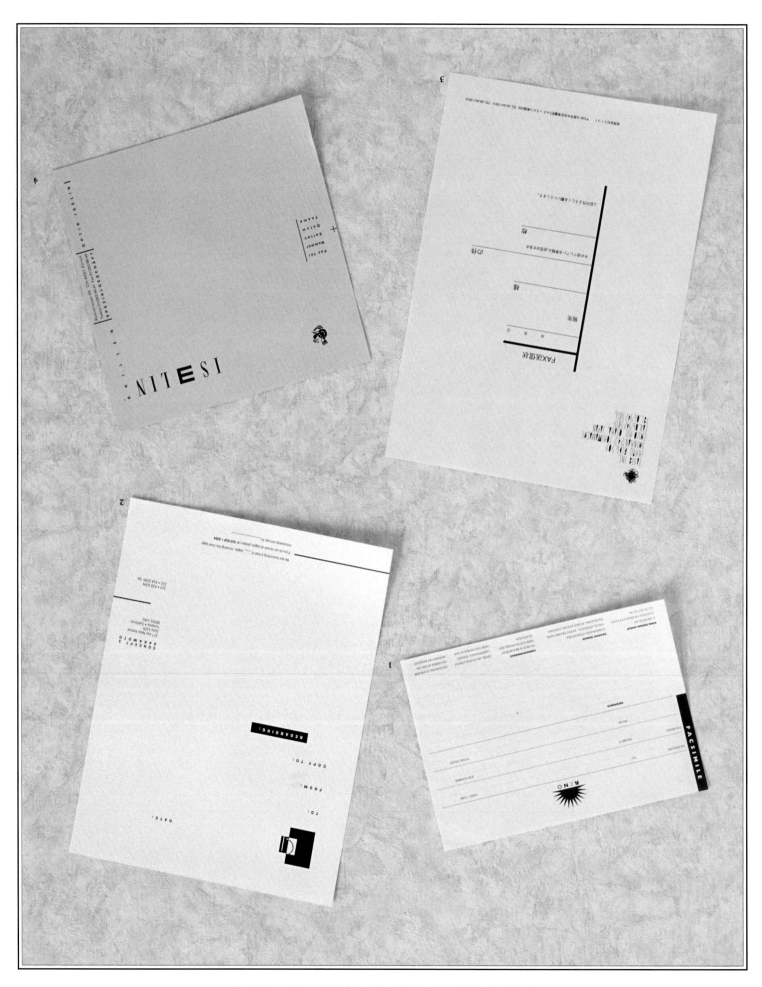

BLEU ELASTIQUE Design チザイン FRANCE 1993 AD, D: Pascal Béjean P: Gilles Marcodini CW: Bleu Elastique DF: Bleu Elastique

TYPO GRAPHIS Typography タイポグラフィ JAPAN 1992 AD, D: Tetsuyuki Kokin DF: Typographis

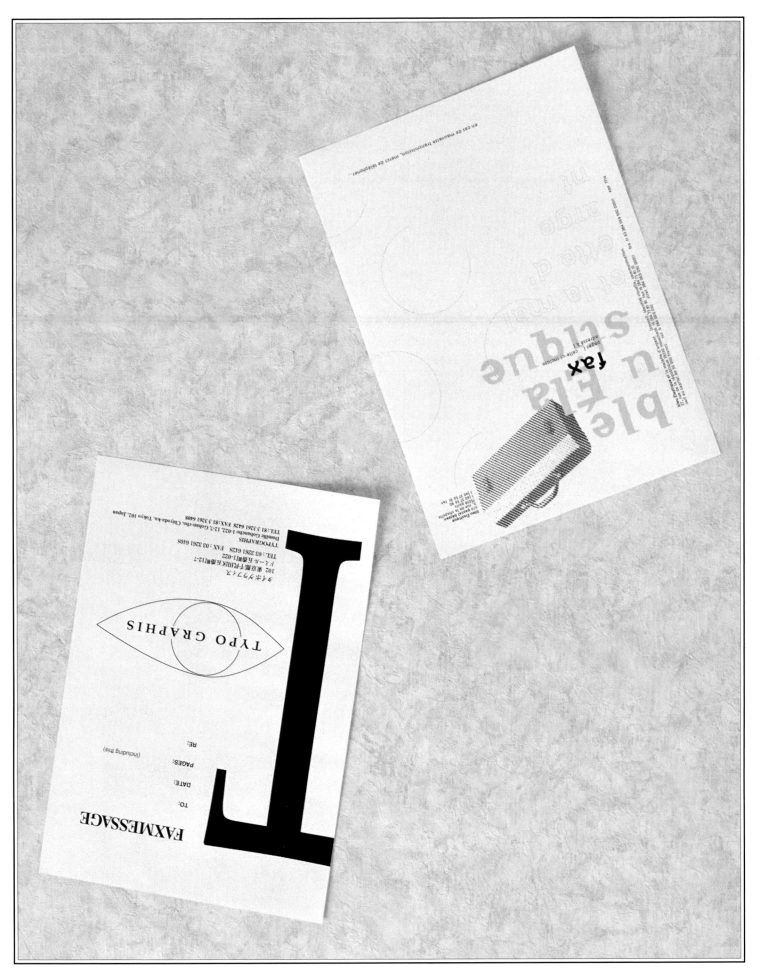

AD: Teun Anders D: Marc Lochs CW: Walter van Lotringen

WALTER VAN LOTRINGEN / TINEKE POSTHUMUS Freelance Illustrator / Art Historian 美術書籍事業部 THE NETHERLANDS 1991

CD: John Staresinic D, I: Ross Gervais CW: Acart Team DF: Acart Graphic Service

ACART GROUP OF COMPANIES Graphics / Communication, Exhibits Service グラフィックデザイン/情報通信、展示サービス CANADA 1990-1991

◆ SPECIAL PROGRAM (Fax headers) ◆

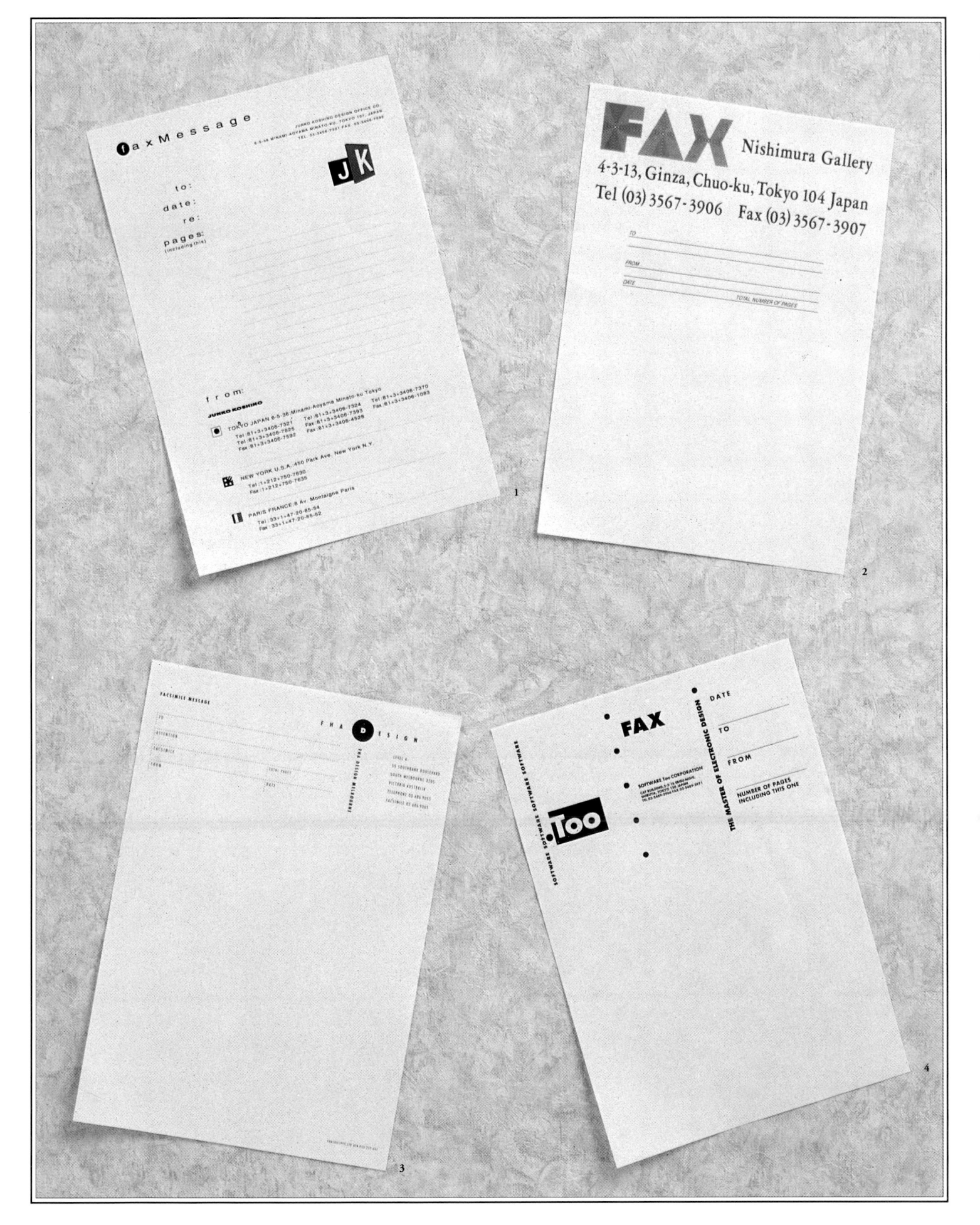

1. **JUNKO KOSHINO DESIGN OFFICE CO.** Apparel Maker アパレルメーカー JAPAN 1993 CD: Hiroyuki Suzuki AD: Junko Koshino D: Tetsuyuki Kokin DF: Typographis

2. **NISHIMURA GALLERY** Gallery 画廊 JAPAN 1991 D: Akihito Tsukamoto DF: Design Club

3. **FHA DESIGN** Graphic Design グラフィックデザイン AUSTRALIA 1993 AD, D: Richard Henderson D: Julia Jarvis DF: FHA Design Australia

4. **SOFTWARE TOO CORPORATION** Computer Related Service コンピューター関連ソフト・ハードウェアの輸入、販売、代理業 JAPAN 1991 AD: Naomi Enami D: Mariko Yamamoto DF: Propeller Art Works

NEVERNEVER ADRIAN　Sportswear Manufacturer　スポーツウエアメーカー　USA 1991　AD, D: Brian Burchfield　DF: Studio Seireni

NICE Graphic Design　グラフィックデザイン　UK 1991　CD: Stephen Male / Neil Edwards / Richard Bonner Morgan　D: Nice　DF: Nice

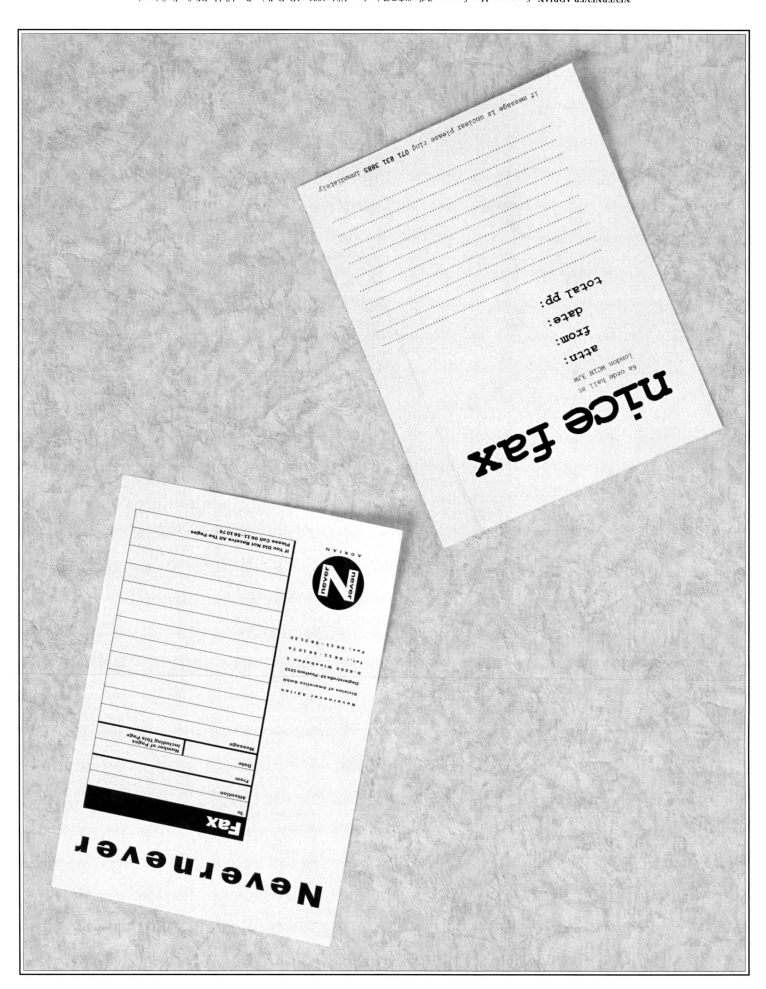

◆ INDEXES ◆

INDEX OF CLIENTS

INDEX OF SUBMITORS

BUSINESS STATIONERY GRAPHICS 2

Art Director, Designer

Sinji Ikenoue

Editor

Kaori Shibata

Photographer

Kuniharu Fujimoto

Business Manager

Masato Ieshiro

English Translator

Write Away Co., Ltd.

Thanks to

Clive Avins

Kaoru Endo

Publisher

Shingo Miyoshi

1994年2月20日初版第 1版発行

発行所 ピエ・ブックス

〒170 東京都豊島区駒込4-14-6-407

TEL: 03-3949-5010   FAX: 03-3949-5650

© 1994 P·I·E BOOKS

製版 （株）飛来社

Plate Making in Japan by Try Sha Co..Ltd.

Printed and Bound in Hong Kong by Everbest Printing Co..Ltd.

ISBN 4-938586-48-7 C3070

P·I·E Books, as always, has several new and ambitious graphic book projects in the works which will introduce a variety of superior designs from Japan and abroad. Currently we are planning the collection series detailed below. If you have any graphics which you consider worthy for submission to these publications, please fill in the necessary information on the inserted questionnaire postcard and forward it to us. You will receive a notice when the relevant project goes into production.

ピエ・ブックスでは、今後も新しいタイプのグラフィック書籍の出版を目指すとともに、国内外の優れたデザインを幅広く紹介していきたいと考えております。今後の刊行予定として下記のコレクション・シリーズを企画しておりますので、作品提供していただける企画がございましたら、挟み込みのアンケートハガキに必要事項をご記入の上お送り下さい。企画が近づきましたらそのつど案内書をお送りいたします。

REQUEST FOR SUBMISSIONS

A. Postcard Graphics

B. Advertising Greeting Cards

C. Brochure & Pamphlet Collection

D. Poster Graphics

E. Book Cover and Editorial Design

F. Corporate Image Design

G. Business Card and Letterhead Graphics

H. Calendar Graphics

I. Packaging and Wrapping Graphics

作 品 提 供 の お 願 い

A.ポストカード・グラフィックス

B.アドバタイジング・グリーティングカード

C.ブローシュア & パンフレット・コレクション

D.ポスター・グラフィックス

E.ブックカバー＆エディトリアル・デザイン

F.コーポレイト・イメージ & ロゴマーク・デザイン

G.ビジネスカード＆レターヘッド・グラフィックス

H.カレンダー・グラフィックス

I.パッケージ＆ラッピング・グラフィックス

Comme toujours, P·I·E Books a dans ses ateliers plusieurs projets de livres graphiques neufs et ambitieux qui introduiront une gamme de modèles supérieurs en provenance du Japon et de l'étranger. Nous prévoyons en ce moment la série de collections détaillée cidessous. Si vous êtes en possession d'un graphique que vous jugez digne de soumettre à ces publications, nous vous prions de remplir les informations nécessaires sur l'étiquette à renvoyer située à la carte postale questionnaire insérée et de nous la faire parvenir. Vous recevrez un avis lorsque le projet correspondant passera à la production.

Wie immer hat P·I·E Books einige neue anspruchsvolle Grafikbücher in Arbeit, die eine Vielzahl von hervorragenden Designs aus Japan und anderen Ländern vorstellen werden. Momentan planen wir eine Serie mit den nachfolgend aufgeführten Themen. Wenn Sie grafische Darstellungen besitzen, von denen Sie meinen, daß sie in diese Veröffentlichung aufgenommen werden könten, geben Sie uns bitte die nötigen Informationen auf der entsprechenden Antwortseite am füllen Sie die beigelegte Antwortkarte aus und schicken Sie sie an uns. Wir werden Sie benachrichtigen, wenn das entsprechende Projekt in Arbeit geht.

DEMANDE DE SOUMISSIONS

A. Graphiques pour cartes postales

B. Cartes de voeux publicitaires

C. Collection de brochures et de pamphlets

D. Graphiques sur affiche

E. Designs de couverture de livre et d'éditorial

F. Designs de logo d'image de société

G. Graphiques pour en-têtes et cartes de visite

H. Graphiques pour calendrier

I. Graphiques pour emballage et paquetage

AUFFORDERUNG ZU MITARBEIT

A. Postkarten-Grafik

B. Werbe-Grußkarten

C. Zusammenstellung von Broschüren und Druckschriften

D. Postergrafik

E. Bucheinbände und redaktionelles Design

F. Corporate-Image-Logo-Design

G.Visitenkarten und Briefkopf-Grafik

H. Kalendergrafik

I. Grafik auf Verpackungen und Verpackungsmaterial

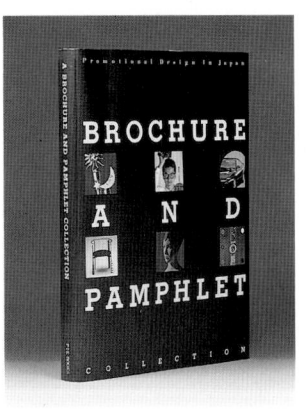

ADVERTISING GREETING CARDS 1
Pages: 224(144 in color) ￥15,000
業種別ダイレクトメールの集大成
A collection of more than 500 direct mail pieces selected from thousands used throughout Japan. Cards were selected for their distinctive design and include 3-D pop-ups, special die-cuts, folds and embossings.

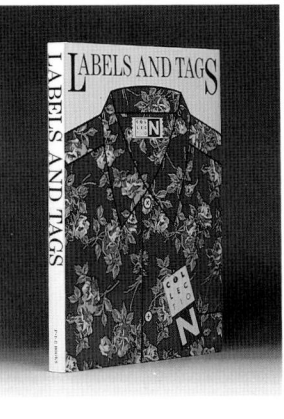

BROCHURE & PAMPHLET COLLECTION 1
Pages: 224(144 in color) ￥15,000
業種別カタログ・コレクション
Here are hundreds of the best brochures and pamphlets from Japan.
This collection will make a valuable sourcebook for anyone involved in corporate identity advertising and graphic design.

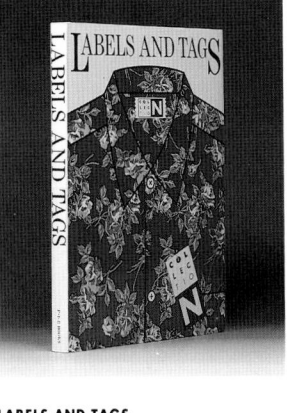

LABELS AND TAGS
Pages: 224(192 in color) ￥15,000
ファッションのラベル&タグ・コレクション
Over 1,600 garment labels representing 450 brands produced in Japan are included in this full-color collection.

POSTCARD GRAPHICS 2
Pages: 240(208 in color) ￥16,000
好評！ 業種別ポストカードの第2弾
Here are 1,500 promotional postcards created by Japan's top design talent. A wide range of clients are represented including 120 fashion houses and 90 major retailers. Presented in striking full color.

BUSINESS CARD GRAPHICS 1
Pages: 256(160 in color) ￥16,000
世界の名刺&ショップカード集大成
Over 1,200 business cards are presented in this international collection.
Created by 500 of the world's top design firms, designers will discover a wealth of new ideas in this remarkable collection.

FASHION INSIGNIA
Pages: 224(208 in color) ￥16,000
ファッションのワッペン・コレクション
One thousand full-color emblems have been gathered in this beautiful and sometimes playful collection.
The great variety of color and shape demonstrates the versatility of embroidery art.

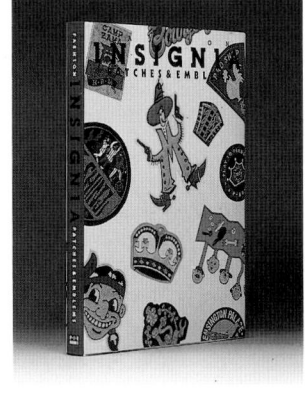

ADVERTISING GREETING CARDS 2
Pages: 224(176 in color) ￥16,000
世界のダイレクトメール・コレクション
500 visually remarkable works representing a variety of businesses. Pieces include new product announcements, invitation cards and direct mail envelopes. An excellent image bank for graphic designers.

BROCHURE DESIGN FORUM 1
Pages: 224(192 in color) ￥15,000
世界のカタログ・コレクション
A large collection of international brochures from a variety of business categories. Showcases more than 250 eye-catching works.

COVER TO COVER
Pages: 240(176 in color) ￥17,000
世界のブック&エディトリアル・デザイン
The latest trends in book and magazine design are illustrated with over 1,000 creative works by international firms.

BUSINESS STATIONERY GRAPHICS 1
Pages: 224(192 in color) ￥15,000
世界のレターヘッド・コレクション
Creatively designed letterheads, business cards, memo pads, and other business forms and documents are included this international collection.

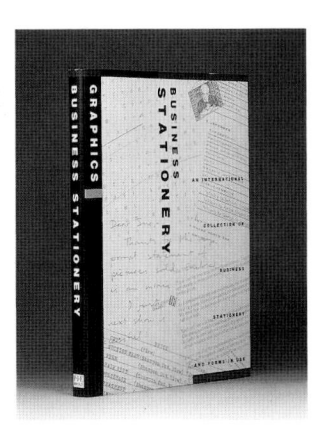

MUSIGRAPHICS 1
Pages: 224(192 in color) ￥16,000
世界のＬＰ&ＣＤグラフィックス
A collection of more than 600 of the world's most outstanding CD and LP covers, featuring design for all musical genres.

BROCHURE & PAMPHLET COLLECTION 2
Pages: 224(192 in color) ￥15,000
業種別カタログ・コレクション、第2弾
Features a selection of 1,000 brochures and pamphlets covering a wide range of products from Japan. The value of brochures in visual communication is demonstrated in this dazzling collection.

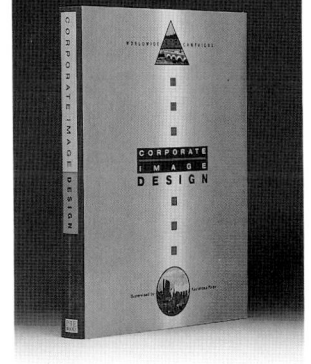

CORPORATE IMAGE DESIGN
Pages: 336(272 in color) ￥16,000
世界の業種別ＣＩ・ロゴマーク
This collection presents the best corporate identity projects from around the world. Creative and effective designs from top international firms are featured in this valuable source book.

POSTCARD GRAPHICS 3
Pages: 232(208 in color) ￥16,000
世界の業種別ポストカード・コレクション
Volume 3 in the series presents more than 1,200 promotional postcards in dazzling full color. Top designers from the world over have contributed to this useful image bank of ideas.

GRAPHIC BEAT London / Tokyo 1 & 2
Pages: 224(208 in color) ￥16,000
音楽とグラフィックのコラボレーション
1,500 music-related graphic works from 29 of the hottest designers in Tokyo and London. Features Malcolm Garrett, Russell Miles, Tadanori Yokoo, Neville Brody, Vaughn Oliver and others.

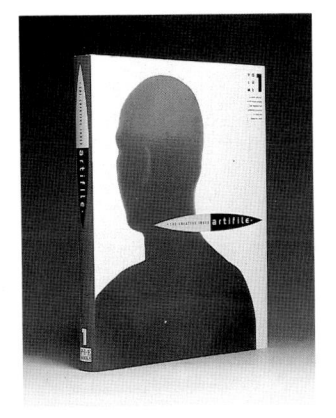

The Creative Index ARTIFILE 1
Pages: 224(Full color) ￥12,500
実力派プロダクション104社の作品集
Showcases the best works from 104 graphic studios in Japan and abroad. A variety of fields included such as advertising design, corporate identity, photography and illustration.

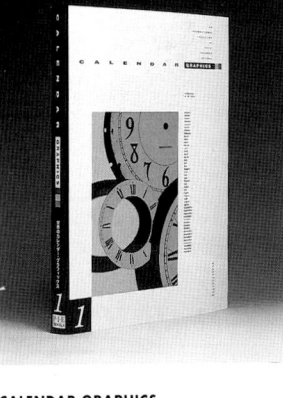

CALENDAR GRAPHICS
Pages: 224(192 in color) ￥16,000
世界のカレンダー・グラフィックス
An exciting collection of creatively designed calendars from around the world. A wide variety of styles included such as poster, book and 3-D calendars. Clients range from large corporations to retail shops.

BUSINESS CARD GRAPHICS 2
Pages: 224(192 in color) ￥16,000
世界の名刺&ショップカード、第2弾
This latest collection presents 1,000 creative cards from international designers. Features hundreds of cards used in creative fields such as graphic design and architecture.

T-SHIRT GRAPHICS
Pages: 224(192 in color) ￥16,000
世界のTシャツ・グラフィックス
This unique collection showcases 700 wonderfully creative T-Shirt designs from the world's premier design centers. Grouped according to theme, categories include sports, casual, designer and promotional shirts among others.

DIAGRAM GRAPHICS
Pages: 224(192 in color) ￥16,000
世界のダイアグラム・デザインの集大成
Hundreds of unique and lucid diagrams, charts, graphs, maps and technical illustrations from leading international design firms. Variety of media represented including computer graphics.

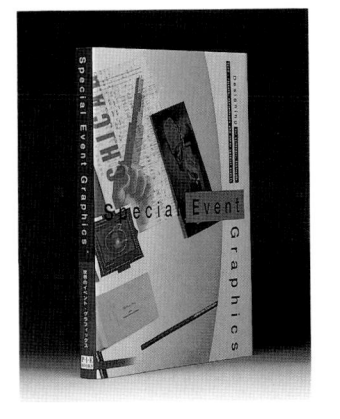

SPECIAL EVENT GRAPHICS
Pages: 224(192 in color) ￥16,000
世界のイベント・グラフィックス特集
This innovative collection features design elements from concerts, festivals, fashion shows, symposiums and more. International works include posters, tickets, flyers, invitations and various premiers.

PACKAGING DESIGN & GRAPHICS 1
Pages: 224(192 in color) ￥16,000
世界の業種別パッケージ・デザイン
An international collection featuring 400 creative and exciting package designs from renowned designers.

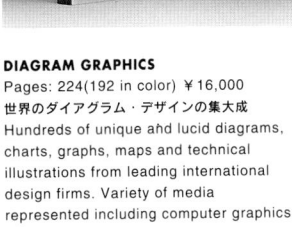

RETAIL IDENTITY GRAPHICS
Pages: 208(176 in color) ￥14,800
世界のショップ・グラフィックス
This visually exciting collection showcases the identity design campaigns of restaurants, bars, shops and various other retailers. Wide variety of pieces are featured including business cards, signs, menus, bags and hundreds more.

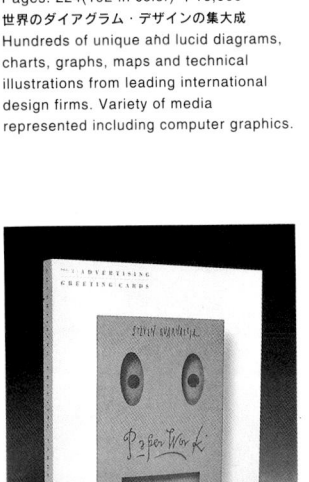

ADVERTISING GREETING CARDS 3
Pages: 224(176 in color) ￥16,000
世界のダイレクトメール集大成、第3弾
The best-selling series continues with this collection of elegantly designed advertising pieces from a wide variety of categories. This exciting image bank of ideas will interest all graphic designers and direct mail specialists.

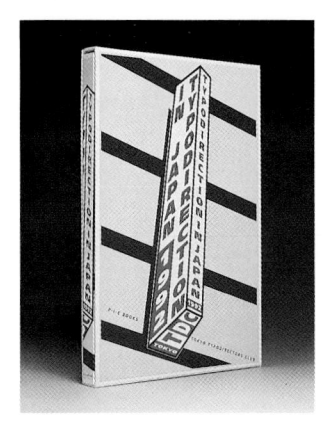

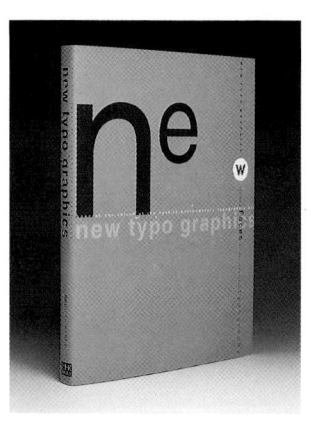

TYPODIRECTION IN JAPAN 4
Pages: 254(183 in color) ￥17,000
年鑑 日本のタイポディレクション '92
314 award-winning works of outstanding typographical art from Japan and abroad. Included, you will find up-to-the-minute examples of concept-development works and previously unpublished typefaces from top art dirctors and graphic designers.

NEW TYPO GRAPHICS
Pages: 224(192 in color) ￥16,000
世界の最新タイポグラフィ・コレクション
New and innovative typographical works gathered from top designers around the world. A wide variety of type applications are shown including posters, brochures, CD jackets, calendars, book designs and more.

The Production Index ARTIFILE 2
Pages: 244(240 in color) ￥13,500
活躍中！ 最新プロダクション年鑑、第2弾
A design showcase featuring the best works from 115 graphic design studios, photographers, and creators in Japan. Works shown include print advertisements, corporate identity pieces, commercial photography and illustration.

CREATIVE FLYER GRAPHICS
Pages:224(176 in color) ￥16,000
チラシ・グラフィックス
Features about 500 rigorously screened flyers and leaflets. You see what superior graphics can accomplish on a single sheet of paper. This is an invaluable reference to all your advertising production for years to come.

1·2 & 3 COLOR GRAPHICS
Pages:208(Full Color) ￥16,000
１・２・３色 グラフィックス
See about 300 samples of 1,2 & 3 color artworks that are so expressive they often surpass the impact of full 4 color reproductions. This is a very important book that will expand the possibilities of your design works in the future.

LABELS AND TAGS 2
Pages:224(192 in color) ￥16,000
世界のラベル＆タグ・コレクション　2
This long-awaited second volume features 1500samples representing 400 top name-brands from around the world.

BROCHURE DESIGN FORUM 2
Pages:224(176 in color) ￥16,000
世界の最新カタログ・コレクション　2
Features 70 businesses and 250 reproductions for a complete overview of the latest and best in brochure design.

カタログ・新刊のご案内について
総合カタログ・新刊案内をご希望の方は、はさみ込みのアンケートはがきを
ご返送いただくか、７２円切手同封の上、ピエ・ブックス宛にお申し込み下さい。